In the Shadow of Freedom

Perspectives on the History of Congress, 1801–1877

Donald R. Kennon, Series Editor

In the Shadow of Freedom

The Politics of Slavery in the National Capital

Edited by Paul Finkelman and Donald R. Kennon

PUBLISHED FOR THE
UNITED STATES CAPITOL HISTORICAL SOCIETY

BY OHIO UNIVERSITY PRESS • ATHENS

Ohio University Press, Athens, Ohio 45701
www.ohioswallow.com
© 2011 by Ohio University Press

To obtain permission to quote, reprint, or otherwise reproduce or distribute material from
Ohio University Press/Swallow Press publications, please contact our rights and permissions
department at (740) 593-1154 or (740) 593-4536 (fax).

Ohio University Press books are printed on acid-free paper ∞ ™

18 17 16 15 14 13 12 11   5 4 3 2 1

Library of Congress Cataloging-in-Publication Data

In the shadow of freedom : the politics of slavery in the national capital / edited by Paul
Finkelman and Donald R. Kennon.
     p. cm. — (Perspectives on the history of Congress, 1801–1877)
Papers from the U.S. Capitol Historical Society meeting held in 2006.
Includes bibliographical references and index.
ISBN 978-0-8214-1934-2 (acid-free paper) — ISBN 978-0-8214-4349-1 (electronic)
1. Slavery—Washington (D.C.)—History—19th century—Congresses. 2. Slavery—
Political aspects—Washington (D.C.)—History—19th century—Congresses. 3. Antislavery
movements—Washington (D.C.)—History—19th century—Congresses. 4. United States.
Congress—History—19th century—Congresses. 5. Slavery—Law and legislation—United
States—History—19th century—Congresses. 6. Washington (D.C.)—Race relations—
History—19th century—Congresses. 7. Washington (D.C.)—Politics and government—To
1878—Congresses. I. Finkelman, Paul, 1949- II. Kennon, Donald R., 1948- III. United
States Capitol Historical Society.
E445.D6I6 2010
305.8009753—dc22
                         2010052956

Contents

PART 2: THE POLITICS OF SLAVERY IN THE DISTRICT OF COLUMBIA

Preface

THIS VOLUME stems from the U.S. Capitol Historical Society Meeting in 2006, the third conference I had the privilege of organizing with my coeditor, Don Kennon. Every spring the United States Capitol Historical Society (USCHS) holds a scholarly conference on an aspect of American history that focuses on Congress, the nation's capital, and the federal government. My work with the USCHS began in 2004 with a conference on Congress in the 1820s followed by a conference in 2005 on Congress in the Age of Jackson. The papers from those two conferences were combined in *Congress and the Emergence of Sectionalism: From the Missouri Compromise to the Age of Jackson.* This volume follows, with essays on how slavery affected life in Washington, D.C., and how slavery affected politics in the capital.

The issues are interrelated. Congress met in a slaveholding city. Antislavery congressmen had to face the reality of slavery every day, and make compromises with the institution, even when they did not want to do so. Slaves were everywhere, working in the places congressmen lived, serving in the restaurants at which they ate, and driving the horse-drawn carriages in which they rode. Southerners also had to face the reality of a slave city with a growing free black population and an increasingly discontented slave population. The constant attempts of slaves to escape bondage—illustrated by the story of *The Pearl*, which is set out in this volume—illustrates how southerners could not easily and comfortably live in Washington with the myth that their slaves were happy and contented. This social reality of slavery affected the congressional debates over slavery in the territories, the annexation of Texas, and southern demands for a new fugitive slave law. *In the Shadow of Freedom: The Politics of Slavery in the National Capital* explores all of these interrelated themes.

As always, it was an enormous pleasure working with Don Kennon on the conference and on the book. Don is a thoughtful, careful scholar and editor. His staff at the USCHS makes our conference run smoothly. Both Don and I owe a great debt to his staff, especially Lauren Borchard and Felicia Bell. We are also greatly indebted to our editor at Ohio University Press, Gillian Berchowitz. She is smart, helpful, and creative. And, as with all great editors, she knows just how to cajole late authors and editors to get their work in. Working with her is always an enormous pleasure. The staff at Ohio University Press, especially our project editor, Rick Huard, rounds out a great team.

Most of all, we are indebted to the colleagues who come to our conference to share their ideas and knowledge and to interact with each other and with the audience. Their papers—published here—reflect their dedication to interdisciplinary scholarship, history, and the life of the mind. Some of these papers are the work of younger scholars, offering new ideas and new research; some reflect a lifetime of work by some of the great masters of our profession. The authors come from different disciplines, but all are historians dedicated to the craft of understanding, explaining, and learning from our past. Don and I learned much from organizing the conference and editing these chapters. We hope our readers will as well.

Paul Finkelman

In the Shadow of Freedom

Paul Finkelman

Slavery in the Shadow of Liberty

The Problem of Slavery in Congress and the Nation's Capital

Few images of early America were more striking, and jarring, than that of slaves in the nation's capital. Every day thousands of slaves moved around Washington, laboring on behalf of the city's white community and the nation's government. In the capital city of the world's most important free republic, slaves were everywhere. Hotels, restaurants, carriages —even houses of prostitution—used slave labor. The homes of the city's most prosperous residents were staffed by slaves rather than hired servants, as was common in the North. Livery stables used slaves to care for horses, and stores used slaves to carry goods to patrons. Black slaves waited on the senators and representatives who made the laws for the American Republic. In almost all ways slaves served and maintained the legislators, bureaucrats, jurists, cabinet officials, military leaders, and even the presidents who lived and worked in the seat of power of the world's most prominent democratic republic.

Southern politicians, jurists, military officers, bureaucrats, and entrepreneurs brought their favorite servants—and often their slave mistresses—with them when they represented their states, dedicated themselves to national service, or journeyed to the nation's capital to seek fame and fortune. For the southerners who dominated Washington society and made the city work, the presence of slaves seemed normal and even comforting. The national capital reminded them of their southern homes and their southern way of life. Slavery in the District of Columbia also reinforced a sense that their "peculiar institution" remained secure in the nation, despite the growing northern opposition to human bondage and after the 1830s the emergence of militant abolitionism. Indeed, as England and other European nations ended slavery and denounced its immorality, American masters were secure in their national capital, where slavery was the rule. Despite growing opposition in the North to slavery, for most of the antebellum period northerners tolerated the capital city's slave culture, although often with a sense of disgust. Foreign visitors must have been confused, bewildered, or perhaps bemused by the sight of so many black bondsmen in a nation that arrogantly proclaimed itself to be the guardian of liberty and the embodiment of freedom, but they also were invariably forced to accommodate it. After all, northerners, diplomats, and other foreigners could rarely escape slave culture, even if they abhorred it. Slavery inevitably affected their lives, and they were served by slaves in boardinghouses, laundries, restaurants, theaters, and almost every establishment they patronized.

Other sights of slavery were less comforting to southerners, while confirming to many northerners and foreign visitors the horrors of slavery. Slaves, after all, were whipped, jailed, and chastised in public. More important, they were sold and sent south. Washington was never a large slave market, but, as Don E. Fehrenbacher noted, the city was "an important depot in the interstate slave trade," as local slaves were purchased and others, from Maryland, Delaware, or Virginia, were marched across the District of Columbia in chains on their way to southern markets. Even southern politicians and leaders found this aspect of slavery unpleasant or worse. In 1802 a grand jury complained about nonresidents coming to the city "for the purpose of purchasing slaves, where they exhibit to our view a scene of wretchedness and human degradation, disgraceful to our characters as citizens of a free government." So offensive was this trade that in the wake of the War of 1812 Congressman John Randolph, a slave-owning Virginian, proposed a congressional investigation into this "inhuman and illegal traffic."[1] From the founding of the city until the passage of the Compromise of 1850 the nation witnessed persistent demands for an end to open commerce in slaves in the nation's capital.

Yet, despite Randolph's protest, and those of various slaveholding residents of the city, slave trading was inseparable from slavery itself. It is impossible to have a regime based on property without providing a market for that

---

[1]Don E. Fehrenbacher, *The Slaveholding Republic: An Account of the United States Government's Relations to Slavery* (New York, 2001), pp. 66–67.

property. Slaves were property, and Washington, D.C., was a slave city, to the satisfaction of its southern residents and to the disgust of many northerners who came to do business in the national seat of government.

THUS WASHINGTON, D.C., embodied the great contradiction of American life. The nation *was* indeed born in freedom. Self-consciously Americans declared that all people were "created equal" and "endowed . . . with certain unalienable rights," which included "Life, Liberty, and the pursuit of Happiness."[2] Equality, liberty, freedom, and similar words were fundamental to the American political lexicon. America was a beacon of freedom even before the Statue of Liberty beckoned new immigrants; it was an icon for all who hoped for a better future well before Lincoln declared the nation was "the last best hope of earth."[3] How was it, then, that slavery was everywhere in the capital city of the land of the free? And how did that affect the culture of the city and the culture of national politics?

The shock of a slave society in the national capital becomes more obvious when we remember the extraordinary level of political freedom that whites achieved in early America. This freedom also contrasts dramatically with the lack of freedom in most of Europe, where there were few democracies, very limited suffrage, and at best religious toleration, with religious minorities almost always denied access to political power and often economic liberty. From the end of the Revolution until the Civil War the nation created a remarkably free political culture for whites and, at least in some parts of the North, for free blacks. The United States was the world's first modern Republic with fundamental rights spread across the population. At the time of the American Revolution, and for much of the period after it, religious discrimination was the rule in Europe and most New World colonies. In most of Europe's Protestant nations Catholics and Jews had almost no political rights and often had limited economic and social rights. At best they might be free to quietly worship as they wished. Most of Catholic Europe had expelled its Protestants and totally disfranchised (or expelled) its Jews. Universities, learned professions, and positions of authority in civilian or military life were bounded by religion.

Such conditions simply did not exist in America. After the Revolution there were no religious tests for voting, property ownership, entrance to professions,

---

[2] Preamble, Declaration of Independence.
[3] Abraham Lincoln, "Annual Message to Congress," Dec. 1, 1862, in *The Collected Works of Abraham Lincoln*, ed. Roy P. Basler (New Brunswick, N.J., 1953), 5:537.

or attendance in schools and universities. Although the new United States was overwhelmingly Protestant, during the Revolution Jews and Catholics had served honorably, not merely as cannon fodder but also as officers and diplomats. Most of the postrevolutionary state constitutions had religious tests for office holding—with some states limiting the right to Protestants and others to "Christians." But this, too, changed quickly. In 1801 Jefferson could brag in his first inaugural that Americans had "banished from our land that religious intolerance under which mankind so long bled and suffered."[4] When Jefferson took office a few states still maintained established churches and some states still had religious tests for office holding, but by the beginning of the antebellum period most of these limitations had disappeared. In the Revolution, Jews and Catholics held military commissions, and by the antebellum period Jews and Catholics had held appointed and elected office throughout the Republic.

Along with religious tests for officeholding, most states abolished economic tests for both voting and officeholding. By the 1830s universal adult white male suffrage was the rule almost everywhere in the nation. This was something simply unknown in Europe. In a few northern states blacks and Indians were also able to vote. Most white male Americans imagined they lived in the freest nation on earth.[5]

Even before the expansion of the franchise in the 1820s and 1830s, Americans secured freedom of thought and expression in political debate. The transition from the Federalists, under Adams, to the Republicans, under Jefferson, was truly remarkable. After a nasty and vicious election campaign, the opposition party peacefully took office, and the defeated chief executive quietly left the capital without any fanfare. Never before had such a peaceful revolution in political power taken place. Jefferson acknowledged as much in his extraordinarily conciliatory inaugural address, declaring, "All, too, will bear in mind this sacred principle, that though the will of the majority is in all cases to prevail, that will to be rightful must be reasonable; that the minority possess their equal rights, which equal law must protect, and to violate would be oppression."[6] He proudly argued that the true political ideology of

---

[4]Thomas Jefferson, First Inaugural Address, March 4, 1801, http://avalon.law.yale.edu/19th_century/jefinau1.asp.

[5]Women, of course, were excluded from the political process, but this made America no different than Europe. In other areas of life, such as the emergence of married women's property acts and access to education, American women probably saw themselves as far freer than their European counterparts.

[6]Ibid.

the new nation was support for the Constitution and a love of liberty. Thus he proclaimed that "every difference of opinion is not a difference of principle. We have called by different names brethren of the same principle. We are all Republicans, we are all Federalists. If there be any among us who would wish to dissolve this Union or to change its republican form, let them stand undisturbed as monuments of the safety with which error of opinion may be tolerated where reason is left free to combat it."[7]

This magnanimous rhetoric was not an entirely accurate portrayal of early politics. Under Adams the national government had persecuted the political opposition with a federal sedition act. Jefferson denounced the act as a violation of states' rights, but as president he could not live up to his own rhetoric about not persecuting the minority. He urged his supporters to prosecute his critics under state laws, and thus Federalist printers in New York, Pennsylvania, and other states were hauled into state courts by Jefferson's local allies. In Connecticut, where the Federalists were still in power, his handpicked U.S. district attorney prosecuted Jefferson's critics, claiming that there was a federal common law of seditious libel. This was done with the acquiescence of a newly appointed federal district judge, who was also a Jefferson ally.[8]

This rejection of true political debate by both the Adams administration and Jefferson was short lived. Public reaction to the suppression of political speech by either the Federalists or the Republicans was decidedly negative, and most scholars believe that the Sedition Act prosecutions by the Adams administration helped lead to his defeat in 1800. By the time Jefferson left office the political system had evolved. Never again would the government use its power to prosecute the mainstream political opposition.

Indeed, by the 1830s white Americans had more liberty and political rights than any other people in the Atlantic world. Party politics were vigorous, and debate in Congress and the newspapers was more open than anywhere else. For most people America was truly "the land of the free."

BUT OF COURSE underneath this patina of liberty was the striking reality, from the very beginning of the nation, that the United States was a slaveholders' republic. At the time of the Revolution slavery was legal in all of the thirteen colonies. The prominence of slave owners in the movement

---

[7]Ibid.

[8]In *United States v. Hudson and Goodwin*, 11 U.S. 32 (1812), the Supreme Court would rule that there was no federal common law of crimes and thus there could be no seditious libel prosecutions unless Congress passed a law allowing them.

against royal authority—George Washington, Patrick Henry, George Mason, Edward Rutledge, Charles Cotesworth Pinckney, Charles Carroll of Carrollton, Richard Henry Lee—led the English intellectual Samuel Johnson to neatly sum up the irony of the Revolution and especially Thomas Jefferson's authorship of the Declaration of Independence: "How is it that we hear the loudest *yelps* for liberty among the drivers of negroes?"[9] The question was reasonable. The United States offered the odd example of a slaveholding society in which the master class had led a revolution against a hereditary monarch, even though that master class believed deeply in the legitimacy of enslaving people based on inherited status.

By the end of the Revolution the four New England states as well as Pennsylvania had either ended slavery outright or taken steps to gradually abolish it by guaranteeing that the children of all existing slaves would be born free.[10] But in the rest of the nation—all the southern states as well as New York and New Jersey—slavery was secure, viable, and profitable. At the Constitutional Convention the southern delegates were enormously successful in winning explicit protections for slavery. The three-fifths clause gave them seats in Congress based on the number of slaves in their states, and this carried over to the Electoral College, because electoral votes were based on congressional representation. In two separate places (Article I and Article IV) the new government pledged to use the national army to suppress slave rebellions. Article I, Section 9, of the Constitution prohibited Congress from ending the African slave trade before 1808 but did not require that the trade ever end. The fugitive slave clause of Article IV gave masters a constitutional right to recover runaway slaves who fled to free states. Most important, the structure of the Constitution gave slavery important protections. As a government of limited and enumerated powers, Congress lacked the authority to interfere with the domestic institutions of the states. In theory the Constitution could be amended to give Congress such powers, but any amendment would require the endorsement of three-quarters of

[9] Quoted in Donald Robinson, *Slavery in the Structure of American Politics, 1765–1820* (New York, 1971), p. 80. On Jefferson, see Paul Finkelman, *Slavery and the Founders: Race and Liberty in the Age of Jefferson*, 2d ed. (Armonk, N.Y., 2001).

[10] Massachusetts and New Hampshire abolished slavery by constitutional provisions (as did the fourteenth state, Vermont), while Pennsylvania, Connecticut, and Rhode Island passed gradual emancipation acts. See Arthur Zilversmit, *The First Emancipation: The Abolition of Slavery in the North* (Chicago, 1967) and Paul Finkelman, *An Imperfect Union: Slavery, Federalism, and Comity* (Chapel Hill, 1981).

the states. This gave the slave states a perpetual veto over any constitutional amendment.[11]

After the convention southern supporters of the new system of government proudly urged their states to ratify the Constitution because it would protect their most important social and economic institution. When Antifederalists in the Virginia ratifying convention insisted that the new Constitution threatened slavery, Edmund Randolph, who had headed the Virginia delegation in Philadelphia, asked "*Where* is the part that has a tendency to the *abolition of* slavery?" He answered his own question, asserting, "Were it right here to mention what passed in [the Philadelphia] convention . . . I might tell you *that the Southern States, even South Carolina herself, conceived this property to be secure*" and "There was not a member of the Virginia delegation who had *the smallest suspicion of the abolition of slavery.*"[12] General Charles Cotesworth Pinckney, who led the South Carolina delegation, told his state legislature, "We have a security that the general government can never emancipate them, for no such authority is granted and it is admitted, on all hands, that the general government has no powers but what are expressly granted by the Constitution, and that all rights not expressed were reserved by the several states." Thus he proudly told his fellow planters and slave owners, "In short, considering all circumstances, we have made the best terms for the security of this species of property it was in our power to make. We would have made better if we could; but on the whole, I do not think them bad."[13]

THIS VOLUME EXPLORES two aspects of the implementation of the "security of this species of property": how slavery operated in the nation's capital and how slavery affected congressional debates in the crucial years between the emergence of radical abolition in 1831 and the debates over the Compromise of 1850. Most of these essays focus on the domestic nature of slavery in Washington, D.C., the debates over slavery in Congress, and the way each affected the other. The political debates over slavery were affected by the fact that they took place in a slaveholding city. Similarly, the day-to-day reality of

---

[11]In 1860 there were fifteen slave states. It would take forty-five free states to outvote them to end slavery by constitutional amendment. Thus, even in the modern fifty-state Union it would be impossible to end slavery by constitutional amendment.

[12]Jonathan Elliot, *The Debates in the Several State Conventions on the Adoption of the Federal Constitution*, 5 vols. (1888; reprint ed., New York, 1987), 3:598–99.

[13]Pinckney quoted in Elliot, *Debates*, 4:286.

slavery in Washington was affected by the fact that it was the national capital and that the U.S. Constitution and the Bill of Rights directly affected what would otherwise have been local law. All of these issues were also affected, as David Brion Davis demonstrates in the opening chapter of this book, by the international context of emancipation and antislavery. As Davis shows, the British abolitionist movement affected not only how American opponents responded to slavery, but also how southerners responded to the opposition to slavery. As slavery came to an end in the former Spanish colonies of Mexico and South America, and then the British Caribbean, the slaveholding South became increasingly isolated in the Atlantic world. These outside events, as Davis has taught us for more than four decades, and reminds us here, affected American politics and slavery in the district, just as they helped shape the American antislavery movement.[14]

While outside forces and ideas affected the discussion of slavery in Congress and the day-to-day workings of slavery in the district, the Constitution and the political structure of the nation were more directly at issue. The Constitution gave Congress plenary power to govern the national capital, which became the District of Columbia. This meant that Congress at least theoretically had the power to end slavery there. In his only term in Congress, 1847–49, Abraham Lincoln drafted legislation to do precisely that, but this quixotic plan from an obscure first-term congressman never reached the floor. In fact, such a bill would never have passed. Southerners would have blocked it in the Senate and any debate in the House would have led to threats of secession from the slaveholders in that body. In the 1840s opponents of slavery in Congress hoped they might limit the spread of slavery into the territories and restrict the admission of new slave states. At best, they wanted to stop slavery from spreading; they understood that there was no realistic possibility of ending slavery where it was already entrenched, even in the national capital, where Congress had the political power to do so.

Indeed, rather than threaten slavery in the District of Columbia, Congress almost always protected it. The district had been carved out of land from Virginia and Maryland, and initially Congress simply adopted the laws of those states as the local law of the nation's capital. Thus, in Washington

---

[14]See generally David Brion Davis, *The Problem of Slavery in Western Culture* (Ithaca, N.Y., 1966), and David Brion Davis, *The Problem of Slavery in the Age of Revolution, 1779–1823* (Ithaca, N.Y., 1975).

County (which constitutes the present-day district), Maryland's slave laws were in force, while in Alexandria, Virginia law was in force—until 1846, when Congress gave that part of the city back to Virginia. Indeed, as Glenn Crothers shows in his essay "The 1846 Retrocession of Alexandria: Protecting Slavery and the Slave Trade in the District of Columbia," one reason for returning Alexandria to Virginia was to protect the slave trade there and give residents of the district easy access to buying and selling slaves. At its creation in 1800, Washington was a slave city and the law of slavery was everywhere. It would remain that way until the Civil War.

In the antebellum period opponents of slavery were able to gain one right in the national capital that they did not have had in any other slave city. Like most southern cities, Washington lived in fear of slave revolts and sought to limit free speech that might undermine slavery or encourage slave unrest. Thus, in 1836 a Connecticut physician, Reuben Crandall, was prosecuted for bringing antislavery pamphlets into the district. Ignoring the idea that the First Amendment protected freedom of speech and freedom of the press, the district attorney secured his indictment. Perhaps because Washington was a national city, and not all residents were either southerners or proslavery, a jury acquitted him. Ironically, the prosecutor in this case was Francis Scott Key, the author of the Star Spangled Banner, which would ultimately become the national anthem. The spectacle of Key prosecuting someone for the mere possession of antislavery material underscores the proslavery culture of the national capital and how deeply slavery was embedded in American political culture. Crandall's acquittal, on the other hand, illustrates that however much Washington was a slave city, it was also a national city.[15]

Crandall's acquittal helped differentiate Washington from cities in slave states. Before the Civil War the First Amendment did not apply to the states, but it did apply to the national capital, and thus there was more free speech there than in other slave cities. By the 1840s and 1850s there was relative free speech in the district and opponents of slavery were free to attack the institution, as long as their rhetoric was mild and could not be construed as encouragement to slave revolts. Thus the abolitionist Gamaliel Bailey even published an antislavery newspaper there, the *National Era*. This would have been impossible in any other slave city in the nation. The two essays in this

---

[15]On Crandall, see Paul Finkelman, *Slavery in the Courtroom* (Washington, D.C., 1985), pp. 164–70.

volume on Bailey by Jonathan Earle and Stanley Harrold illustrate his importance to both the national antislavery movement and the antislavery community. The Bailey household, which was at the center of antislavery activity and agitation, could not have operated in any other southern city. But as a national city, there was significant freedom of speech and press, at least for whites.

However, any other abolitionist activity might lead to severe punishment. In 1848 Daniel Drayton and Edward Sayers were captured for attempting to help slaves escape from the district aboard their ship, the *Pearl*. The district attorney, Philip Barton Key—the son of Francis Scott Key—secured 115 separate indictments against each man. Unlike his father in the Crandall case, Philip Key was able to win a conviction of Drayton, who was then sentenced to twenty years in prison for conviction on one of the indictments. Key's plan was to prosecute each man on each indictment, if necessary, to ensure they spend time in prison. Key could not get the jury to convict Sayers in his first two trials, and Drayton's conviction was later reversed on appeal. Still facing multiple indictments, the two men agreed to pay fines and court costs totaling more than $20,000. When they could not raise this money, they were sent to prison, where they remained until they were pardoned in 1852.[16] The chapter by Mary K. Ricks in this volume helps us better understand the story of the *Pearl* in the context of the city of Washington and thus illustrates the connection between the city's free black community, the slave community, and antislavery. Mary Beth Corrigan, meanwhile, explores the family connections of the city's slave community, which also helps us understand how the life of slaves and free blacks in the national capital was affected by the southernness of the city and also how life in this slaveholding city was affected by the fact that it was a national city.

Despite the relative free speech for antislavery whites, and the greater opportunities for slaves and free blacks than in the rest of the South, the nation's capital remained a slaveholders' city and the capital of the slaveholding Republic. Only once before the Civil War would Congress limit slavery in any way. Congress banned the public sale of slaves in the district as part of the Compromise of 1850. However, this was hardly more than a symbolic

[16]See ibid., pp. 179–81, and Fehrenbacher, *Slaveholding Republic*, pp. 49–53; Stanley Harrold, "The Pearl Affair: The Washington Riot of 1848," *Columbia Historical Society Records* 50 (1980):140–60.

loss for the South, since masters could still privately buy and sell slaves. And, as Professor Crothers reminds us, they could also take them across the river to sell them in Alexandria, which had recently been ceded back to Virginia. Most important, southerners also understood that the ending of the public slave trade was a small—and mostly symbolic—price to pay for the huge gain that came from the passage of the draconian Fugitive Slave Act of 1850. David Zarefsky's discussion of the debates over the annexation of Texas, as well as James B. Stewart's chapter on Joshua Giddings, remind us that understanding slavery in the district cannot be divorced from politics. Similarly these three essays remind us that the politics of slavery cannot be understood without remembering that the debates over slavery took place in a slave city.

Whether slaves were publicly sold in the district or not, slavery remained an important social and economic institution in Washington throughout this period. This was true even though the number of slaves declined. In 1830 there were about 4,500 slaves in the district, constituting about 15 percent of the total population. Another 4,500 or so free blacks also lived in the district, making the nation's capital about 30 percent black. While not subject to the harsh regulations of slavery, these nonslaves were hardly free in any traditional sense. They were restricted by all sorts of laws, regulations, and informal rules that limited their opportunities and left them vulnerable to the whims of white law enforcement and congressional regulation. Moreover, many of the free blacks had slave relatives. Slave status in America was matrilineal. Thus, if a slave woman married a free black man, their children were also slaves, and conversely the children of an enslaved man were free if his spouse was free. Complicating these many unions between free blacks and slaves was another legal reality: no slave could ever be legally married. Thus, black families in the district were often complicated mixtures of slaves and free people, none of whom might be legally married. Furthermore, since any slave might be sold at a master's whim, any unions between slaves and free blacks were always vulnerable to destruction through sale.

From 1830 to 1850 the white population of the district grew much faster than the slave or free black population. Thus in 1850 blacks constituted about 26 percent of the city's 51,700 people, but of the 13,700 blacks in the city only 3,700 were slaves. The relative decline in the slave and free black population was in part a result of returning Alexandria to Virginia. But, this changing demographic also suggests that some Washington masters were selling their slaves further South, just as other masters in the Chesapeake region were doing. For example, many of the 76 slaves found on the *Pearl* were immediately sold and removed from the city, perhaps with some of their relatives. The fact that free blacks were also implicated in this attempted mass escape illustrates the complex relationship of free blacks to slaves in the nation's capital. Finally, in the 1840s more northerners may have been moving into the district, and they would not have brought slaves with them. Still, even with this shrinking of the slave population, the city remained very much a southern city and a slave city.

Slavery in the district exacerbated increasing tensions over the problem of slavery in the nation. For northerners, slavery in the district symbolized how much the "slave power" controlled the nation. The sight of slaves in chains, in the shadow of the national Capitol, underscored that the United States was not really the land of the free. On the other hand, for southerners slavery was key to the social and economic order of Washington society. At the political level, for southerners to openly hold slaves in the national capital symbolized the legitimacy of what they increasingly recognized as a peculiar institution.

These symbolic issues were important, as was slave labor to the Washington community, especially because from 1820 to 1850 Congress constantly debated slavery. Western expansion, which included the acquisition of new territory and the admission of new states, was a central aspect of American public policy between 1820 and 1850. Slavery complicated these issues. As David Zarefsky demonstrates, for northerners the annexation of Texas was an unconstitutional and dangerous acquisition of a vast and useless tract of land solely to allow for a new slave state. Opponents of Texas annexation correctly predicted it would lead to war with Mexico, which would lead to demands for new slave territories. The debates over Texas annexation were fierce. Initially President John Tyler negotiated a treaty with the Republic of Texas, but he could not obtain the necessary two-thirds vote in the Senate to ratify it. He then asked for a regular bill, with a simple majority in both Houses of Congress, allowing for the annexation of Texas. Opponents of Texas annexation considered this to be unconstitutional, but the bill passed, Tyler signed it, and Texas became a state.

Soon after that the United States was at war with Mexico, which had never recognized Texas independence. That led to more debate in Congress and, ultimately, to the Compromise of 1850. That compromise did not, of course, solve the problem of slavery in the West or in the nation. It only exacerbated the conflicts, setting the stage for more failed compromises, the collapse of both major political parties, and ultimately the collapse of the Union itself. The issues discussed here illustrate how slavery corroded politics and public life in the national capital. Politics is often called the "art of the possible." Slavery, as the essays in this volume illustrate, undermined real freedom in the nation's capital and, in the end, made politics impossible.

1: Congress and Slavery in Context

David Brion Davis

The Impact of British Abolitionism
on American Sectionalism

IT IS DIFFICULT for us historians to free ourselves from at least the unconscious assumption that American slavery was doomed from the start,
that it was destined to collapse when confronted with the liberal forces of
inevitable progress that supposedly lie at the heart of Western civilization. It
is therefore hard for us to take seriously the detailed argument of the major
southern leader James Henry Hammond, who on February 1, 1836, assured
Congress that because of its extraordinary economic value and importance,
southern slavery "could never be abolished." "The thing is physically impossible," Hammond stressed.[1]

I will return in a moment to the kind of evidence Hammond presented.
Despite this seeming confidence, Hammond's own outbursts of insecurity on
the floor of the House and later in the Senate, along with the fears of most
of his southern colleagues, point the way to my central question: Why did
southern leaders feel so threatened, vulnerable, and potentially weak and
then overreact in counterproductive ways when they actually enjoyed such
immense political and economic power, when they were protected by the
national two-party system, to say nothing of blatant northern racism and
strong northern allies, and were opposed, at least before the 1850s, by a small,
weak, and divided abolitionist movement?

---

[1] William Lee Miller, *Arguing about Slavery: The Great Battle in the United States Congress* (New
York, 1996), pp. 9–10.

My answer, in large part, points to Great Britain, even though—and this magnifies the problem—there was much agreement in Britain by the 1840s and 1850s that Parliament's so-called mighty experiment of slave emancipation had been an economic disaster.[2]

Turning first to political power, southern slaveholding presidents governed the nation for fifty of the seventy-two years between the inaugurations of Washington and Lincoln, and before Lincoln none of the northern presidents challenged the slaveholding interests (except, of course, John Quincy Adams when he was a congressman). In the U.S. Senate, where senators from slave states roughly balanced those from free states, the president pro tempore was almost always a slaveholder. Slaveholders also constituted the majority of cabinet members and Supreme Court justices. It is hardly surprising that what the late Don Fehrenbacher terms "the Slaveholding Republic" conducted a proslavery foreign policy, exemplified in 1842 by Secretary of State Daniel Webster's suggestion of possible war against Britain following the British treatment of the black insurgents who had revolted and captured the American slave ship *Creole*. Nor is it surprising that the succession of major political compromises, beginning with the Missouri Crisis of 1819–21, largely favored the South.[3]

As for economic realities, Hammond noted that even the British government had not dared to emancipate its 800,000 colonial slaves without giving their owners some compensation. He estimated that the staggering £20 million came to about 60 percent of the slaves' value, but failed to add that, together with the money paid to slaveholders or their creditors, the continuing forced and uncompensated labor of the so-called West Indian apprentices, which would not end until 1838, would come close to equaling the slaves' value.[4]

---

[2]Unfortunately, the best and most informative studies of the effects of British abolitionism on American sectional politics have not yet been published. I have learned a great deal from Joe Bassette Wilkins, Jr., "Window on Freedom: The South's Response to the Emancipation of Slaves in the British West Indies, 1833–1861," Ph.D. diss., University of South Carolina, 1977; Steven Heath Mitton, "The Free World Confronted: The Problem of Slavery and Progress in American Foreign Relations, 1833–1844," Ph.D. diss., Louisiana State University, 2005; and Edward Bartlett Rugemer, "The Problem of Emancipation: The United States and Britain's Abolition of Slavery," Ph.D. diss., Boston College, 2005.

[3]Don E. Fehrenbacher (completed and edited by Ward M. McAfee), *The Slaveholding Republic: An Account of the United States Government's Relations to Slavery* (New York, 2001); I am also drawing on my own *Inhuman Bondage: The Rise and Fall of Slavery in the New World* (New York, 2006).

[4]Robert William Fogel, *Without Consent or Contract: The Rise and Fall of American Slavery* (New York, 1989), p. 228.

The crucial point, Hammond stressed, was that the value of America's 2.3 million slaves in early 1836 "would amount to upwards of nine hundred millions," that the value of the annual increase of 60,000 slaves would come to another $24 million, and that therefore the cost of freeing all slaves in one hundred years "would require an *annual* [my italics] appropriation of be-tween thirty-three and thirty-four millions of dollars." That amount was at least equal to all the annual revenue collected by the federal government and did not include, Hammond noted, any costs of transporting the freed slaves outside the United States—an issue the British had no need to face, but a necessary requirement, in the minds of most American leaders and probably most American whites, for any viable emancipation.[5] Even the grad-ual emancipation of slaves in the North increased the degree and intensity of racism in the northern states, the depth of which is difficult for us today to imagine.

I should add that by 1860 most New World emancipations had included a form of compensation to slaveholders. By then the nearly four million southern slaves' value came to an estimated $3.5 billion in 1860 dollars. That would be about $68.4 billion in 2003 dollars. But a more revealing figure is the fact that the nation's gross national product in 1860 was only about 20 percent above the value of slaves, which means that as a share of to-day's gross national product, the slaves' value would come to an estimated $9.75 trillion.[6]

As investment capital, the value of the nation's slaves in 1860 far ex-ceeded (by perhaps a billion dollars) the cash value of all the farms in the South, including the border states of Delaware, Maryland, Kentucky, and Missouri. In 1860 the southern slaves were also worth three times the cost of constructing all the nation's railroads or three times the combined capital invested nationally in business and industrial property.[7]

Of course this highly valued property was closely tied in with national productivity, exports, imports, investment, trade, insurance, banking, textile manufacturing, and a host of other activities I have no time to discuss. From the 1820s to 1860 racial slavery was such a deeply integral part of America's society and economy that it was reasonable for even an optimist like the well-informed Abraham Lincoln to predict in 1858 that any peaceful abolition of

---

[5]Miller, *Arguing about Slavery*, p. 10.
[6]I am much indebted to Professor Stanley L. Engerman for providing and verifying these numbers in personal correspondence.
[7]Davis, *Inhuman Bondage*, p. 298.

the institution would take at least one hundred years; Lincoln, in other words, was thinking of what we now term the civil rights era![8] When considering the seeming security of the South's expanding and not so peculiar institution, we should remember such diverse things as the anti-abolitionist mobs and riots in the North; the persistence of legal slavery in New York until 1827, in Connecticut until 1848, and in New Jersey until the Civil War; the total absence of southern slave revolts after 1831, despite the rise of radical abolitionism, John Brown's raid, and even multiple Union invasions of the South in the Civil War. Let me add the thriving if illegal nineteenth-century Atlantic slave trade and the lack of any prospects for slave emancipation in Cuba or Brazil before the American Civil War. In fact, it was only because of the Revolution of 1848 that France and Denmark freed their colonial slaves; Holland took action only in 1863, partly as a result of the American Civil War; and the enslavement of blacks persisted in the Middle East to at least the 1960s and can be found in parts of Africa to the present day.

Further, the widespread assumption that justifications for slavery had been wholly repudiated in the nonslaveholding world is at least partially questioned by a 1853 decision of a joint commission, established by Britain and America to deal with a list of private claims against both governments. One key issue concerned the American rebel slaves who in 1842 had steered the slave ship *Creole* to British Nassau. The commission's umpire finally ruled that Britain, which had validated the freedom of the insurgents, had to pay $110,330 in compensation to the American claimants.[9]

These thoughts bring me back to my initial question and to Anglo-American relations. In the celebrated year 1808, Britain and the United States simultaneously outlawed their countrymen's involvement in the African slave trade. But these landmark actions occurred in entirely different historical contexts and conveyed entirely different implications. Since the 1680s, the British had been the leading carriers of African slaves to the New World, and the slave populations in the British Caribbean could not begin to reproduce themselves without a large and continuing influx of African coerced labor. Parliament's law of 1807 abolishing the slave trade in 1808 was the climax of twenty years of abolitionist agitation, petitioning, and public mobilization—

---

[8]Abraham Lincoln, "Fourth Debate with Stephen A. Douglas at Charleston, Illinois, September 18, 1858," in *The Collected Works of Abraham Lincoln*, 9 vols., ed. Roy P. Basler (New Brunswick, N.J., 1953), 3:181.

[9]Fehrenbacher, *Slaveholding Republic*, pp. 108–10.

a humanitarian triumph that reformers saw as the first and essential step toward the gradual emancipation of all British colonial slaves.[10]

In America it was the slaveholding President Thomas Jefferson who in 1807 called upon Congress to enact a slave-trade abolition law which the Constitution of 1787 had absolutely prohibited for the next twenty years. In America there had been nothing comparable to Britain's strong, national abolitionist movement, but there was also no need, as in Britain, to overcome the formidable political power of groups like the West India planters and merchants. Most important, the slave population in the American South had long been rapidly increasing by natural means. In Upper South states like Virginia there was a great desire to keep the state's population as white as possible by reducing the growing black/white ratio and also by ensuring a continuing market for their own surplus slaves in the Deep South and Southwest.[11]

Moreover, in terms of moral ideology, outlawing the slave trade enabled the more scrupulous planters to build a mental wall separating them from the violence of African "slave-making" and from the publicized horrors of the Middle Passage. By 1820 Virginia congressman Charles Fenton Mercer could even be hailed as "the American Wilberforce" when he helped secure a law that made participating in the African slave trade a crime punishable with death.[12]

Despite the striking differences between the meaning and implications of the British and American abolition laws, exemplified by the two countries'

---

[10]See especially Seymour Drescher, *Econocide: British Slavery in the Era of Abolition* (Pittsburgh, 1977); Roger Anstey, *The Atlantic Slave Trade and British Abolition, 1760–1810* (London, 1975); and Adam Hochschild, *Bury the Chains: Prophets and Rebels in the Fight to Free an Empire's Slaves* (Boston, 2005).

[11]In Virginia the natural increase in the slave population began by the 1720s; a similar increase began in South Carolina in the 1770s. While the national census did not begin until 1790 and 1800, leaders in the Chesapeake had long been aware of the increasing black population and had even tried to limit or cut off slave imports before the American Revolution.

[12]Davis, *Inhuman Bondage*, pp. 274–75; Douglas R. Egerton, *Charles Fenton Mercer and the Trial of National Conservatism* (Jackson, Miss., 1989), pp. 164–68. Significantly, the southern critique of British abolitionism sometimes exempted Wilberforce, who had devoted most of his efforts to ending the slave trade. Thus the influential *Southern Literary Messenger* conceded in 1842 that Wilberforce and his associates were "as pure philanthropists as the world ever saw." Yet this writer added that men in the British government had converted "this noble and generous feeling of the *people* at large" into an instrument "of national aggrandizement, and . . . a cloak for their designs upon America" ("Our Relations with England," *Southern Literary Messenger* 8 (1842):381, 387–96.

wholly opposite policies with respect to their own *internal* slave trading within the British Caribbean, and within the southern American states and coast-lines, abolitionism itself had acquired a transatlantic character from the very beginning, in the 1780s. The early history of these reform movements owed much, on both sides of the Atlantic, to such Americans as Anthony Benezet, Benjamin Rush, and William Dillwyn—an American Quaker expatriate who became a key organizer of the British movement—as well as to Britons like Granville Sharp and Thomas Clarkson.[13]

James Cropper, a wealthy British Quaker who became an initiator and central figure in the British antislavery movement of the 1820s and early 1830s, maintained close ties with pioneer American abolitionists like Benjamin Lundy, also a Quaker. Lundy, who opposed the movement to colonize blacks outside the United States and would later have a decisive role in preparing William Lloyd Garrison for his famous antislavery crusade, reprinted in his magazine in the mid-1820s the radical appeal for "immediate, not gradual emancipation" by the English Quaker Elizabeth Heyrick. It was Cropper who raised funds to send the British abolitionist agent Charles Stuart to America, where he converted to the cause such crucial figures as Theodore Dwight Weld. Meanwhile, Garrison sailed to Liverpool, where he stayed in Cropper's mansion and raised funds for the American cause while helping Cropper undermine the American colonization movement in Britain.[14]

Southern politicians and writers were especially alarmed by the arrival in America of British militant speakers like George Thompson, who was confronted and physically threatened by angry mobs in the North, as well as by the number of free black abolitionists who continued to tour the British Isles. And given the global outreach of the British and Foreign Anti-Slavery Society, to say nothing of the World Anti-Slavery Conventions held in London in

---

[13]For a new and brilliant analysis of the origins of British abolitionism, which had much to do with Britons' responses to the success of Americans in winning independence in 1783, see Christopher Leslie Brown, *Moral Capital: Foundations of British Abolitionism* (Chapel Hill, 2006).

[14]David Brion Davis, *The Problem of Slavery in the Age of Revolution, 1775–1823* (1975; rev. ed., New York, 1999), pp. 49–50, 62–63; Davis, "The Emergence of Immediatism in British and American Antislavery Thought," "James Cropper and the British Anti-Slavery Movement, I: 1821–1823, II: 1823–1833," in *From Homicide to Slavery: Studies in American Culture* (New York, 1986), pp. 238–89; Richard J. Blackett, "The Global Garrison: America's Premier Radical Abolitionist and the International Response," Fifth David Brion Davis Lecture, sponsored by the Gilder Lehrman Center for the Study of Slavery, Resistance, and Abolition, Yale University, Apr. 3, 2006.

1840 and 1843, it was easy for southern leaders like John C. Calhoun and James Henry Hammond to conclude that American abolitionists had become the tools of a monarchic, imperialistic country that was searching for methods to undermine the world's only democracy while ignoring the plight of women and children working in the British mines, to say nothing of the starving Irish. Indeed, by the 1840s many proslavery writers implied that there would be no difficulty in disposing of native abolitionists if it were not for the support they received from a foreign power, from what many Americans had long perceived as America's "natural enemy."[15]

Meanwhile, moving back in time, three massive slave revolts in the British Caribbean, in 1816, 1823, and 1831, seemed to confirm the subversive causal connection between ANY abolitionist agitation and slave uprisings. This lesson had been etched in slaveholders' minds throughout the New World by the incredible Haitian Revolution of 1791–1804, the only time in human history when hundreds of thousands of slaves succeeded in winning their own freedom and independence by overthrowing their masters and defeating the best armies of the time—British, Spanish, and French.[16] According to widely accepted mythology, this unprecedented slaughter of the master race had originally been ignited by the propaganda of French abolitionists, or the Amis des Noirs. Despite the efforts of British abolitionists to refute this theory, it badly damaged their cause from 1794 to the early 1800s, when Napoleon's reinstitution of slavery and the slave trade gave a patriotic stamp to British abolitionism. Many decades later Gov. George McDuffie of South Carolina could remind his legislature of the fearful consequences of what he called "*amis des noirs* philanthropy," which like later antislavery movements had had a "small and contemptible beginning." In McDuffie's judgment, this meant that "the laws of every community should punish this species of interference with death, without benefit of clergy."[17]

Before commenting on the later revolts in the British Caribbean, I should emphasize that the Amis des Noirs theory seemed to be substantiated in

---

[15]Miller, *Arguing about Slavery*, pp. 33–39, 127–38; David Brion Davis, *The Slave Power Conspiracy and the Paranoid Style* (Baton Rouge, 1969), pp. 43–47. While proslavery speakers and writers identified abolitionists with the older monarchic enemies of democracy, they also linked abolitionism with such modern heresies as Fourierism, "free-loveism," socialism, and communism.

[16]The best recent study is Laurent Dubois, *Avengers of the New World: The Story of the Haitian Revolution* (Cambridge, Mass., 2004).

[17]Reprinted in William Goodell, ed., *Anti-Slavery Lecturer* (Sept. 1839).

many southern minds by the connection between the furious and fiery congressional debates in 1820 over admitting Missouri as a slave state and the bombshell of the Denmark Vesey conspiracy in South Carolina two years later. According to Secretary of State John Quincy Adams, the most explosive point in the Missouri debates came when the southern senators "gnawed their lips and clenched their fists" as they heard New York senator Rufus King not only denounce slavery but declare that "all laws or compacts imposing any such condition upon any human being, are absolutely void, because contrary to the law of nature, which is the law of God."[18] King, who had also fought against slavery in the Constitutional Convention of 1787, could be unfairly dismissed as a self-serving, monarchic, pro-English Federalist who had become a political relic, but his speech immediately encouraged more serious predictions of disunion and civil war.[19]

The import of King's words increased significantly two years later when some of the African American testimony at the Denmark Vesey trials alleged that Vesey or other insurgents knew about and had been inspired by King's speech. As slave informers enabled South Carolina authorities to uncover the alleged conspiracy by interrogating scores of slaves and free blacks, this nonevent became the largest and most momentous symbol of slave resistance in North American history. Significantly, Vesey, now a free black, had briefly worked as a slave in Haiti, then Saint-Domingue. And after burning Charleston and killing most whites, the conspirators by some accounts were planning to escape to Haiti, whose president, Jean-Pierre Boyer, had reportedly been addressed by Vesey. While these outside connections were clearly important, the central message of the blacks' testimony conveyed the

---

[18] *The Diary of John Quincy Adams, 1794–1845*, ed. Allan Nevins (New York, 1951), p. 226; Miller, *Arguing about Slavery*, pp. 179–80; Davis, *Problem of Slavery in the Age of Revolution*, p. 332.

[19] According to Secretary of State John Quincy Adams, Henry Clay, who later played a central role in negotiating the Missouri Compromise, "had not a doubt that within five years from this time the Union would be divided into three distinct confederacies." But Secretary of War John C. Calhoun, who was very close to Adams on a personal level, did not think "the slave question pending in Congress . . . would produce a dissolution of the Union, but, if it should, the South would be from necessity compelled to form an alliance, offensive and defensive, with Great Britain" (*Diary of John Quincy Adams*, pp. 227–28). This remark of Calhoun's is startling until one remembers that Wilberforce had been defeated in 1816 regarding a central registration of slaves and that in 1820 there were no antislavery organizations in Great Britain (James Cropper would not found the first major antislavery society in Liverpool until 1822). In 1820 the antislavery cause in Britain seemed virtually dead, and Calhoun showed a willingness for the South to return "to a colonial state" in order to acquire sea power to cut the North off "from its natural outlet upon the ocean" and presumably to maintain British markets for southern cotton.

secret thoughts, hatred, and desire for revenge internalized by at least some slaves who in everyday life appeared to accept and even appreciate the paternalism of whites.[20]

South Carolinians could only speculate about the actual behavior of nineteenth-century slave rebels, but many British planters came face to face with insurgent reality. What I have called the Amis des Noirs causal thesis seemed to be starkly confirmed when the British abolitionists' parliamentary debates for a centralized registry of slaves sparked a massive uprising in Barbados in 1816, and when new and more radical developments in the British antislavery movement were supposedly the cause of even larger slave revolts in Demerara (part of later British Guiana) in 1823 and Jamaica in 1831. Southern critics ignored the fact that in all three colonies slaves had exercised extraordinary self-discipline in sparing the lives of whites. They burned and gutted hundreds of plantation houses, set fire to many acres of sugarcane, and locked prominent whites in wooden stocks intended for slaves. But in Barbados the rebels killed only one white civilian and one black British soldier; in Demerara the number rose to no more than two or three white men; and in the enormous and prolonged Jamaican rebellion, only fourteen whites were killed, in contrast to 540 slaves. I have argued elsewhere that the elite slaves who led these uprisings were well aware that any widespread killing of whites would undermine their cause in antislavery Britain.[21]

Nevertheless, America's consul in Jamaica, Robert Monroe Harrison, who experienced the 1831 rebellion but seldom strayed from his home in Kingston, wrote to Secretary of State John Forsyth, a fellow proslavery southerner, that Forsyth should try to imagine the feelings of the friends and relatives of murdered husbands who had "their secret parts" cut off and placed in the mouths of their wives and daughters, who themselves were "afterward violated in the most cruel manner." This obsessive conviction that rebellious slaves would rape all the wives and daughters of white men stemmed at least in part from some accounts of the Haitian Revolution and was widely accepted, at least by males, in the antebellum South.

American historians have seldom noted that the massive slave warfare in Jamaica erupted only months after Nat Turner's traumatic killing of nearly sixty whites in Virginia, mostly women and children (there was no evidence

---

[20]For a review of the recent debate among historians over the reality of the Vesey conspiracy, see Davis, *Inhuman Bondage*, pp. 170–71, 210–11, 222–23, 371 n. 38, 385 n. 55, 386 n. 60, 400 n. 33.

[21]Davis, *Inhuman Bondage*, pp. 212–13, 217–21.

of any rapes). Both events also coincided in 1831 with Garrison's inaugura-
tion of a wholly new, radical stage of American abolitionism. Many American slaveholders were also aware of some other seeming coincidences in the
transatlantic world. Beginning in 1830, as the British reformers succeeded in
using itinerant agents to mobilize a vast public movement demanding "immediate slave emancipation," various British West Indian leaders threatened
to secede from the British empire and perhaps join the United States. This
was exactly when South Carolina attempted to prove that an American state
could nullify a law of the federal government (in this case, a tariff, though a
conflict closely related to the slave economy). And South Carolina's initial
failure to nullify a federal law and to mobilize southern support for possible
secession coincided in 1833 with news that Britain had emancipated some
800,000 slaves, and that in Philadelphia white and even some black reformers from various northern states had organized an American Anti-Slavery
Society committed to the immediate emancipation of all slaves in the South.

Accordingly, the years 1830 through 1833 heightened the southern fear
that abolitionists would provoke bloody slave revolts and also dramatized
the danger of centralized governmental power, especially, as seen by slaveholders—a kind of power that could be taken over by abolitionist fanatics if
they could mobilize enough public opinion with their self-righteous propaganda, including highly volatile visual imagery that could directly influence
and inflame illiterate slaves. By 1836 most southern leaders had acquired an
almost paranoid determination to protect the South from abolitionist mail
and to prevent the reception in Congress of abolitionist petitions of any kind.

By the same token, southern eyes focused no less on Britain and the British West Indies. Ironically, the old British "Mother Country," rejected and
castigated from the time of Jefferson's list of indictments in the Declaration
of Independence, continued to be the major market for most of the South's
slave-grown cotton. Yet, as one southern woman wrote to her cousin in England in 1861, the British West Indies had provided the South with a "window" for twenty-seven years—a window for viewing the total disaster of slave
emancipation when British abolitionists won their way. By watching the British since 1834, she added, the South had learned that only resistance, even
the resistance of war, could prevent a West Indian–like collapse into social
and economic ruin.[22]

---

[22]Wilkins, "Window on Freedom," pp. 317–18. Wilkins's work has now been richly extended and reinforced by Rugemer's important dissertation, "The Problem of Emancipation," and by Mitton's no less informative "Free World Confronted."

Even in the 1820s a few South Carolina planters and publicists like James Robert Turnbull, who had been educated in London and had served on the special court in 1822 for the trial of the Denmark Vesey conspirators, scrutinized the emerging British antislavery movement. As a result, they discovered a wholly new phenomenon in the world. It appeared that the original efforts of Granville Sharp, Wilberforce, Clarkson, and their supporters, who seemed to call for nothing more than the outlawing of the African slave trade, had led to an irreversible concatenation of events that included imperialistic interference in the commerce of other nations, dictatorial treatment of the so-called Crown colonies, and then a massive and unprecedented popular outcry for the overthrow of colonial slavery itself. In other words, in the eyes of Turnbull and various others, once a small group of reformers succeeded in hammering in an "entering wedge" and in inflaming a public that had no knowledge of plantation life or of the capacity of Africans for freedom, nothing could prevent the destruction of millions of dollars worth of property and of entire social systems.[23]

But as matters developed, the period of coerced labor "apprenticeship" from 1834 to 1838 gave even American southerners the impression that Britain's mighty experiment had been an economic success. "Mighty experiment," implying a decision based on scientific economic knowledge, was the term Colonial Secretary Edward Stanley (later Lord Derby) had used when he presented the government's emancipation resolution to Parliament.[24] By 1840 the British started to buy slaves in West Africa and then nominally free and redefine them as indentured servants to be sent to the West Indies. But this policy was soon limited by abolitionist protest and apparently received little publicity.[25] The British government did privately acknowledge the extent of the West Indian disaster in 1843 when the conservative Peel ministry secretly approached America's proslavery Secretary of State Abel P. Upshur with a proposal to allow agents to recruit large numbers of American free blacks to replace the former plantation slaves, who in such colonies as Jamaica, Trinidad, and British Guiana were now refusing to work on

---

[23]Manisha Sinha, *The Counterrevolution of Slavery: Politics and Ideology in Antebellum South Carolina* (Chapel Hill, 2000); Wilkins, "Window of Freedom"; Frederick Merk, *Slavery and the Annexation of Texas* (New York, 1972); Brit. Emp. E 1/19, 10–11, MSS, British Library, London.

[24]For the motivations and consequences of this landmark decision, see Seymour Drescher's brilliant *The Mighty Experiment: Free Labor versus Slavery in British Emancipation* (New York, 2002).

[25]See the sources I cite in Davis, *Slavery and Human Progress* (New York, 1984), p. 351 n. 165.

plantations. As the British minister put it to Upshur, Britain's most important colonies were suffering "severely in their productive industry from a dearth of agricultural laborers."[26]

After Upshur and his successor, John C. Calhoun, grasped the full meaning of this rejected proposal (and England ultimately turned to so-called coolies from India to replace many thousands of slaves), southern leaders became convinced that Britain was now determined to undermine all competitive slave societies, a plan exemplified by Britain's intervention in Texas and Cuba, and use of Canada as a refuge for American fugitives.

Meanwhile, the Anglo-Texans' declaration of independence from Mexico in 1836 aroused British fear that an independent slaveholding Texas republic could quickly become, like contemporary Cuba, a vast new market for slaves transported from Africa. When it became apparent that the immediate annexation of Texas by the United States was not politically expedient, Britain secretly made it clear to Texan leaders that slave-trade prohibition would be the price for any treaty with Texas or mediation with Mexico. Indeed, by 1843 Britain's foreign secretary, Lord Aberdeen, tried to sound out Mexico on a proposal linking recognition of Texan independence with slave emancipation. Aberdeen went further in seeming to confirm the worst southern fantasies when he privately acknowledged that "Great Britain desires and is constantly exerting herself to procure, the general abolition of slavery throughout the world." As secretary of state, John C. Calhoun was able to publicize this statement as evidence of a British plot to destroy the Union. He also lectured the British on the blessings of black slavery as opposed to British factory labor.[27]

During the 1830s and 1840s, Britain and America veered toward war a number of times as a result of disputes over the Canadian border, the slave ship *Caroline*, America's annexation of Texas, and conflicts over the bound-

---

[26]For this recent discovery, I am much indebted to Dr. Steven Heath Mitton for sending me a copy of his dissertation, "The Free World Confronted: The Problem of Slavery and Progress in American Foreign Relations, 1833–1844," Ph.D. diss., Louisiana State University, 2005, pp. 133–45. I have also learned from Stanley L. Engerman that the British plantation colony of Mauritius, off the east African coast, began importing East Indian labor soon after the emancipation act of 1834, and that from 1839 to 1845, Trinidad imported some 1,300 subsidized free blacks from the United States. For detailed information on the economic failure of British West Indian emancipation, see Drescher, *Mighty Experiment*, pp. 158–237.

[27]Frederick Merk, *Slavery and the Annexation of Texas* (New York, 1972), pp. 82, 187–92, 257–64, 281–88; Brit. Emp. E 1/19, 10–11, MSS, British Library, London; David M. Pletcher, *The Diplomacy of Annexation: Texas, Oregon, and the Mexican War* (Columbia, Mo., 1973), pp. 122–27, 134, 142–53; David Brion Davis, *The Slave Power Conspiracy and the Paranoid Style* (Baton Rouge, 1969), pp. 43–47.

aries of territory in the Pacific Northwest. After President Tyler finally secured the annexation of Texas as a huge slave state in 1845, his expansionist successor, James K. Polk, was careful to settle the Oregon boundary issue with Britain before provoking the Mexican War.[28]

But this continuing tension with Great Britain enabled southern leaders to keep alive memories of the War of 1812 and the Anglophilic and traitorous Hartford Convention of 1814–1815, whose leaders had included such early radical abolitionists as Theodore Dwight. As I have already suggested, the fantasy that American abolitionists were in effect agents of a British conspiracy received some credence from Garrison's publicized trip to Britain in 1833; from the arrival in New England of British antislavery agitators like George Thompson; and from the attendance at the 1840 World's Anti-Slavery Convention in London of a handful of American male and female abolitionists. One should also note that American abolitionists and literary figures like Ralph Waldo Emerson did their best to honor and celebrate the August 1 anniversaries of British slave emancipation. They also circulated positive accounts of the social and religious consequences of freeing West Indian slaves. But it was not until the 1840s and especially the 1850s that a more political brand of American antislavery began to pull free from the British stigma, thanks in part to the southern self-defeating attacks on civil liberties and demands that slavery should be legitimate and acceptable in all the Western territories.

Many southerners had expected that British emancipation would lead to almost immediate black insurrections, presaged by the great Jamaican slave revolt of 1831. When no news arrived of black uprisings, even as years passed, southern leaders and commentators concentrated their attention on four consequences of the mighty experiment: the refusal of many blacks to work on plantations, at least in the larger colonies where enough land was available for subsistence agriculture; the resulting plummet in sugar production and land values; the alleged increase in crime and racial hostility; and Britain's desperate efforts to find alternative plantation labor, eventually in distant India.

As abolitionists tried to counter the depressing reports of economic failure following the end of apprenticeship, the southern-controlled U.S. Department of State received statistics showing that by 1843 the price of freeholds in Jamaica had declined by half; coffee and sugar production had declined

---

[28]Most of this material is taken from my *Inhuman Bondage*, pp. 281–86.

by one-quarter to one-half of their former yield, and some large plantations were worth less than 10 percent of their preemancipation value.[29] Since many southern writers were convinced that this economic disaster had been predictable—as well as being an enormous boon for competitive slaveholders in Cuba, in parts of the South, and in Brazil—the question of Britain's motives became even more central.[30]

Duff Green, the influential editor of the *U.S. Telegraph* and a close friend of John C. Calhoun, contended that British philanthropy was a mere screen for British industrialists and East India interests, groups convinced that free laborers would consume more British produce and that populous India would become Britain's major consumer market. If the British had any genuine humanitarian concerns, Green asked, why did they continue to brutalize and starve Ireland? *Niles Weekly Register* also pointed to the British neglect of starving, impoverished whites in Ireland while great sums were being raised to free and teach religion to West India Negroes.

Writing at length to America's minister to France, Secretary of State Calhoun acknowledged that Britain had initially acted on humanitarian motives, assuming that tropical products could be produced more cheaply by free African and East Indian labor than by slaves. West Indian emancipation had been "calculated to combine philanthropy with profit and power, as is not unusual with fanaticism." But this experiment had proved to be catastrophic. Calhoun noted that British statesmen could read the statistics that showed how far Cuba, Brazil, and the United States had outstripped all the British tropical possessions in the production of coffee, cotton, and sugar.

In order to regain and keep her financial superiority, Calhoun affirmed, Britain was now pursuing two simultaneous objectives. First, she aimed to

---

[29]Wilkins, "Window on Freedom," pp. 143–45.

[30]James Henry Hammond won acclaim throughout the South when in 1845 he brilliantly and respectfully published two letters to the eighty-five-year-old Thomas Clarkson, arguably the great founding father of all abolitionism, and an Englishman no less. Hammond then seemed to demolish point by point the entire intellectual edifice on which Clarkson had based his life's work. Hammond disarmingly admitted at the outset that he had no wish to defend the African slave trade, which Clarkson had devoted almost a half century of sustained effort to suppress. But then Hammond correctly observed that an illegal slave trade from Africa was still thriving and apparently could not be abolished by force (though the trade to Brazil would be stopped in five more years). James Henry Hammond, *Two Letters on Slavery in the United States, Addressed to Thomas Clarkson, Esq.* (Columbia, S.C., 1845); Drew Gilpin Faust, *James Henry Hammond and the Old South: A Design for Mastery* (Baton Rouge, 1982), pp. 278–84.

restore her own capacity to produce tropical staples by exploiting only nom-inally free labor in the West Indies, East Africa, and her East India posses-sions. But this capital investment could never succeed unless Britain also *destroyed* the rival and superior slave societies that "have refused to follow her suicidal policy" and that could therefore keep the prices of tropical staples "so low as to prevent their cultivation with profit, in the possessions of Great Britain, by what she is pleased to call free labor."[31]

Britain's increasing reliance on the importation of contract laborers from India, after an ocean passage of some 131 days to the West Indies, seemed to lend support to the arguments of people like Calhoun and Duff Green. The southern press was especially elated when the *London Times* not only supported Indian "coolie labor" in a series of editorials in 1857, but also proclaimed that slave emancipation had been a colossal failure, destroying immense amounts of property and degrading Negroes still lower than they had been as slaves. Southern papers gleefully reprinted the *Times's* demand that abolitionist fa-natics go to the British West Indies and view the Negro in his "idleness, his pride, his ingratitude, contemptuously sneering at the industry of that race which made him free, and then come home and teach" other fanatics.[32]

While some British and northern writers praised the peacefulness, Chris-tianization, and desire for education exhibited by the former slaves, many previous advocates of emancipation had assumed that the freed people would continue to work with even higher productivity on plantations, and were thus unprepared for the reports of economic decline, subsistence agricul-ture, and local markets. For former slaves, however, nothing was more im-portant than freeing their women, especially, from constant heavy field labor under the threat of the lash.

The South's fixation on British abolitionism and the declining economy of Haiti as well as the British Caribbean helps to explain the southerners' almost paranoid and disproportionate response to critics in the North. Here I have in mind such measures as the gag rule in Congress, which violated the North's highly cherished right of petition and the right of free speech. A few wise southerners like Georgia's Senator John King pointed out that sup-porters of this extremist position could not have served the purposes of

---

[31]Wilkins, "Window on Freedom," pp. 44–49, 82; Calhoun to William R. King, Aug. 12, 1844, reprinted in Merk, *Slavery and the Annexation of Texas*, pp. 281–88.
[32]Wilkins, "Window on Freedom," pp. 254–55, 302–3; Drescher, *Mighty Experiment*, pp. 179–237.

the abolitionists any more effectively than if they had been paid to do so.[33] Then there was the seizure and destruction of abolitionist or suspected abolitionist mail; the radical and extreme measures for enforcing the Fugitive Slave Act of 1850, when the small number of fugitives in no way threatened the slave economy; and the excessive demands regarding the federal sanction of slavery in the territories—demands that would lead even a cautious moderate like Abraham Lincoln to fear that Stephen Douglas's "popular sovereignty" or a "Second Dred Scott decision" would legalize slavery throughout the nation.[34]

For those convinced that abolitionism was a British-sponsored crusade to destroy their society and transform the South into another Haiti, it was only a short step to contemplate disunion and even to accept Leonidas Spratt's "global mission" of founding a "slave republic" based on the revival of the African slave trade. According to the Charleston editor Spratt, restrictions on the slave trade necessarily implied that slavery itself was wrong—and had historically served to isolate the South, sap its morale, and retard its economic and political growth.

Since Britain had made slave-trade abolition into a kind of totem symbolizing legitimate commercial power, there was a certain brilliance in throwing off all restraints and violating "civilization's" most pious taboo. For some southerners who saw themselves besieged by an ideologically hostile world, defending the slave trade became a self-vindicating ritual that would test the integrity of their cause as well as the expected opportunism of capitalist nations like Britain that could not survive without King Cotton and whose tenderness for human rights, as Spratt put it, did not prevent them from crushing India, Algeria, and Poland or from tolerating the trade in white Circassian slaves to the markets of Constantinople.[35]

---

[33]Miller, *Arguing about Slavery*, p. 121.

[34]Lincoln actually felt that a second Dred Scott decision was less dangerous, because less imminent, in September 1859 than "that insidious [Stephen] Douglas Popular Sovereignty," which saw no wrong in slavery and would swiftly extend slavery into every state of the Union (Lincoln, "Fourth Debate," in Basler, *Collected Works*, 3:404–5, 423, 425–26). I am indebted to my friend John Stauffer for this reference.

[35]L. W. Spratt, *The Foreign Slave Trade the Source of Political Power—of Material Progress, of Social Integrity, and of Social Emancipation to the South* (Charleston, 1858), pp. 3–31; Spratt, "The Philosophy of Secession," reprinted in John Elliott Cairnes, *The Slave Power: Its Character, Career and Probable Designs*, 2d ed. (London, 1863), pp. 390–410; Sinha, *Counterrevolution of Slavery*, pp. 125–52; Ronald T. Takaki, *A Pro-Slavery Crusade: The Agitation to Reopen the African Slave Trade* (New York, 1971).

Despite this defiance of Britain, once the southern states had seceded they had to face political reality. The Confederacy's war for independence would depend in good part on gaining the recognition of Great Britain. It was surely for that reason that the Confederate Constitution prohibited any possible reopening of the African slave trade while guaranteeing the permanent legality and security of racial slavery. Ironically, especially in view of the major argument I have been making, Britain by the 1860s was beginning to absorb much pseudoscientific racism and for various reasons came very close to recognizing and aiding the Confederacy in the Civil War.

Nevertheless, the overreaction of southern extremists had made it much easier for moderate northerners to rally broad support in a political campaign against the so-called slave power, a home-grown tyranny that threatened the very survival of democracy in America.

James B. Stewart

Christian Statesmanship, Codes of Honor, and Congressional Violence

The Antislavery Travails and Triumphs of Joshua Giddings

THINK ABOUT "proslavery violence in Congress" and the name that springs to mind is Charles Sumner. As we all know, this Massachusetts legislator was driven to the Senate floor in 1857, blood-soaked and unconscious while enduring a vicious beating by South Carolina's Preston Brooks. Two days before, the abolitionist-minded Sumner had concluded a lurid speech assailing slaveholders for practicing immoral perversions. Brooks responded to what he considered Sumner's personal "insults," first by gathering support from close congressional friends and then by thrashing Sumner senseless with a lethally heavy cane. An explosion of personal vengeance had suddenly subverted the legislative deliberations so vital to sustaining a democracy. The nation had taken a sudden, lurching step toward Civil War.

That's the familiar way to tell the story of congressional violence—as a fast, brutal shift in Washington politics from peaceful disputation to naked aggression. Today, however, I want to recount this story differently. In this telling, the caning of Sumner represented not a sudden rupture in 1857. Instead, it represents the most extreme enactment of rituals of violence that first began in Congress in the late 1830s and that continued right up to the Civil War.

Some of the motives for this dangerous behavior were rooted in Congress's immediate environment, Washington, D.C., a city alive with enslaved workers, slavedealers, antislavery insurgents, and deeply cliquish, highly com-

Reprinted in revised form with permission from *Antislavery Violence: Sectional, Racial and Cultural Conflicts in Antebellum America* (Knoxville, 1999), pp. 167–92.

petitive politicians. Other motivations, closely related, involved congressmen's conflicting codes of ethics and behavior, values that pitted slaveholding men of "honor" against Yankee exponents of Christian "conscience." The catalyst that transformed these volatile elements into an explosive mixture was the behavior of a very small minority of northern congressmen. These were politicians who understood themselves as Christian statesmen, men whose deepest spiritual insights compelled them to face their slaveholding colleagues in Congress and vocally condemn the institution of slavery.

The best known of these, of course, was tenacious John Quincy Adams, the ex-president who created extraordinary legislative conflict by insisting that the House of Representatives debate petitions from the abolitionists. The most provocative and disruptive "Christian statesman" of all, however, was not Adams. Instead, it was Ohio's Joshua Reed Giddings, representative from Ohio's Western Reserve, the Midwest's most deeply "abolitionized" district—the congressman who, before the Civil War, served more consecutive terms than any other member of the House. Giddings's political longevity, his deep evangelical piety, and his ceaseless congressional attacks on slavery make him an exceptional figure. His career also illuminates how Christian statesmanship, Washington, D.C.'s, slaveholding environment and codes of congressional honor combined to foster violence in Washington politics during the pre–Civil War era.

To historians of the American conflict over slavery Giddings is a familiar figure. In 1842 the House of Representatives censured him by a huge majority for presenting resolutions that defended the right of slaves on ships in international waters to rise in bloody insurrection. Giddings then resigned his seat and appealed to his constituents. They reelected him by a crushing majority and gave him an explicit mandate to offer his resolutions again. This he did successfully, in defiance of House rules, his Whig party's wishes, and slaveholders' demands. His actions opened a new phase in the sectional conflict in which it was no longer possible for House rules to stifle attacks on slavery.[1]

---

[1] For standard treatments of the "gag rule" controversy and for Giddings's role in it, see James Brewer Stewart, *Joshua R. Giddings and the Tactics of Radical Politics* (Cleveland, 1970); Leonard R. Richards, *The Life and Times of Congressman John Quincy Adams* (New York, 1986); George R. Rable, "Slavery, Politics and the South: The Gag Rule as a Case Study," *Capitol Studies* 3 (1975):69–87; James M. McPherson, "The Fight against the Gag Rule: Joshua Leavitt and Antislavery Insurgency in the Whig Party, 1839–1842," *Journal of Negro History* 48 (1963):177–95; William Lee Miller, *Arguing about Slavery: The Great Battle in the United States Congress* (New York, 1996); and Michael Kent Curtis, "The Curious History of Attempts to Suppress Antislavery Speech, Press and Petition in 1835–37," *Northwestern University Law Review* 89 (1995):785–869.

The key to understanding the full importance of this well-known event is Giddings's blunt insistence that black Americans had the right to use violence to liberate and defend themselves. In this respect Giddings's censure and reelection were only parts (albeit crucial parts) of a much more volatile drama played out over two decades between himself and his slaveholding counterparts, men who loathed his advocacy of black people's rights of revolution.

We know a great deal about why slaveholding congressmen would despise Giddings's behavior and why he would despise theirs. Much has been written about the colliding values of Yankees inspired by evangelical "conscience" and slaveholding "men of honor" driven by a need for personal dominion. Little is known, however, about the impact of these conflicting ethical systems on the nation's legislative processes as civil war drew closer.[2] Giddings's repeated confrontations with angry southern congressmen speak directly to this question. They illustrate that long before Brooks beat Sumner senseless, debate in Congress over slavery was being significantly undermined by violence-tinged rituals of defiance and retribution

Giddings brought a truly disturbing version of northern religious radicalism to the House of Representatives. In national politics there was no more ardent a "Yankee saint" than he. On some topics Giddings professed an abiding hatred of violence typical of Christian reformers. He advocated pacifism in the treatment of Indians and in the conduct of foreign policy. Yet he also emphatically defended the right of freedom-seeking slaves to shed their oppressor's blood. He commended fugitives who slew their pursuers, and he lauded whites who assisted escapees.[3]

Even Giddings's defense of the supremacy of "the law" itself seemed to invite armed conflict. He couched it in terms that appealed beyond statutes

---

[2]See Bertram Wyatt-Brown, *Southern Honor: Ethics and Behavior in the Old South* (New York, 1982); Steven M. Stowe, *Intimacy and Power in the Old South: Ritual in the Lives of Planters* (Chapel Hill, 1987); Dixon D. Bruce, *Violence and Culture in the AnteBellum South* (Austin, 1979); Drew G. Faust, *James Henry Hammond: A Design for Mastery* (Baton Rouge, 1982); Edward L. Ayres, *Vengeance and Justice: Crime and Punishment in the Nineteenth Century American South* (New York, 1984); James Brewer Stewart, "A Great Talking and Eating Machine: Patriarchy, Mobilization and the Dynamic of Nullification in South Carolina," *Civil War History* 27 (1981):198–220; Kenneth Greenberg, *Honor and Slavery: Lies, Duels, Noses, Masks, Dressing as a Woman, Gifts, Strangers, Humanitarianism, Death, Slave Rebellions, the Proslavery Argument, Baseball, Hunting, and Gambling in the Old South* (Princeton, 1996). Two recent works that introduce Yankee "saints" are Robert Abzug, *Cosmos Crumbling: American Reform and the Religious Imagination* (New York, 1994), and James Brewer Stewart, *Holy Warriors: The Abolitionists and American Slavery* (New York, 1996).

[3]For a full treatment of Giddings's early career and beliefs, see Stewart, *Joshua R. Giddings*, pp. 1–83.

to overriding moral absolutes. Though he insisted, for example, that he upheld the master's "legal rights" of ownership, in the next breath he informed slaveholding congressmen that they had absolutely no "moral right" to retain their slaves. This lack of "moral right," according to Giddings, made slave revolts, though technically illegal, entirely justifiable in God's sight.[4]

Giddings's day-to-day behavior in the House of Representatives also seemed to incite slaves to violence. As southern congressmen listened from their desks close by, Giddings laced his speeches with commentaries on slavery so scathing and endorsements of slave resistance so enthusiastic that they drew Frederick Douglass's applause. And when tempers flared, Giddings invariably responded to slaveholders' threats with bitter disparagement of their "codes of chivalry." In the opinion of one his most acid political critics, fellow Whig Robert C. Winthrop of Massachusetts, Giddings's bellicose style seemed to put him "at war with Washington" itself.[5]

Winthrop's observation suggests still more about the origins of Giddings's personal combativeness and his justifications of slave violence. In part the roots of both lay, in part, in the shock and disgust Giddings experienced as he observed slavery first hand as it was practiced so openly in the District of Columbia and as it was represented so domineeringly in the halls of Congress. Shocking scenes of enslavement he encountered on Washington's streets mocked the evangelical convictions of the people he represented and ripped at the core of his personal beliefs. The slaveholding politicians he observed in the Congress seemed to behave like petty tyrants, not like republican lawmakers.

In faraway Ohio, Giddings had spoken against slavery as a matter of religious conviction and as a political necessity. Upon arriving in Washington, however, he suddenly sensed that a vile institution and the overbearing politicians who practiced it violated his deepest moral sensibilities. The slavery he had once opposed in principle he now instinctively hated as flesh and blood evil.

Yet Giddings was also a practicing politician. He knew that his terrible insights into slavery had to be reconciled with his loyalty to the national Whig party—the party whose platforms he supported—the party that had sponsored his election. This deep Whig commitment pledged him to ally closely with the same slaveholding politicians he so deeply distrusted and to

[4] Ibid.

[5] Robert Charles Winthrop to Nathaniel Appleton, Feb. 7, 1848, in Robert Charles Winthrop, ed., *A Memoir of Robert C. Winthrop* (Boston, 1897), pp. 156–57.

uphold the laws that protected their human property. Giddings knew full
well that he could never rise from his seat in the House of Representatives,
demand immediate emancipation, and expect to continue his congressional
career. He could, however, put a bridle on his conscience and make statements just short of outright abolitionism that still conveyed as much of his
outrage as possible.

Undergirding all Giddings's responses to slavery was his conviction that
he was entering Washington politics as person who had undergone a profound spiritual transformation. Only eighteen months before his arrival in
the district he had successfully emerged from a protracted crisis. Through
an evangelical conversion experience he had found himself able to overcome extreme depression triggered by fiscal bankruptcy, family estrange-
ment, betrayal by close friends, and frustrated political ambitions. At age
forty-two, he now tenaciously embraced a newly acquired belief in God's
redemptive power of spirituality that had finally restored his equilibrium.

Once at ease in the local tavern, he now espoused strict temperance. Once
a lukewarm critic of slavery, he now added his sponsorship to the Ashtabula
County Anti-Slavery Society, a group dedicated to "immediate emancipation." Once a headline-seeking criminal attorney, he now visited his jailed
former clients, supporting revivals of faith among them and urging a repen-
tance similar to his own.[6] His budding career as a legislator and his sacred
new calling as a Christian believer were now one. By voting as his conscience dictated, he automatically furthered God's larger plans for humanity. Early in his career he remarked privately that "I must do my political
duty and leave the consequences to God," since "the wisdom of providence
. . . is manifestly to be seen in any subject brought before our Congress." This
idea, he further disclosed, was one upon which he "love[d] to meditate."[7]

But though Giddings now lived to serve higher purposes, one crucial trait
remained unchanged—his feelings of debilitating depression in the absence
of ambitious challenges. When he was not challenged by hard and reward-
ing tasks, he succumbed to "hypochondria," as he called it, a physically painful melancholy that overtook him "till all was blue." His remedy lay in setting
and achieving formidable new goals, and he expressed deep fears about his

---

[6]For confirmation of the information in the foregoing paragraphs, see Stewart, *Joshua R. Giddings*; for his vocational crisis and its resolution, see pp. 22–33.

[7]Joshua R. Giddings to James A. Briggs, Apr. 29, 1843, James A. Briggs Papers, Western Reserve Historical Society, Cleveland.

depression returning just as he began congressional duties. But once Giddings discovered congressional antislavery as his lifelong calling, his "hypochondria" vanished forever.[8]

Settling into unfamiliar quarters in the district, Giddings naturally identified people and places that made him feel closer to home. In seeking such welcoming accommodations, Giddings was hardly unusual. Nearly all congressmen came to Washington without their families and roomed with "messmates" who shared their regional roots. The boardinghouses where groups of congressmen roomed and ate together created a spirit of brotherhood that reinforced cultural homogeneity. Southerners hived together just as Yankees did, and congressmen habitually referred to one another by mess group affiliations, such as "Dowson's crowd" or the "Army mess." For his part, Giddings found welcoming quarters at Mrs. Sprigg's boardinghouse.[9]

By joining a mess with like-minded northerners and by immediately befriending John Quincy Adams, Giddings, like many representatives, instinctively reinforced his own parochialism.[10] He and new friends from the House of Representative ("two Presbyterians and one Methodist") observed temperance vows and avoided Washington's "gay and social circle" of strong drink, cigars, and conviviality, where Giddings believed himself "allmost [*sic*] a stranger." Instead of attending soirees, they met for devotional services. And once Giddings had decided that he must bring himself to witness a local slave auction, two of his new friends proved their loyalty by going along with him.[11]

In late January 1839, Giddings had his first direct encounter with slavery when happening upon a "coffle of about sixty slaves . . . chained together on their way south." They were being driven, he reported, by "a *Being* the shape of a man . . . on horseback . . . with a huge bullwhip in his hand," who occasionally cracked it as he "chastised" laggards. As the group passed before

---

[8]Giddings to Laura W. Giddings, June 28, 1836; Apr. 27, 1837; Dec. 9, 1838, Joshua R. Giddings Papers, Ohio Historical Society, Columbus.

[9]Barbara Jeanne Fields, *Slavery and Freedom in the Middle Ground: Maryland in the Nineteenth Century* (New York, 1986). Giddings Diary, Jan. 1, 1839, Giddings Papers.

[10]For a detailed description of Washington boardinghouse culture and its relationship to the national legislative process, see James Sterling Young, *The Washington Community, 1800–1828* (New York, 1966), especially pp. 1–109. Though Young's study ends in 1828, it is clear that his analysis also applies to the period of Giddings's Washington career, from 1839 to 1859. For documentation on this point, see note 35.

[11]Giddings Diary, Jan. 1, 1839; Giddings to Laura W. Giddings, Jan. 3, Dec. 1, 16, 1839, Jan. 1, 1840, Giddings Papers.

him, Giddings could do no more than to stand by helplessly and "to view the barbarous spectacle."[12] By the next day, he had seen still more and had grown all the more disturbed, reporting hotly to his wife: "We have public auctions where slaves are sold right before the Capitol, and in sight of the door, And a number of slave prisons. In allmost [*sic*] every walk I take I pass some of them."[13]

Two weeks later, Giddings again found himself part of a horrifying drama that seemed to demand his intervention. Once again, as he recorded in his diary, he could only look on, feeling enraged and shamefully ineffectual:

> In the evening we were alarmed by a thrilling cry of distress which continued for some minutes. It proved to be the outcry of a slave who was undergoing the chastisement of his master; and fearing that he would die in the operation, broke from him and ran. He was pursued, knocked down & pounded by the master & son till he appeared lifeless; and the spectators, interfering, were told that he was the property of his master and that he had the right to kill him if he pleased. The master and his son then took him & dragged him through the street as they would have done a dead hog to a stable and there left him.[14]

When he next encountered slavery, Giddings could no longer bear to sustain the agonizing role of silent observer. Only two days later, Giddings and his two messmates watched a twenty-six-year-old black man being put up for auction at the Pennsylvania Avenue Slave Stand. This time, Giddings sought out a direct confrontation. When he entered the room, Giddings reported the auctioneer "became exceedingly embarrassed . . . the moment he saw me," a reaction suggesting that Giddings had made his disapproval obvious. Yet his naive thought that his presence might somehow make a difference ultimately meant nothing. A painfully outraged Giddings empathized deeply with the captive. "As the bidders one after another raised the price of their fellowmen, his eyes followed them and the deep horror and agony of his soul was portrayed in the contortions of his countenance."[15]

Had Giddings voiced objections as the price rose, he surely would have recorded this in his diary. But for this loyal Whig, any such heartfelt protest was clearly an act of political suicide. Once again Giddings retired in si-

---

[12]Lawrence J. Friedman, *Gregarious Saints: Self and Community in American Abolitionism* (New York, 1982); Stewart, *Joshua R. Giddings*, chap. 4.

[13]Giddings Diary, Jan. 30, 1839; Giddings to Laura W. Giddings, Jan. 31, 1839, Giddings Papers.

[14]Giddings Diary, Feb. 14, 1839, Giddings Papers.

[15]Ibid., Feb. 16, 1839.

lence, a "man of conscience" as disturbed by his inability to act as by the "horror and agony" he had witnessed. At times like these, the morally supportive world of the Western Reserve could hardly have seemed more remote to him.

Painfully conscious of this chasm, Giddings took quick steps to attempt to connect the two. He met with his antislavery messmates, seeking their help in a plan to attack the slave trade on the floor of the House.[16] He also conveyed to his family back home in Ohio news of the terrible things he had witnessed. Though he had not been able to help the slave on the auction block, he surely could lead his children to detest such atrocities. To his ten-year-old son, Grotius, he wrote moralistically of a slave girl of eighteen he had met who was "well dressed, well behaved and appears as well informed a girl as any other. But her master can sell her when he pleases. What think you, is it right?" Soon after this his elder daughter, Lura, also received fatherly interrogations that requested her judgments on the buying and selling of slaves. Though Giddings could never bear witness in public to his fullest abolitionist "conscience," he privately exercised it widely when tutoring his children to meet that higher standard.[17]

While Giddings explored the slavery in the district, House proceedings opened. Debate turned quickly to an abolitionist petition requesting diplomatic recognition for Haiti, the Caribbean republic born of black insurrection in 1793. This was Giddings's first chance to assess congressional discussions on slavery, and everything he heard upset and angered him: "Northern men appear afraid to come out and declare their sentiments. . . . They keep a distance from the subject," he reported. Still more tellingly, he quickly sensed in slaveholders' remarks their deepest fears, those of slave violence. Though he himself flatly dismissed such forebodings as unfounded, Giddings had actually pinpointed the most sensitive emotion in the ethic of southern honor, fears that a man of "conscience" might directly address to produce a transformative impact. It was "amusing and astonishing," Giddings wrote privately, that in "the South the general impression [of abolition] is that it is designed to create a general rebellion among the slaves & and have them cut their masters' throats." It was, in his view, long past time for someone to "come forth & with plainness set forth the claims of the north."[18]

---

[16]Ibid., Jan. 30, 1839; Giddings to Laura W. Giddings, Feb. 1, 1831, Giddings Papers.

[17]Giddings to Grotius Giddings, Dec. 29, 1839; Giddings to Lura Maria Giddings, Feb. 17, 1839, Giddings Papers; Stewart, *Joshua R. Giddings*, pp. 50–51.

[18]Giddings Diary, Dec. 17, 1838.

As Giddings saw the "stalwart" Adams silenced when presenting anti-slavery petitions, he quickly concluded that, in the House of Representatives, arrogant slaveholders called the tune. Everyone else bowed to their wishes when it came to matters of slavery. As Giddings judged it, slaveholders went out of their way to intimidate "diffident, taciturn and *forbearing*" northerners with their "high and important bearing . . . their confident and bold assertion, their overbearing manners."[19] Moreover, Giddings now believed that the southerners' authoritarianism and his own horrifying encounters with slavery explained each other. The House itself was being "enslaved" by haughty planters, coarsened by their power as masters: "Our Northern friends are in fact afraid of these southern Bullies," he observed. Even Adams doubted the wisdom of Giddings's plan to confront the issue of slavery in the District of Columbia. But for Giddings, in stark contrast to his agonizing position at the slave auction, this was a situation in which he could surely speak out. To choose otherwise would be to submit to the enslavement of his Christian conscience, and to the enslavement of his constituents' feelings as well: "We have no northern man who can boldly and forcibly declare his abhorrence of Slavery and of the slave trade," Giddings emphasized. "This kind of fear I have never experienced nor shall I submit to it now."[20]

First Giddings considered the idea of demanding a House report on how many slaves in the district had committed suicide or killed their own children rather than endure further debasement. Then, two weeks later he rose from his seat, delivered a stinging attack on slavery in the district, and spoke feelingly about his recent experiences: "On the beautiful avenue in front of the capitol, members of Congress, during this session, have heard the harsh voice of the auctioneer, publicly selling human beings, while they were on their way to the capitol. They also have been compelled to turn aside from their path to permit a coffle of slaves, males and females, chained to each other by their necks, to pass on their way to this National slave mart."[21] "I felt that forbearance ceased to be a virtue and my national pride was humbled," Giddings recalled after the speech. "I no longer felt myself the Representative of *Freemen* while I was compelled to remain silent and witness my country's disgrace."[22]

---

[19]Ibid., Dec. 14, 1838.

[20]Ibid.

[21]*Congressional Globe*, 25th Cong., 3d sess., 1839, pp. 179–81.

[22]Giddings to "Dear Sir," Feb. 26, 1839, Joshua R. Giddings Miscellaneous Papers, New York Historical Society, New York.

The politician of Christian "conscience" now set about to discover the furthest congressional limits for expressing his hatred of slavery. Doctrines that endorsed slave violence, and behavior that invited direct confrontation on the floor of the House were soon to become his hallmarks. They also forced him to struggle with the obvious contradiction between detesting slavery and remaining loyal to the national Whig party.

Giddings addressed these conflicting allegiances in his own way by simply denying their existence. Instead, he flatly insisted that antislavery action and Whig party loyalty amounted to the same thing. "True Whigs" must espouse the antislavery position, he decided, and "true antislavery" meant support-ing the Whig party. Citing House votes on the "gag rule," which Democrats solidly supported while Whigs split along sectional lines, Giddings concluded that the Democrats, as a party, were fundamentally responsible for every proslavery measure. Whigs, on the other hand, even southern ones, ought to agree with his antislavery creeds. To this dubious assertion Giddings added a second, disturbing claim that the Whig programs of economic national-ism actually forwarded the cause of emancipation by disseminating wealth and knowledge throughout the nation. This, Giddings insisted, was a pro-gram deeply "dangerous to the interests of slavery, which must ever depend [on] ignorance and stupidity . . . , [and] is ever jealous of the progress of knowledge, which teaches man to know the rights that God has given him."[23]

In asserting the harmony between Whig economic ideology and anti-slavery, Giddings was perfectly serious. He proved this throughout most of the 1840s by voting for slaveholding Whigs to be Speaker of the House by and campaigning vigorously for slaveholding presidential candidates. Yet from any critical perspective, Giddings's attempts to reconcile his conscience with his claims of Whig loyalty were fraught with sectional danger. His de-mand that southern Whigs accept his antislavery doctrines defied intricate sectional understandings that held his party together. His assertion that Whig programs of economic nationalism led people in the slave states to learn "the rights that God has given [them]" seemed to imply to some sensitive listeners an interest in promoting unrest among the slaves.

Reasons for suspicion became still more apparent once Giddings started to expound his constitutional doctrines. And when he began by asserting

---

[23]Giddings's fullest expositions of antislavery constitutional theory are found in his seven essays, published under the pseudonym "Pacificus," which were originally published in the *Western Reserve Chronicle*, Nov. 8, 15, 22, 27 (quotation), 30, Dec. 6, 13, 1842. The essays are also reprinted in George W. Julian, *The Life of Joshua Giddings* (Chicago, 1892).

that his ideas were ones that slaveholders had always agreed to, one can easily imagine how rapidly resentments compounded. As Giddings emphasized
time and again, his constitutional doctrines respecting slavery were "not new,
as they are as old as the Constitution, nor are they *antislavery* for they have
been, for a half a century, agreed to by the southerner."[24] When making this
stunning assertion, he meant, as he explained, that the "reserved powers"
clause of the Tenth Amendment explicitly denied Congress any legislative
power over slavery in parts of the Union where state law already permitted
it. Put another way, neither the federal government nor the citizens of the
free states had the slightest constitutional obligation to support the peculiar
institution. With his hatred of slavery now validated by the Constitution,
Giddings could with a clear conscience occupy his seat in the House and attack slavery as his conscience dictated.[25]

Giddings's weapons of constitutional warfare rendered full justice to his
deepening militancy. Since he held that the federal government had no power
to involve the free states with slavery, his constituents could and should aid
escaping slaves and impede the fugitives' pursuers—peacefully if possible, but
violently if necessary. And though he granted insurrections could be suppressed under federal laws of treason, southern slaves nevertheless retained
their moral warrant to rebel. But where federal statutes alone prevailed,
constitutional law and God's justice supported fleeing slaves and their white
defenders when taking up arms and slaying the pursuers. Under these circumstances, Giddings stated unequivocally, the Constitution plainly upheld
the shedding of the masters' blood. His bald challenge to "southern honor"
could hardly have been stated more provocatively.[26]

Clearly this was exactly Giddings's intention. As he well knew, the impact
of his assertions guaranteed tempers would flare. "The Federal Government
has no right to interfere with our domestic institutions!" declared slave-owning
politicians time and again. Heartily agreeing, Giddings invariably exhorted
his southern colleagues to follow their own logic to its bitterest antislavery

[24]*Western Reserve Chronicle*, Nov. 30, 1839.
[25]For a complete evaluation of Giddings's antislavery constitutionalism, see Stewart,
Joshua R. Giddings, pp. 43–49. For the Whig Party's actual relationship to the problem of slavery in both national and regional contexts, see Michael Holt, *The Political Crisis of the 1850s*
(New York, 1978); Daniel Walker Howe, *The Political Culture of the American Whigs* (New York,
1979); James Brewer Stewart, "Abolitionists, Insurgents, and Partisan Politics in Northern
Whiggery, 1836–1844," in *Crusaders and Compromises: Essays on the Relationship of the Antislavery
Struggle to the Ante-bellum Party System*, ed. Alan M. Kraut (Westport, Conn.: 1983).
[26]See Stewart, *Joshua R. Giddings*, pp. 43–49, and citations in note 23 above.

conclusions: (1) abolish slavery in the District of Columbia; (2) never expend a penny of national revenue to recapture fugitives or to compensate masters for the loss of their escapees; (3) endorse the obligation of citizens in the free states to protect and arm fugitive slaves; and (4) guarantee the right of slaves who escaped to defend that freedom by killing their pursuers.

It took Giddings over a year to elaborate these doctrines fully. But by 1841 he was fully prepared to challenge slavery, and with it "southern honor," on the floor of the House. He did so by specifically connecting the issue of violent resistance by escaped slaves to the congressional debate on the ongoing war in Florida against the Seminole Indians. His provocative remarks and the slaveholders' enraged responses revealed for a moment the violence that lay just below the surface when southern codes of "honor" and Yankee creeds of "conscience" clashed openly in the House of Representatives. A close examination of this initial incident reveals a sequence of volatile interactions that would repeat itself throughout Giddings's long career.[27]

As Giddings spoke against the war appropriation, slaveholders discovered to their shock that he was basing his objections on a defense of the Florida maroons, an armed insurgency of slave escapees who had fled from Georgia plantations and who now fought with the Seminoles. As everyone listening knew, these escapees were conducting a bloody resistance to their reenslavement by the U.S. Army that was unprecedented in cost and duration. Yet here was a congressman unabashedly taking their side.

The nature of this war, Giddings insisted, had "prostituted" the military "to the base purpose of leading an organized company of negro catchers." But if, as the "gentlemen from the south who hold to a strict construction" insisted so endlessly, the federal government must never meddle with slavery, why, Giddings queried, was the army trying to reenslave people whose freedom was clearly guaranteed by "the laws of nature and nature's God"? Indeed, Giddings added hotly, "if the negroes had quietly suffered themselves to be trailed with bloodhounds or had supinely permitted themselves to be hanged for their loss of liberty, they would have deserved the name of slaves." Expending taxpayers' dollars to subsidize the army as "man-stealers" tainted his constituents with the "sin" and "guilt" of slavery, Giddings insisted further. The $40,000 in question would be much better spent on internal improvements for the benefit of the nation as a whole rather than being used

---

[27]The entire incident, as recounted below, is documented in the *Congressional Globe*, 26th Cong., 2d sess., 1841, pp. 157–72, and app., pp. 346–52.

to turn the people of his district into "the purchasers of human beings." The army should withdraw, he concluded, leaving slaveholders daring enough to risk their own lives to face the maroons by themselves.

More than an hour long, the speech displayed Giddings's unusual talent as a researcher, filled as it was with references and quotations from War Department documents, Claims Committee reports, and clauses from Indian treaties. Over the decades, Giddings became so fascinated by the history of the war against the maroons that in 1858 he published an impressive volume on the subject of value to scholars even today. His lifelong attraction to the subject of black resistance seems to have engaged him intellectually as well as emotionally.[28] For the slaveholding congressmen, however, emotional responses took an altogether different form; insulted southern honor was quick to enforce its claims.

One witness to the developments after Giddings's speech wrote that "the House was nearly all the time agitated like the waves of the sea"—"a peaceful riot," as Giddings himself described it.[29] One after another, slaveowning congressmen, all from districts close to the Seminole War, rose to repulse Giddings's assaults by inflicting him with shame and intimidation. From their point of view Giddings had utterly flouted parliamentary etiquette by assaulting their values so openly. They, in turn, were now entirely justified in administering their rites of humiliation. In an instant, civility evaporated. Conflict between slaveholding "pride" and evangelical "conscience" exploded on the floor of the House.

Giddings sat quietly as William Cooper, a Georgian, began the assault "in a very agitated manner." He scorned Giddings's honesty and hotly denied that his constituents would "steal . . . Negroes from Indians." Giddings continued silent when next Edward Black, also from Georgia, swore that had Giddings uttered his "violent, inflammatory abolition speech" in Georgia, "he would most certainly be subjected to the infliction of lynch law . . . we would give him an elevation of which he little dreams." Black then yielded the floor to his South Carolina colleague Waddy Thompson, who concluded the day's assault by attempting to read Giddings out of the Whig party. This, Thompson stated, was an enterprise in "which every Southern man should

---

[28]Joshua R. Giddings, *The Exiles of Florida: A History of the Seminole War* (Columbus, Ohio, 1858).

[29]Joshua Leavitt to "Readers," *Emancipator*, Feb. 18, 1841; Giddings to Laura W. Giddings, Feb. 14, 1841, Giddings Papers.

only feel as a Southern man." He next took care to insult Giddings to his face by scorning him in front of his colleagues as the *"very obscurest of the obscure."*[30]

To close the proceedings with "honor" satisfied, Thompson took pains to have the last word. He successfully moved adjournment. This prevented Giddings from making any response to the abuse heaped upon him, a humiliating conclusion for Giddings, as the Georgian saw it. The upstart Ohio "firebrand" now stood shamefully silent before Congress, made mute by slaveholders' rebukes. And just to make certain that Giddings's humiliation would be more infamous still, Thompson arranged for his insulting remarks to be printed verbatim in the next day's *National Intelligencer*, the Whigs' leading national newspaper, putting in italics his reference to Giddings as being *"the very obscurest of the obscure"* of all Whigs.

By trying so elaborately to humiliate Giddings, slaveholders obviously meant to break his will. But Giddings had promised himself several years before never to give in to "these southern bullies." So when the House opened the next morning, he immediately rose to respond to "a matter personal to himself." Thompson's published remarks, Giddings stated, "are printed in italics and I suppose they are intended as a direct personal insult." As a matter of "personal privilege," he demanded the right to reply. Instead of submitting to the slaveholders' chastisements, Giddings stood defiant. Realizing this, another Georgia planter seated near Giddings, Julius Alford, suddenly exploded, swearing that he would "sooner spit on Giddings than listen further to his abolitionist insults."[31]

The formal record of Giddings's response captures him vividly as he asserted his "strength of conscience." Spurning his tormentor's challenge: "Mr. G. said that it was once related of a veteran marshal, who had grown old in the service of his country, and who had fought a hundred battles, that he happened to offend a fiery young officer, who spat in his face for the purpose of insulting him. The General, taking his handkerchief from his pocket, and wiping his face, remarked: 'If I could wash your blood from my soul as easily as I can this spittle from my face, you should not live another day.'"[32] Killing him would be easy, Giddings was telling Alford. All that stayed his hand was a devotion to conscience that left him contemptuous of lesser men

---

[30]*Congressional Globe*, 26th Cong., 2d sess., 1841, pp. 158–59, 165–67, 170–72, contains documentation on the exchanges described below. See also Julian, *Life of Giddings*, pp. 92–96.

[31]*Congressional Globe*, 26th Cong., 2d sess., 1841, pp. 170–72.

[32]Ibid.

like Alford. Alford immediately leapt to his feet, began shouting threats, and headed straight for Giddings. Onlookers quickly intercepted him and steered him back to his seat.

With Alford forcibly silenced, Giddings now commanded the field. An imposing physical presence—six feet two inches tall, 225 pounds, an expert marksman and wrestler—he turned to his original tormenter, Waddy Thompson, and lectured him on what honor really meant: "I claim no station superior to the most humble, nor inferior to the most exalted," Giddings assured Thompson. Men who tried to slander him, moreover, would never be able to bait him into defending his honor with force. "At the North," Giddings emphasized, "we have a different mode of punishing insult from what exists in the South. With us," he lectured Thompson, "the man who wantonly assails another is punished by public sentiment." For the moment, at least, the "man of conscience," his honor intact, stood triumphant over those who had sought to demean him.[33]

Historians have demonstrated that competing definitions of masculinity held powerful influence throughout the antebellum era. This skirmish between Giddings and the southern Whigs displayed one form of this male competitiveness, expressed through assertions of abolitionist "conscience" and slaveholding "honor." Among Giddings and his antagonists, men who embodied these conflicting self-understandings, angry competition on the floor of the House became almost inevitable. Driving this process forward, moreover, was the powerful influence of the various Washington boardinghouse subcultures that were mentioned earlier.[34]

While Giddings broke bread and prayed at Mrs. Sprigg's boardinghouse with antislavery evangelicals like William Slade and John Mattocks of Vermont and Seth Gates from New York's "Burnt-Over-District," slaveholders like Waddy Thompson, Julius Alford, Edward Black, and Mark Cooper also lived together with other Deep South messmates. These were fraternities as intensely loyal to the values of the plantation as were Giddings and his friends to their culture of Yankee piety. Over the next decade, at Mrs. Sprigg's boardinghouse, Giddings presided over an ever more visible antislavery brotherhood with whom he could enjoy the "good company." Planters, meanwhile, grouped together in boardinghouses of their own, where strong drink and

---

[33]Ibid.

[34]See note 2 above and also Mark C. Carnes and Clyde Griffin, *Meanings for Manhood: Constructions of Gender in Victorian America* (Chicago, 1990).

religious indifference often prevailed. In legislative processes that brought together such antagonistic fraternities, it was hardly surprising that the militant Giddings and volatile slaveholders drove each other toward confrontation.[35]

Other features of life in the nation's capital added to these frictions. In the streets of the District of Columbia, a "pedestrian's city," congressmen happened upon one another time and again. Chance encounters and impromptu observation took place constantly. It was easy to notice Giddings in the company of nationally prominent immediate abolitionists like Theodore Weld, Gamaliel Bailey, and Joshua Leavitt. These same "fanatics" (from a slaveholder's perspective) could also be seen openly consulting with the Ohioan and his messmates just outside the House, and for a time several of these abolitionists also became messmates at Mrs. Sprigg's boardinghouse. Worse still, from the planters' perspective, Giddings also felt no reluctance to be seen in public with African Americans or to entertain them privately, and he was justly suspected of having assisted local fugitive slaves in their passages to freedom.[36] Little wonder that slaveholding congressmen saw Giddings, the organizer of maddening "abolitionist conspiracies," as someone whose daily actions purposely inverted the southern social order. So they shunned him whenever they met him by chance. The snubbing upheld their honor. It also prevented the loss of tempers and perhaps worse.

---

[35]Giddings to Lura Maria Giddings, Dec. 1, 1839, Dec. 15, 1844; Giddings to Laura W. Giddings, Dec. 1, 1839 (quotation). The evidence of the southern boardinghouse arrangements indicates that in 1839–40 all of Giddings's southern antagonists lived together either at Mrs. Ballard's or Dr. Jones's boardinghouses and that all their messmates, with one exception, represented districts deep in the cotton or rice South (see Faust, *James Henry Hammond*, pp. 166–67, and Perry M. Goldman and James Sterling Young, *The United States Congressional Directories, 1789–1840* (New York, 1973), 356–61, which lists congressmen by boardinghouse addresses). In the next session (the last reported in the directories) the mix and locations changed somewhat, but the general pattern from the previous session remained (pp. 370–75). Throughout all this, Giddings remained at Mrs. Sprigg's with other "yankees."

[36]For evidence of Mrs. Sprigg's antislavery activities, see Joshua R. Giddings to Joseph Addison Giddings, Aug. 13, 1842, Giddings Papers. In addition to this evidence, it seems inconceivable that abolitionist purists such as Theodore Weld or Joshua Leavitt would have permitted themselves to rent rooms from a serious slaveholder. For discussions of Washington, D.C., as an intimate, pedestrian's city, see Young, *Washington Community*, pp. 87–110; Constance McLaughlin Green, *Washington: Village and Capitol, 1800–1878* (Princeton, 1962). For confirmation of slaveholder's streetcorner snubbings of Giddings, see Julian, *Life of Giddings*, p. 76. A flavor of Giddings's streetcorner abolitionist activism is conveyed in Giddings's letter to Theodore D. Weld, Jan. 28, 1844: "We want a man to go among the people of the city, get up petitions, hold meetings, prepare the minds of the people of both Blacks and Whites" (Gilbert Hobbs Barnes and Dwight L. Dumond, *The Letters of Theodore Weld, Angelina Grimké Weld and Sarah Grimké*, 2 vols. [Washington, D.C., 1934], 2:990–91).

From the late 1830s onward Giddings and his slaveholding enemies played out on the floor of the House of representatives a consistent ritual of intimidation and defiance inspired by these hostile dynamics . Every incident began with Giddings adamantly defending the slaves' constitutional right to revolt, his constituents' right to remain untainted by slavery's sin, and his personal right to speak his conscience. Next, enraged slaveholders made strenuous efforts to silence him that ranged from the famous attempt to censure him to attempts to attack him physically on the House floor. As each of these dramas closed, Giddings invariably stood once more in the House again to face down his adversaries. In this manner controversy over slave violence and Congress's inability to maintain common civility became connected in one self-reinforcing process.

On a political level, Giddings encouraged these confrontations as "cheering signs of the times" that foreshadowed the slaveholders' total capitulation. His expressions of optimism, however, also revealed some of the deeper satisfactions he derived from his disruptive behavior. "We are forming a phalanx that will drive slavery into the Atlantic or the Gulf of Mexico," he reported to his eldest son in 1843. The planter politicians were finally receiving their due, Giddings believed: "Thank God I have lived to see those fellows tremble before northern influence." On a still more personal level, he drew deep exhilaration from the atmosphere of confrontation that he, his messmates, and John Quincy Adams were creating. Nothing excited him more than "with my own eyes [to] see the southern slaveholders literally shake and tremble through every nerve and joint." Baiting "arrogant" planters was a challenge that Giddings relished: "I enjoyed the sport yesterday first-rate," he once confided. His reflexive personal animosity toward southern "bullies" cannot be doubted. Slaveholding congressmen certainly sensed it.[37]

Between 1841 and 1858, when Giddings retired, slaveholding congressmen attempted to goad him into physical combat on the House floor on at least seven occasions. Sometimes the moment came suddenly, as it did in 1843 when Charles Dawson of Louisiana pushed Giddings from behind, threw him into the desks on the House floor, and reached for the bowie knife concealed beneath his coat. On another occasion, in 1845 Georgia's Edward Black interrupted Giddings while he was speaking against slavery, yelled out that the Ohioan ought to be hanged, and then charged, with cane upraised,

---

[37]Giddings to Laura W. Giddings, Feb. 6, 1842, Jan. 23, 1843; Giddings to Joseph A. Giddings, June 1, 1842, Dec. 25, 1843, Jan. 7, 1844, Giddings Papers.

swinging fiercely but inaccurately at Giddings's head. During the tense debates over the Wilmot Proviso in March 1849, a drunken Richard Meade of Virginia seized Giddings by the collar and, according to Giddings, "shaking his fist in my face began to threaten me." Even advancing age offered him no protection from these spontaneous outbursts. Mississippian Lucius Q. C. Lamar proved this in 1858 when he called the sixty-three-year-old Giddings a "damned old scoundrel" and "with a countenance filled with rage" tried to attack.[38]

On other occasions, however, slaveholders attempted to enrage Giddings into making the first move, which of course he never did, by subjecting him to insult after insult. During the well-known "Pearl Affair" in 1848 (a failed attempt to smuggle escaped slaves out of the capital in which Giddings was personally involved), proslavery rioters roamed the streets. Meanwhile, within the House of Representatives slaveholders taunted Giddings with threats to hang him or to "deliver him bodily to the mob."[39] Edward Stanly, however, went furthest in telling the world in 1852 why slaveholders so hated Giddings by castigating him for his "disreputable habit" of associating with black people. At bottom, it was Giddings's genuine racial egalitarianism, which he practiced so visibly so consistently and on such a personal level, that disturbed planter politicians most of all: "He receives visits in his home from free negroes," Stanly complained. "He gives them money and treats them as close friends, entertaining them in his private quarters." Giddings had to be an "insane man," Stanly charged, the equivalent of a "bad nigger" who should be hung for "stealing and [for] slandering his neighbor."[40]

---

[38]*Congressional Globe*, 27th Cong., 3d sess., 1843, pp. 140–58, and app., pp. 194–98; Giddings to "Daughter," Feb. 13, 1843, Giddings to Laura W. Giddings, Feb. 19, 1843, Giddings Papers. *Congressional Globe*, 28th Cong., 2d sess., 1845, pp. 250–56; Giddings Diary, Mar. 2, 3, 4, 1849, Giddings Papers; Giddings to Lura Maria Giddings, Jan. 24, 1858, George W. Julian Papers, Indiana State Library.

[39]Joshua R. Giddings, *A History of the Rebellion: Its Authors and Causes* (Columbus, Ohio, 1864), pp. 273–77; *Congressional Globe*, 30th Cong., 1st sess., 1848, pp. 641, 652–59, 667–70; Giddings to Seth M. Gates, Apr. 27, 1848, Gerrit Smith-Miller Papers, Syracuse University Library; Giddings to Joseph Addison Giddings, Apr. 25, 1848, Giddings to Laura W. Giddings, Apr. 20, 1848, Giddings Papers; Joshua R. Giddings, *Speeches in Congress* (New York, 1968), pp. 220–49. The best scholarly treatments of the Pearl Affair are Stanley C. Harrold, Jr., "The Pearl Affair: The Washington Riot of 1848," *Records of the Columbia Historical Society* 50 (1980):140–60.

[40]*Congressional Globe*, 32d Cong., 1st sess., 1851, pp. 160–82, 187–96, 200, and for Stanly's remarks and Giddings's response, see pp. 531–35. Giddings to Lura Maria Giddings, Feb. 15, 1852, Joshua R. Giddings-George W. Julian Papers, Library of Congress.

Unless Giddings protected his "manhood" by defending himself against these attacks, every code of southern honor marked him as a coward, and he knew it. Invariably, however, he met these challenges by scorning his attackers to their faces as morally stunted people who were to be pitied, not fought with, since they were literally beneath his contempt. In short, he heaped dishonor on southern honor itself. To Stanly he replied scornfully: "When a man descends to the vulgarities of barroom blackguards he gets lower down than a man can go. . . . I cannot follow him so far as to throw the mantle of charity over him." And when Dawson pushed him into the desks and reached for his knife, Giddings repelled him, saying that he was a "perfectly harmless" drunkard who deserved "pity" instead of a thrashing. To his wife, however, Giddings also observed that "had I struck him, his bowie knife would have been of little avail." The imposing, well-muscled Giddings found his assailants easy to restrain until peacemakers intervened.[41]

But while order could be patched back together, each of these incidents ruptured a bit more seriously the tissues of civility upon which peaceful deliberation depended. Viewed in this manner, Preston Brooks's assault on Charles Sumner in 1857 was a predictable next step in the rituals of attack and defiance that had so often involved Giddings for nearly two decades.

A brief comparison between Giddings's case and Sumner's is instructive. Giddings's consistent intransigence ultimately protected him when expressing his hatred of slavery. In the midst of the uproar over the "*Pearl* affair," Giddings made certain that everyone remembered this: "I will inform the gentleman that it is too late in the day to attempt to seal the lips of any northern representative," Giddings emphasized. "I give notice to the gentleman, and to all others, that I shall say just what I think on any and every subject that comes before us. It is my intention to call things by their right names, and to speak, so far as I am able, in such direct, plain and simple language as to be understood."[42]

In the more decorous Senate, Sumner had established no such protective boundaries before delivering his philippic on "The Crime against Kansas." Unlike Giddings, moreover, whose speeches never singled out a single individual, Sumner carefully subjected one particular slaveholding senator to an

---

[41] *Congressional Globe*, 32d Cong., 1st sess., 1852, pp. 531–35; Giddings to Laura W. Giddings, Feb. 13, 1843, Giddings Papers; Giddings to "Daughter," Feb. 13, 1843, Giddings-Julian Papers.

[42] Giddings, *Speeches in Congress*, p. 231.

elaborate pattern of insults. Thus, while Giddings no less than Sumner trans-
gressed the etiquette of civility, they did so under different circumstances with
very different consequences. The disabled Sumner became a martyr in the
North and an embarrassment to moderates in the South. The untrammeled
Giddings, by contrast, confirmed slaveholders' most terrifying suspicions
about the insurrectionary goals of the new Republican party that began forming in the mid-1850s.

The 1856 remarks to the House by Henley Bennett from Mississippi suggest just how profoundly unsettling Giddings's long-accumulating impact
had actually been. The Republican party stood indicted of endorsing slave
insurrections, Bennett charged. To prove it, all one needed to do was refer
to Giddings's speeches in Congress. According to Bennett, Giddings had
stated only two years earlier that he would welcome the day when "the black
man, armed with British bayonets and led on by British officers shall assert
his freedom and wage a war of extermination against his master, when the
torch of the incendiary shall light up the towns and cities of the South and
blot out the last vestiges of slavery. . . . I will hail it as the dawning of the
millenium."[43]

While Giddings immediately denied that he had ever "uttered such sentiments," the truth of his rebuttal rested on narrowest literalism. In the speech
to which Bennett referred, Giddings actually had been protesting what he
had taken to be the Pierce administration's policies to bolster slavery in Cuba.
But as he had done so, he had pushed his "states' rights" theories of slavery
to an extreme that made Bennett's warnings, accurate or not, perfectly un-
derstandable. The "popular sentiment [against slavery] which is now rolling
on in the north" would, Giddings predicted, soon sweep the institution away:
"When the contest shall come . . . when the slaves shall rise in the South;
when in imitation of the Cuban bondsmen the slaves shall feel that they are
men; when they feel the stirring emotions of immortality . . . entitled to the
rights that God had bestowed upon them . . . the lovers of our race will
stand forth and exert the legitimate power of the Government for freedom.
. . . Then we will strike off the shackles . . . and make peace by giving freedom to the slave.[44]

Soon other slaveholders began joining in with still other damning examples
of Giddings's presumably insurrectionary intent. One speech in particular

---

[43] *Congressional Globe,* 34th Cong., 3d sess., 1856, pp. 53–56, 78–80.
[44] Ibid., 33d Cong., 1st sess., 1854, app., pp. 986–89.

that Virginia's John Letcher cited before the House told slaveholders all they felt they needed to know. Giddings had delivered this speech in 1846, when supporting the annexation of all of British-held Oregon. Annexation, he had argued, would not only increase the number of free states but also would lead to a British invasion of the South and the liberation of the slaves. Though denying that he desired "servile insurrection," he nevertheless had emphasized his belief that slaveholders had already become terrorized by the "prospect of black regiments of the British West Indian Islands. Servile insurrection torments their imaginations; rapine and murder dance before their affrighted eyes." As for his own feelings about this prospect, as well as those of his constituents and the people of the North in general, Giddings could not have been clearer: "hundreds of thousands of honest and patriotic men will 'laugh at your calamity and will mock when your fear cometh.' If blood and massacre should mark the struggle for liberty of those who for ages have been oppressed and degraded, my prayer to the God of Heaven shall be that justice, *stern unyielding justice* be awarded to both master and slave."[45]

Technically speaking, Giddings had not actually advocated that the slaves rebel. Instead, as he emphasized in rebuttal to the slaveholders, he had simply described his feelings *should* insurrection occur. After all, as he had argued for so many years, neither Congress nor the northern states had any right whatever to be involved with slavery in the South; as an upholder of the Constitution it was certainly not his place to interfere with the "peculiar institution."

Repeated yet again was the same "states' rights" distinction in support of slave violence that had so angered slaveholding congressmen for so many years. As they heard Giddings explain it once more, it revolted them, just as it always had. Here, in their view, was hypocrisy so transparent that it offended their intelligence and mocked their deepest values. Giddings, as slaveholders saw him, had always been a self-aware insurrectionist who dissembled by speaking constitutional nonsense. Yet, despite their most strenuous efforts to drive him into silence, for two full decades he always succeeded in having his way with them. Ever defiant and eager to traffic in violence, Joshua Giddings, the Yankee of Christian "conscience," stood as a sustained, unavenged rebuke to southern honor.

---

[45]Ibid., 34th Cong., 3d sess., 1856, pp. 159–60. Here Giddings read into the record part of the actual speech he had given in 1846 during the debate over the annexation of Oregon.

To conclude, it is useful to speculate on the thoughts of Giddings and his antagonists upon the occasion of the Ohioan's retirement after twenty years of continuous service. At a private reception to which all in Congress were invited in March 1859, 104 Republican senators and representatives presented to "Father Giddings" (as many Republicans now called him) a solid silver tea set that bore this inscription: "To Joshua R. Giddings as a token of his Moral Worth and Personal Integrity." Not a single southern representative attended the event, and Giddings, one suspects, took pride in their gesture of contempt.[46]

---

[46]Julian, *Life of Giddings,* p. 363.

Stanley Harrold

Gamaliel Bailey, Antislavery Journalist and Lobbyist

IN MAY 1846 the American war against the Republic of Mexico began. As American armies captured the Mexican provinces of New Mexico and California and advanced deep into Mexico itself, increasing numbers of northerners opposed the war. They were either abolitionists or antislavery members of the Whig party who feared southerners intended to extend slavery into these lands, regarded the war as unjustly aggressive, and rejected territorial expansion. Gamaliel Bailey, an abolitionist from Cincinnati, was among the war's more outspoken opponents. In January 1847 he became editor of the *National Era*—a new antislavery weekly newspaper published in Washington, where he continued to denounce the war.[1] But in October of that year the *Richmond Whig* noticed that Bailey's weekly had joined leading proslavery Democratic newspapers in advocating the acquisition of more territory from Mexico. The *Whig* commented, "We see but one Abolition paper—and that is the *National Era,* recently established as the metropolitan organ and champion of the fanatics—and that paper is just as eager for more territory, and for as much of it as possible, as the [Richmond] *Enquirer* and the [Washington] *Union*." Bailey responded, "We certainly have no objection to more territory, provided it be acquired by peaceful and honorable cession, and then consecrated to Freedom, and we would as lief have it on

---

[1]John H. Schroeder, *Mr. Polk's War: American Opposition and Dissent 1846–1848* (Madison, 1973); *Cincinnati Weekly Herald and Philanthropist,* Apr. 29, May 20, June 10, Aug. 12, 1846; *National Era,* Jan. 14, 28, Feb. 25, 1847.

the South as on the North." He then added mildly, "By the way, the Whig will permit us to suggest that the frequent application of the epithet 'fanatics' to Anti-Slavery citizens, is in bad taste, to say the least."[2]

This relatively cordial exchange between Bailey and a radically proslavery newspaper, aligned with John C. Calhoun, reflects two significant facts. First, Bailey—who had been chosen to edit the Washington paper by leaders of the American and Foreign Anti-Slavery Society and the northwestern wing of the abolitionist Liberty party—was not a typical abolitionist. Second, proslavery southerners who disdained more radical antislavery papers, such as William Lloyd Garrison's *Liberator,* Joshua Leavitt's *Emancipator,* and Frederick Douglass's *North Star,* read Bailey's *National Era.* In fact, white southerners regarded the *National Era* as less threatening than Horace Greeley's nonabolitionist *New York Tribune.* Bailey was therefore a good choice to hold a journalistic outpost of northern abolitionism in the determinedly *southern* national capital. Many abolitionists wondered, however, if Bailey— seeking acceptance and survival—conceded too much to represent the cause of the slave effectively and honorably.

BAILEY WAS BORN in Mount Holley, New Jersey, in December 1807. His father, Gamaliel Bailey, Sr., was a silversmith and itinerant Methodist minister. His mother, Sarah Page Bailey, belonged to a locally prominent family that included several physicians. In 1816 the Baileys moved to Philadelphia, where young Gamaliel developed what became a lifelong interest in literature. Nevertheless, practical considerations, as well as family tradition, led him to attend the city's Jefferson Medical College, where he graduated in 1828. Bailey, who was under average height and extremely thin, suffered from poor health and physical breakdowns throughout his life. When one of these episodes followed his graduation, he shipped as a seaman aboard a China trader. Many nineteenth-century Americans assumed that sea voyages were therapeutic. But Bailey had to assume duty as ship's surgeon during a cholera epidemic that spread among vessels at port in Canton, China. While treating others, he contracted the disease himself.[3]

The suffering he observed and endured led Bailey during the long voyage home to undergo a profound religious experience that made him a committed

[2]*National Era,* Oct. 28, 1847.
[3]Stanley Harrold, *Gamaliel Bailey and Antislavery Union* (Kent, Ohio, 1986), pp. 1-4.

evangelical.[4] When he returned to Philadelphia in 1830, the religious, social, and moral controversies of the time drew him almost by happenstance into reform and into life on the border between the North and South. His father had become a leader in the new Methodist Protestant Church, which had its headquarters in Baltimore. Bailey went there in 1831 as the editor of the church's weekly journal—the *Methodist Protestant.* In this post he learned journalism and also became moderately opposed to slavery.[5]

The following year Bailey traveled to St. Louis, where he hoped to join an expedition to Oregon. When the expedition either failed or turned out to be fraudulent, he walked to Cincinnati, where his parents had settled and where he hoped to establish a medical practice. In 1833 he married Margaret Lucy Shands, a young woman whose family had moved to Cincinnati from Virginia. Margaret shared Bailey's literary and religious interests and his increasingly abolitionist inclinations. The couple had twelve children, six of whom survived infancy.[6] Bailey concentrated on medicine until 1834. That year, while lecturing on physiology at Lane Theological Seminary, he joined in the debate organized by American Anti-Slavery Society agent Theodore D. Weld. Like others who attended the debate sessions, Bailey at first favored the American Colonization Society's plan to encourage gradual emancipation by sending free African Americans to Liberia in West Africa. But the arguments of Weld and others that the Colonization Society perpetuated slavery convinced him that for moral and practical reasons slavery must be abolished immediately and free African Americans be accorded citizenship rights in the United States. Soon Bailey became an Ohio Anti-Slavery Society leader and assistant editor of the *Philanthropist,* an abolitionist weekly newspaper that James G. Birney, a former Alabama slaveholder, brought from Kentucky to Cincinnati in 1836. That year Bailey stood with Birney, other abolitionists, and local African Americans against an anti-abolitionist, anti-black mob that included a large contingent from slaveholding Kentucky.

[4][Joseph Evans Snodgrass], "A Pioneer Editor," *Atlantic Monthly* 17 (1886):744; G[amaliel]. B[ailey]., "From the Journal of a Physician at Wampoa," *Methodist Protestant* (Baltimore), Feb. 11, 18, 1831.

[5]*Methodist Protestant,* Jan. 7, 28, Feb. 18, 225, Mar. 4, 25, Apr. 22, May 27, Aug. 12, Sept. 2, Nov. 4, 25, 1831.

[6]*Methodist Protestant,* Nov. 4, 1831; Bailey to Mr. Pro Tem, May 12, 1846, in *Cincinnati Weekly Herald and Philanthropist,* May 27, 1846; [Snodgrass], "Pioneer Editor," p. 745; *Cincinnati Directory for 1831* (Cincinnati, 1831), p. 13; Margaret L. Bailey to Rufus Griswold, Oct. 16, 1848, Griswold Papers, Boston Public Library; Grace Greenwood, "An American Salon," *Cosmopolitan* 8 (1890):437, 440, 445.

Unlike Birney and his sons, however, Bailey did not take up arms against the mob that succeeded in destroying the *Philanthropist* press.[7]

In 1837, when Birney left Cincinnati for a position with the American Anti-Slavery Society in New York City, Bailey became editor of the *Philanthropist*. In that capacity, and as corresponding secretary of the Ohio Anti-Slavery Society, he became the leading abolitionist in the Old Northwest and an advocate of a brand of antislavery politics that could appeal to voters beyond abolitionist ranks. As the principal founder of the Ohio Liberty party in 1840, he contended that an antislavery party must restrict its efforts to ending slavery within the exclusive jurisdiction of the federal government— in Washington, D.C., in the territories, and in interstate commerce. He left moral appeals to antislavery societies and abolition in the South to state action. In this policy the Ohio party differed substantially from a more radical Liberty faction centered in upstate New York, which declared slavery illegal everywhere. The New Yorkers advocated federal action against slavery, the right of slaves to escape, and the right of northern abolitionists to go south to help them. In 1841, after a second mob attack on the *Philanthropist*, Bailey, seeking survival and to influence white southerners, explicitly renounced the New Yorker's potentially violent program.[8]

Bailey also differed from William Lloyd Garrison and his New England associates who dominated the American Anti-Slavery Society after 1840. The Garrisonians relied on agitation in the North, rejected formal involvement in politics, called for disunion between the North and the South, and became radical advocates of women's rights. Bailey appealed to white southerners, emphasized party politics, endorsed a spread-eagled nationalism, and had a more traditional understanding of women's role in society. Unlike the Garrisonians *and* the New York Liberty Party, he avoided harsh rhetoric in his criticisms of slaveholders and his advocacy of emancipation. Moderation helped him extend the circulation of the *Philanthropist* into Kentucky

[7][Snodgrass], "Pioneer Editor," p. 745; Robert H. Abzug, *Passionate Liberator: Theodore Dwight Weld and the Dilemma of Reform* (New York, 1980), pp. 89–94; *Philanthropist* (Cincinnati), Apr. 22, 1836; Executive Committee of the Ohio Anti-Slavery Society, *Narrative of the Late Riotous Proceedings Against the Liberty of the Press in Cincinnati* (Cincinnati, 1836), p. 12; Betty Fladeland, *James G. Birney: Slaveholder to Abolitionist* (Ithaca, N.Y., 1955), pp. 125–42; David Grimsted, *American Mobbing, 1828–1861: Toward Civil War* (New York, 1998), pp. 58–63.

[8]Harrold, *Bailey*, pp. 18–19; *Philanthropist* (Cincinnati), June 30, Dec. 16, 1840; Jan. 6, Sept. 22, Oct. 13, 1841, Apr. 13, June 15, Oct. 15, 1842, Aug. 30, 1843; Stanley Harrold, *American Abolitionists* (Harlow, UK, 2001), pp. 65–66.

and expand its influence in the Northwest. In 1843 he added a daily edition called the *Morning Herald* and changed the weekly's name to the *Weekly Herald and Philanthropist*.[9] By 1846 Bailey's diplomatic language, his ability to weather mob attacks, and the growing circulation of his newspaper (rather than his increasingly conservative conduct) led Lewis Tappan of the American and Foreign Anti-Slavery Society to propose that he edit in Washington what became the *National* Era—a newspaper that would serve as the national voice of non-Garrisonian abolitionists.[10]

BAILEY WAS NOT the first northern abolitionist to reside in Washington. Benjamin Lundy published his *Genius of Universal Emancipation* in the city from 1830 until he was indicted for libel in 1833. From the late 1830s into the early 1840s, Theodore Weld and Joshua Leavitt lived in Washington to lobby Congress on slavery issues. Leavitt (a Bostonian), Charles T. Torrey, and William L. Chaplin (both of Albany, New York) served consecutively as Washington correspondents for abolitionist newspapers between 1840 and 1850. But none of these men brought their families to live in Washington or purchased a home there. In December 1836 Bailey did both as he, his wife, six children, and his elderly parents settled in the city. Their first Washington residence was on E Street, not far from the *National Era* office, in a two-story brick building opposite the southern end of the Patent Office.[11]

As he initiated publication on January 7, 1847, Bailey had numerous goals. First, he wanted to survive physically and financially. Second, he hoped the *National Era* would become the newspaper of record for the antislavery cause. To that end he made it a superior product in appearance, editorial

[9]Harrold, *Bailey*, pp. 21–24, 72–73, 85; Stanley Harrold, *Abolitionists and the South 1831–1861* (Lexington, Ky., 1995), pp. 141–43. Bailey on women's rights: *Philanthropist* (Cincinnati), June 11, 1839; *National Era*, Feb. 18, 1851. Circulation in Upper South: SCOBLE to Joshua Leavitt, Aug. 6, 1845, in *Emancipator*, Aug. 20, 1845. Daily edition: Bailey to Stanley Matthews, Feb. 9, 1847, Matthews Papers, Rutherford B. Hayes Library, Fremont, Ohio. Circulation in Northwest: *Philanthropist* (Cincinnati), Sept. 18, 1844, Jan. 22, 1845. Avoids harsh rhetoric: Bailey to Zebina Eastman, June 11, 1847, J. Frank Aldrich Papers, Chicago Historical Society.

[10]Harrold, *Bailey*, pp. 81–85.

[11]Merton L. Dillon, *Benjamin Lundy and the Struggle for Negro Freedom* (Urbana, Ill., 1966), pp. 121–26, 148, 186; Weld to Lewis Tappan, Dec. 14, 1841, Weld to Angelina G. Weld, Jan. 1, 2, 1842, in Gilbert H. Barnes and Dwight L. Dumond, eds., *Letters of Theodore Dwight Weld, Angelina Grimké Weld, and Sarah Grimké, 1822–1844*, 2 vols. (New York, 1934), 2:879–87; Leavitt to Joshua R. Giddings, Aug. 7, 1842, Giddings Papers, Ohio Historical Society; *Emancipator*, Aug. 18, 1847; Greenwood, "American Salon," 439; Lewis Tappan to Joshua Leavitt, Feb. 28, 1847, in *Emancipator*, Feb. 10, 1847; *National Era*, Jan. 7, 1847.

independence, and literary selections. He used large sheets of high-quality paper and the best type, which he replaced frequently. Third, he sought to reach a white southern audience, especially in the border slave states. Fourth, he wanted to enhance antislavery politics. Among his objectives in this last regard was the formation of a broad-based antislavery party that would supplant either the Whig or Democratic Party and extend into the South. He also wanted to increase the number and influence of antislavery congressmen and establish a local political organization that could serve as a national antislavery coordinating committee. Bailey used the *National Era* to advocate the abolition of the slave trade and slavery itself in the district. He also denounced local ordinances that discriminated against free African Americans. But he avoided public cooperation with local black leaders or the few radical white abolitionists in the city. Publicly, at least, he was more interested in national politics than in a practical local struggle for black rights.

Bailey knew he had placed his family and himself in a dangerous situation. Washington's white population, embarrassed as it was by the local slave trade, upheld slavery, opposed black rights, and held abolitionist *fanatics* in contempt. Plenty of southern senators, congressmen, and federal employees would do all they could to keep Washington a slaveholding city. Bailey also knew that previous attempts to establish antislavery newspapers in the Border South had aroused mob action. The most recent incident involved Cassius M. Clay's *True American* in Lexington, Kentucky. Clay's bombastic rhetoric, threats of defensive violence, and his apparent cooperation with slaves had precipitated mob action in August 1845.[12] Bailey learned from this. He trusted that his previous experience in southern-oriented Cincinnati, his diplomatic skills, and his doctrinal flexibility would allow him to either avoid violence or blunt its impact.

Bailey arrived in Washington with letters of introduction "to some of the [city's] most influential citizens," including the editors of its leading newspapers. He presented a letter from Supreme Court Justice John McLean to Joseph Gales and William Seaton of the moderately proslavery *National Intelligencer.* He carried a letter from a Virginia son-in-law of William Henry

[12]Lewis Tappan to Joshua Leavitt, Feb. 28, 1847, in *Emancipator*, Mar. 10, 1847; *National Era*, Jan. 7, 1847; Tappan to A. A. Phelps, Jan. 16, 1847, letter book copy, Tappan Papers, Library of Congress; Bailey to Zebina Eastman, June 11, 1847, J. Frank Aldrich Papers, Chicago Historical Society; Lewis Tappan to Bailey, Sept. 2, 1845, letter book copy, Tappan Papers; Grimsted, *American Mobbing*, pp. 129–33.

Harrison to Thomas Ritchie, the staunchly proslavery Virginian who edited
the *Union*. When Bailey met with Ritchie, he went so far as to mention that
his wife's family included prominent Virginia slaveholders. Bailey also established rapport with the national press corps at the Capitol and—to placate
anti-black and anti-abolitionist Irish workingmen—helped organize in the
city a "great relief meeting for Ireland." In his editorials Bailey emphasized
freedom of the press. "The march," he warned, "would be easy from a
ruined press to the Capitol" and to national disgrace. When, during the war
against Mexico, Whig senators opposed to the war banned prowar Ritchie
from attending Senate sessions because he had called them traitors, Bailey
—despite his own opposition to the war—defended Ritchie. "What is the
liberty of the press good for," he asked, "if every expression . . . is to be
nicely criticized."[13]

Bailey's multifaceted, ingratiating strategy helped him avoid disaster in
April 1848 when three nights of rioting followed the failed *Pearl* slave escape
attempt. A local posse onboard a steamboat captured seventy-seven would-
be escapees and their three white would-be rescuers at the mouth of the
Potomac River during the early hours of April 18. As the posse paraded its
prisoners up Pennsylvania to the city jail, a mob formed. By evening it focused its anger on the *National Era* office under the not unreasonable assumption that Bailey and others associated with it had something to do with
the escape attempt. Some southern congressmen praised the mob. Senator
Henry Foote of Mississippi charged that the mere presence in Washington
of an antislavery newspaper encouraged slaves to escape. He said of Bailey:
"The editor of it may be an intelligent man. I have heard that he is. He is
certainly an abolitionist."[14]

After the first night of rioting, when a heavy rainstorm saved the *National
Era* office from serious damage, Bailey—at the urging of Washington mayor
William Seaton—issued a handbill denying that he or anyone associated
with his newspaper had assisted in what he called "the abduction of the
slaves." He reminded influential Washingtonians of his opposition to using
illegal means against slavery, his moderate conduct, and his condemnation

[13]Bailey to Zebina Eastman, June 11, 1847, Aldrich Papers; *National Era*, Jan. 7, 28, Feb.
18, Dec. 30, 1847, June 1, 1848; Bailey to Gerrit Smith, Sept. 2, 1847, Smith Papers, Syracuse
University; Lewis Tappan to Joshua Leavitt, Feb. 28, 1847, in *Emancipator*, Mar. 10, 1847.

[14]Stanley Harrold, *Subversives: Antislavery Community in Washington, D.C. 1828–1865* (Baton
Rouge, 2003), pp. 116–45; *New York Herald*, Apr. 19, 1848; *Emancipator*, Apr. 26, 1848; *Congressional Globe*, 30th Cong., 1st sess., 1848, app., p. 504.

of "invective and denunciation." Nevertheless only overwhelming force presented by city police, deputized "good citizens," and federal marshals ordered
into action by President James K. Polk prevented destruction of the *National
Era* office during the next two nights. Bailey was brave when on each of these
nights he met on his front porch with elements of the mob. In the first instance
he refused a request that he prevent further violence by agreeing to remove his
press from the city. In the second, he charmingly dissuaded a group of 200
Marylanders and Virginians who had come to tar and feather him.[15]

Through the establishment of good community relations, disavowal of
illegal tactics, and steadfast insistence on the observation of constitutional
guarantees, Bailey—with the help of antislavery congressmen Joshua R.
Giddings of Ohio, John P. Hale of New Hampshire, and John G. Palfrey of
Massachusetts—had established a place for abolitionist journalism in the
nation's capital. When the disturbance ended, Giddings observed, "We shall
have no more mobs here for some time to come." Bailey never again faced
a serious mob threat.[16]

BAILEY'S EFFORT to make the *National Era* the nation's leading antislavery
newspaper also succeeded. His long career as a reform journalist had taught
him, he observed, that "the more wants a paper can supply, the more interest it can enlist in its support . . . the better for its main object." Acting on
this insight, Bailey—in the words of a twentieth-century historian—made
the *National Era* "into a sharp well-edited, thoroughly readable newspaper,
one of the best of the period and certainly the best of the antislavery publications." A big step in this direction was activist poet John G. Whittier's
service as the paper's corresponding editor. Whittier lacked Bailey's political
sophistication but surpassed him by far as an essayist. Between 1847 and
1854, Whittier, who was an established literary figure, contributed over
one hundred poems and nearly three hundred essays to the *National Era*.[17]

[15]*New York Herald*, Apr., 19–21, 1848; *National Intelligencer*, Apr., 20, 21, 1848; *Daily Union*,
Apr. 20, 1848; *National Era*, Apr. 20, 27, May 4, 1848; Benjamin B. French to H. F. French,
Apr. 26, 1848, B. B. French Papers, Library of Congress; Washington correspondence of the
New York Tribune, quoted in *Liberator*, Apr. 5, 1848; Bailey to Moses A. Cartland, Sept. 12,
[18]56, Cartland Papers, Harvard University.
[16]Giddings to Joseph A. Giddings, Apr. 26, 1848, Giddings Papers, Ohio Historical
Society.
[17]*National Era*, Jan. 21, 1847; Russell B. Nye, *William Lloyd Garrison and the Humanitarian
Reformers* (Boston, 1955), 135; Lewis Tappan to John G. Whittier, Apr. 21, 1847, Pickard-
Whittier Papers, Harvard University; Thomas Currier, *A Bibliography of John Greenleaf Whittier*
(Cambridge, Mass., 1939), pp. 477–83.

During the newspaper's early years, Bailey also published original work by such well-known literary and political figures as Robert Dale Owen, Harriet Martineau, Oliver Wendell Holmes, Henry B. Stanton, Theodore Parker, Nathaniel Hawthorne, William Cullen Bryant, and Alice and Phoebe Cary. Meanwhile, the paper employed its own congressional reporter and carried a great deal of material on antislavery in the Upper and Border South.[18]

Among the writers the *National Era* published were several promising women. Sarah Jane Clarke, who wrote under the pseudonym Grace Greenwood, began her career with Bailey during the late 1840s and went on to become one of the more celebrated American female journalists of the nineteenth century. Bailey also encouraged Emma (E.D.E.N.) Southworth, who was an impoverished Washington schoolteacher when he began publishing her sentimental, southern-oriented novels in 1847. Much more important was Bailey's literary relationship with Harriet Beecher Stowe, whom he had very likely met years earlier in Cincinnati. Stowe was relatively unknown when the *National Era* published three of her short pieces in 1850. In January 1851 Bailey sent her a check for $100, requesting "that she might write as *much* as she pleased, *what* she pleased, and *when* she pleased." Stowe responded in March that she would submit a series of three or four sketches on slavery, which, she suggested, will "give the lights and shadows of the patriarchal institution." She planned to present a picture of slavery's best side and "something *faintly approaching the worst.*" She informed Bailey that "there is no arguing with *pictures,* and everybody is impressed by them, whether they mean to be or not."[19]

Neither Stowe nor Bailey realized what they were getting into. On May 8 Bailey announced that "Uncle Tom's Cabin; or, The Man that Was a Thing," would begin soon and run for about ten issues. When the serial started on June 5, with its subtitle changed to "Life among the Lowly," it became an instant sensation. As the story grew longer and longer, Stowe

---

[18]*National Era*, Sept. 23, Dec. 23, 1847, Mar. 2, Apr. 27, May 25, 1848, Jan. 24, 1850, Mar. 4, May 13, 1852; *Emancipator,* June 9, 1847.

[19]Greenwood: *National Era*, Dec. 28, 1848, through 1853; Grace Greenwood to Whittier, Jan. 7, 1849, Pickard-Whittier Papers. Southworth: *National Era*, Aug. 19, 1847, through 1853. Southworth, *The Haunted Homestead and Other Novbelles* [sic] *with an Autobiography of the Author* (Philadelphia, 1860), p. 37; Stowe: Stowe to [Calvin E. Stowe], Jan. 12, 1851, in Charles E. Stowe, *Life of Harriet Beecher Stowe, Compiled from Her Letters and Journals* (New York, 1889), p. 146; Bailey to [Joseph Evans Snodgrass], May 27, 1853, in [Snodgrass], "Pioneer Editor," pp. 748–49; Stowe to Bailey, Mar. 9, [1851], TS, William Lloyd Garrison Papers, Boston Public Library.

struggled to keep up the weekly pace. By the time she ended it on April 1, 1852, she had a book contract with John P. Jewett in Boston. Building on the sensation it had created in the *National Era*, *Uncle Tom's Cabin* became the best-selling novel of the century and an extraordinarily effective piece of antislavery propaganda.[20]

In October 1854 Lewis Tappan declared that the *National Era* had an influence "greatly exceeding in magnitude the effect of all other anti-slavery papers in the country." When it began publication in January 1847, the weekly's circulation was 8,000; by the following autumn it had reached 11,000, surpassing the *Intelligencer* and the *Union*. In 1850 it reached 15,000; in 1851, 17,000; by mid-1852, 19,000; and by early 1853 (boosted by *Uncle Tom's Cabin*) it peaked at 28,000. By then it was among the best-selling newspapers in the United States. Nearly half of its subscribers were in the Old Northwest and a third were in New York, but it circulated in every state and territory.[21]

THE *NATIONAL ERA* succeeded because it gained a nonabolitionist audience in the North. But, as Bailey planned, it also reached white readers in the South. Before the Civil War newspaper editors exchanged copies of their papers in order to locate stories and to debate one another. By November 1847, the *National Era* exchanged with over sixty southern newspapers. Although southern postmasters occasionally confiscated Bailey's paper as an "inflammatory sheet," it appealed to white southern readers simply because it was "the best reading paper published in Washington City." In 1849 the *Nashville Gazette*, characterizing the *National Era* as "able and dignified," recommended it to southern politicians.[22]

---

[20]*National Era*, May 11, June 5, 1851, Apr. 1, 1852; Joan D. Hedrick, *Harriet Beecher Stowe: A Life* (New York, 1994); E. Bruce Kirkham, *The Building of Uncle Tom's Cabin* (Knoxville, 1977), pp. 141–44.

[21]Tappan to L. A. Chamerovzow, Oct. 29, 1854, in Annie Heloise Abel and Frank J. Klingberg, eds., *A Side-Light on Anglo-American Relations 1839–1858, Furnished by the Correspondence of Lewis Tappan and Others with the British and Foreign Anti-Slavery Society* (Lancaster, Pa., 1927), 348 (hereafter cited as *Side-Light*). The growth of the *National Era*'s circulation is traced in Joseph A. Del Porto, "A Study of Antislavery Journals," Ph.D. diss., Michigan State University, 1953, pp. 237–74. For comparison, the *New York Weekly Tribune* had a circulation of 39,720 in 1850.

[22]Lewis Tappan to John Scoble, Nov. 14, 1847, in *Side-Light*, pp. 218, 228; Elisha Betts to Editors, Oct. 10, 1850, in *Southern Press* (Washington), Oct. 17, 1850; *Southern Press*, July 3, 1851; *Nashville Gazette*, quoted in *National Era*, Feb. 8, 1849. By the start of 1853, southern subscribers accounted for one-sixth of the *National Era*'s circulation. See *National Era*, Jan. 13, 1853.

Bailey said he wished to "reach the mind of the South." In reality he aimed at the nonslaveholding majority of white southerners. The *National Era* maintained that the antislavery movement was not a sectional but a class struggle. The paper called on southern voters to overthrow "the ruling caste, the Slave Power." It argued that slaveholders cared nothing for democracy or the interests of most white southerners. Instead they identified their aristocratic interests with southern interests and claimed that criticism of slavery amounted to criticism of the South. Abolition, Bailey informed nonslaveholders, would free them from political domination and improve their economic prospects. He joined other abolitionists in warning that, as long as slavery existed, white southerners risked a "war of extermination and anarchy." He called on them to adopt a plan of peaceful emancipation that would align African Americans "with law and order, instead of against it."[23]

The *National Era* published a great deal of material suggesting that effective antislavery activity existed in the Upper and Border South. The paper's columns contained optimistic letters from Joseph Evans Snodgrass of Maryland, John G. Fee of Kentucky, and many others. Bailey wrote editorials on the complexity of legislating emancipation in Virginia, on individual manumissions, and—as the years passed—on Liberty, Free-Soil, and Republican party organization in the border slave states. Although he differed substantially from Cassius M. Clay in demeanor, he supported Clay's emancipation campaigns in Kentucky in 1849 and 1851.[24]

FROM THE TIME Bailey organized the Ohio Liberty party in 1840, he hoped the third party would transform the American party system. It might accomplish this, he believed, either by attracting disaffected northern Whigs and Democrats to its ranks and becoming a major party, or by merging into a broader antislavery coalition designed to challenge slaveholder power in Washington. By 1846 the war against Mexico had intensified fears among hundreds of thousands of northerners that the expansion of slavery into newly acquired territories would hurt the interests of wage labor, lead to the admission of more slave states, and perpetuate what was known as slave

---

[23]*National Era*, Feb. 25, Aug. 26, 1847, Nov. 16, 1848.

[24]Daniel R. Goodloe, MS autobiography, Goodloe Papers, Southern Collection, University of North Carolina; Bailey to Joshua R. Giddings, Sept. 29, 1849, Giddings-Julian Papers, Library of Congress. Bailey and Clay: Harrold, *Bailey*, pp. 78, 86; *National Era*, June 21, July 5, 19, 1849, Apr. 25, 1850; Clay to Bailey, Aug. 4, 1849, in *National Era*, Aug. 16, 1849; Charles Francis Adams, diary entry, Dec. 6, 1851, Adams Papers, Massachusetts Historical Society.

power rule in Washington. These fears encouraged a minority of northern Whigs (called "Conscience Whigs") and a minority of northern Democrats (called "Barnburners") to advocate antislavery policies similar to Bailey's and most Liberty abolitionists'. Bailey made the *National Era* the principal journal in favor of uniting the three antislavery groups. He suggested that the Liberty party make concessions regarding its platform to bring this about. He was not, however, as willing to compromise abolitionist principles as was his Cincinnati friend Salmon P. Chase.[25]

During the summer of 1848, as the Free-Soil party formed out of negotiations among Conscience Whigs, Barnburner Democrats, and Liberty abolitionists, Bailey worked well with such antislavery Whigs as Joshua R. Giddings, Charles Francis Adams, and John G. Palfrey. But, even though his views on national policy were more Democratic than Whig, he had difficulty with the Barnburners. They demanded that former Democratic president Martin Van Buren become the Free-Soil presidential candidate *and* they fell short of Liberty standards in regard to black rights and slavery in the District of Columbia. Because neither the Ohio Liberty party nor the *National Era* had advocated direct political action against slavery in the southern states, Bailey could support a party committed only to opposing slavery within Congress's exclusive jurisdiction. He insisted, however, that the Barnburners and the Free-Soil party endorse the equal rights principles of the Declaration of Independence and that Van Buren disavow his 1835 pledge to veto bills providing for abolition in the district. When in August 1848 the Barnburners along with other delegates at the Free-Soil Convention in Buffalo, New York, endorsed the declaration, and—shortly thereafter—Van Buren repudiated his earlier position on abolition in the district, Bailey welcomed the new party. But he also, as the Liberty party outside of New York disbanded, declared his political independence. Rather than seek to become a party leader, he proposed to work as a journalist and lobbyist to promote an even more inclusive antislavery organization.[26]

As a third party in the 1848 election, the Free-Soilers did well. Organized for just a few months, they were competitive in Massachusetts, Ohio, New

---

[25]Harrold, *Bailey*, pp. 25–123.

[26]*National Era*, Feb. 24, June 15, 29, July 6, 13, Aug. 24, 31, 1848; Bailey to Charles Francis Adams, July 13, 1848, and Adams to John G. Palfrey, July 16, 1848, Adams Papers; Bailey to Van Buren, Aug. 2, 1848, Van Buren Papers, Library of Congress.; Van Buren to Benjamin F. Butler, Joseph L. White, and Salmon P. Chase, Aug. 22, 1848, in *National Era*, Aug. 31, 1848.

York, and Pennsylvania. Although Van Buren came in a distant third behind winning Whig candidate Zachary Taylor and Democratic candidate Lewis Cass, he received 10 percent of the popular vote, and the Free-Soilers elected twelve congressmen—by 1849 they also had two U.S. senators.[27] During the following years, Bailey devoted the *National Era* to keeping the new party united, preventing its platform from being watered down and attracting new supporters. Meanwhile, the Compromise of 1850's failure to settle the slavery issue, the new fugitive slave law's inspiration of widespread northern resistance, and the Kansas-Nebraska Act of 1854 reopening of the slavery expansion issue created new opportunities for forming a major antislavery party. In response, Bailey worked to unite antislavery politicians and encourage party formation.

Shortly after he arrived in Washington, Bailey assumed duties, earlier performed by Weld and Leavitt, as antislavery lobbyist at the Capitol. He searched for documents and helped develop arguments presented in Congress. He attended sessions and influenced northern and border slave state members on slavery restriction and other slavery issues. He made himself a familiar figure on Capitol Hill. The week following the *Pearl* riots, proslavery Indiana Congressmen William W. Wick, on seeing Bailey enter the gallery to listen to Giddings speak, declared, "The Abolitionist is among us, and let him stay. . . . Shall we say that it is dangerous to discuss the dogmas of his paternity because they have been adopted by others?"[28]

Bailey began caucusing with the antislavery delegation in 1847, and he gained a reputation as an unpretentious, soft-spoken, but "singularly well informed, conscientious, clear-sighted" counselor. In December 1848 he moved the *National Era* office to a more central location "on 7th Street a few doors below the General Post Office" so he could be more available to northern congressmen. In July 1849, as Congress considered compromise measures that might permit the expansion of slavery, Whittier reported that "Dr. Bailey is confined to his office; there must be some one always there to supply the

[27]Richard H. Sewell, *Ballots for Freedom: Antislavery Politics in the United States 1837–1860* (New York, 1976), pp. 167–68.

[28]Charles Francis Adams, diary entries, Feb. 15, 16, 1847, Adams Papers; John G. Palfrey to Margaret Bailey, [March 1866], Palfrey Family Papers; Greenwood, "American Salon," p. 440; *National Era*, Feb. 18, 1847; Bailey to Zebina Eastman, Oct. 1, 1849, Aldrich Papers; Bailey to Charles Sumner, [1855], Sumner Papers; George W. Julian, *Political Recollections 1840–1872* (Chicago, 1884), pp. 71–74; Charles Durkee, "On the California Question in the House of Representatives," June 7, 1850, in *National Era*, July 4, 1850.

members with necessary facts, for they are all sadly ignorant in this matter." Bailey told George W. Julian in 1849, "'Tis of no use sending slipper politicians here. They can't stand the blandishments of the slaveholders."[29]

Bailey did not regard Washington as an especially corrupting location. He praised the resident population as "intelligent, moral, and religious." But he realized that northern congressmen, who usually left their families at home, were lonely and easily dispirited. Therefore, in September 1848 he established the Washington Free-Soil Association, administered first by a pious young editorial assistant, and later by his Washington-born clerk, Lewis Clephane. Patterned on similar Democratic and Whig associations and on a book concern Bailey had begun in Cincinnati during the late 1830s, the association maintained reading rooms and published Free-Soil and antislavery tracts in cooperation with the *National Era*'s printers and the American and Foreign Anti-Slavery Society. In 1855 Bailey encouraged his employees to form the Republican Association of Washington, which gained national influence.[30] In addition, from 1848 into the late 1850s Bailey supported efforts to establish a racially integrated antislavery church in Washington. He hoped it would serve northern congressmen and his family, as well as spread an antislavery gospel in the city. In the process he earned the lifelong admiration of two young abolitionist ministers, Josiah Bushnell Grinnell of Vermont (a Congregationalist) and Moncure Conway of Virginia (a Unitarian). These men— as well as George W. Bassett who arrived in 1858—enjoyed Bailey's help and hospitality in what proved to be a very difficult undertakings.[31]

The most memorable of Bailey's efforts to boost the morale of Washington's antislavery politicians and to draw in allies were the social gatherings

---

[29]Bailey to Salmon P. Chase, Sept. 14, 1847, Chase Papers, Historical Society of Pennsylvania; Charles Francis Adams, diary entry, Apr. 29, 1848, Adams Papers; Josiah B. Grinnell, *Men and Events of Forty Years: Autobiographical Reminiscences of an Active Career from 1850 to 1890* (Boston, 1891), p. 60; George W. Julian, *Life of Joshua R. Giddings* (Chicago, 1892), p. 88; *National Era*, Dec. 21, 1848; Whittier to Lewis Tappan, July 14, 1849 (photostat of original in Lewis Tappan Papers, Library of Congress), Whittier Papers, Essex Institute, Salem, Mass.; Bailey to Julian, Mar. 14, 1849, Giddings-Julian Papers.

[30]*National Era*, Mar. 27, 1851; "Declaration of the Free Soil Association of the District of Columbia," in *National Era*, Sept. 28, 1848; Lewis Clephane, *Birth of the Republican Party* (Washington, 1889), pp. 8–9. Bailey never formally joined either association.

[31]*Emancipator*, Mar. 29, 1848; *National Era*, Mar. 27, 1851, May 17, Dec. 11, 1855, Oct. 30, 1856, Feb. 18, 1858; Grinnell, *Men and Events*, pp. 52–55, 75; Conway, *Autobiography, Memories, and Experiences*, 2 vols. (London, 1914), 1:223–41; Bailey to Lewis Tappan, Jan. 13, 1859, American Missionary Association Archives, Amistad Research Center, Tulane University; [Mary Abigail Dodge to her parents], Jan. 24, 1859, in H. Augusta Dodge, *Gail Hamilton's Life in Letters*, 2 vols. (Boston, 1901), 1:221.

he held in his home starting during the spring of 1848. Almost all of the Free-Soil congressmen took boardinghouse rooms. Their early caucuses shifted from one of these rooms to another. As the number of Free-Soilers increased, Bailey encouraged them to meet at his home, where houseguests, including at various times Tappan, Whittier, and Charles Francis Adams, could join in discussions. Bailey formalized the gatherings at the start of the spring 1851 session of Congress by inviting all the Free-Soilers for "talk and a cup of coffee . . . *every* Saturday night of the session." By that time Bailey had moved his residence to C Street, where he had bought one of the "finest houses" for about $10,000.[32]

He and Margaret Bailey excelled at entertaining. Conway recalled that "the serious force and learning characteristic of the *National Era* could hardly prepare one to find Dr. Bailey the elegant and polished gentleman that he was." Similarly Julian remarked, "There was about the presence and per-sonality of the doctor a wonderful charm." "Delicate-looking" in his mid-forties, with a broad forehead and full beard, Bailey exuded honesty and "dignity of character," as well as "an almost boyish lightness of spirit," which encouraged his guests to relax and enjoy themselves. Conway described Margaret Bailey as a "tall, graceful and intellectual woman." She made sure that young women, whom Conway referred to as "bright and pretty 'Yan-kee' ladies," attended the gatherings. Many of them wrote for the *National Era* and added a literary as well as political tone to the Baileys' soirees.[33]

Among the Free-Soil politicians who attended were Chase, who entered the U.S. Senate in 1849, Hale, Giddings, David Wilmot, Preston King, Horace Mann, Robert Rantoul, Palfrey, William Allen, William Slade, Charles Sumner, Norton S. Townshend, and Charles Durkee. But, as Julian recalled, "Dr. Bailey took care to invite sundry men who were not committed to the Free-Soil gospel, but who were tending in that direction, and such were evi-dently helped forward by the influence of these meetings." Whigs who at-tended included the conservative Thomas Corwin, who served as Millard

---

[32]Horace Mann to Mary Peabody Mann, Apr. 30, 1848, Mann Papers, Massachusetts Historical Society; Lewis Tappan to John Scoble, July 3, 1850, in Abel and Klingberg, *Side-Light*, p. 251; George W. Julian to wife, June 26, July 19, 1850, Jan. 2, 11, 1851, in Grace Julian Clarke, "Home Letters of George W. Julian, 1850–1851," *Indiana Magazine of History* 19 (1933):137–38, 141, 153, 156; Julian, *Political Recollections*, p. 112.

[33]Conway, *Autobiography*, p. 186; Greenwood, "American Salon," pp. 438, 440, 447; Grinnell, *Men and Events*, p. 75; John G. Whittier, "Gamaliel Bailey," in *National Era*, July 7, 1859; [Snodgrass], "Pioneer Editor," pp. 746, 748.

Fillmore's secretary of the Treasury, William H. Seward, John McLean, Benjamin Wade, Thaddeus Stevens, and Horace Greeley—all of whom became Republicans in 1855–56.[34]

Initially the affairs were, as Grace Greenwood recalled, "democratically informal, and quite simple in the matters of dress and refreshment." The Bailey children joined the dinner and early evening conversation, much to the annoyance of Charles Francis Adams, who complained about the food and described Bailey's home to be "a very ill regulated house." The young women performed plays and created tableaus. Guests engaged in square dancing, ballad singing, and word games. After the Baileys moved to C Street, the entertaining became more lavish, although British writer William Makepeace Thackeray expressed shock when in 1853 teetotaler Bailey served coffee instead of brandy after dinner. In it all Grinnell recognized "the plotting . . . heart and policy of the great editor, Bailey," binding together antislavery leaders in a still hostile city.[35]

The best known, and perhaps most significant, of Bailey's lobbying efforts occurred in May 1854 at the end of the long congressional struggle over the Kansas-Nebraska bill that had been introduced the previous January by Stephen A. Douglas, the powerful Democratic senator from Illinois. The bill, which repealed the Missouri Compromise and allowed slavery to expand into Kansas Territory, aroused opposition across the North, greatly intensifying the sectional conflict. The Senate passed the bill on March 4. Thereafter, Bailey concentrated on the House of Representatives, which had a large northern majority. The main difficulty was the three-way division among the bill's opponents, including Free-Soilers, Anti-Nebraska Whigs, and Anti-Nebraska Democrats. "Party names & preferences," Bailey advised a fellow journalist, "are the cords that bind the Samson of the North." Working with New York Democrat Preston King, Bailey spent May 19 and 20 at the Capitol talking with opposition leaders as the final vote on the bill

---

[34]Greenwood, "American Salon," pp. 440–47; Grinnell, *Men and Events*, pp. 57–60; Horace Mann to Mary Peabody Mann, Feb. 24, 1853, in Mary Peabody Mann, *Life of Horace Mann* (1937; reprint ed., Miami, 1969), p. 396; William H. Seward to wife, Apr. 10, 1854, in Frederick W. Seward, *William H. Seward*, 3 vols. (New York, 1891), 2:226; Bailey to James S. Pike, Apr. 23, 1848, in Pike, *First Blows of the Civil War: The Ten Years of Preliminary Conflict in the United States from 1850 to 1860* (New York, 1879), p. 418.

[35]Greenwood, "American Salon," pp. 443, 445–46; Charles Francis Adams, diary entries, May 22, Dec. 14, 1851, Adams Papers; Conway, *Autobiography*, p. 186; Grinnell, *Men and Events*, p. 61; Julian to wife, Jan. 22, Feb. 20, 1851, in Clarke, "Home Letters," pp. 157, 160–61.

approached. Just before the House adjourned on the twentieth, he and King succeeded in getting the leaders of the Anti-Nebraska Whigs and Democrats to meet with the Free-Soilers "in a common caucus at eight in the evening." As it turned out, the Kansas-Nebraska bill passed the next day. But at a second caucus meeting, about thirty congressmen endorsed Bailey's larger goal by calling for "an immediate union of all Anti-Nebraska men, and the organization of a new party." There were plenty of state-level meetings that summer that engaged in the grassroots organizing that eventually produced the Republican party. But Israel Washburn, one of the Democrats at the House caucus, later praised Bailey as the "earliest and ablest and most influential advocate" of antislavery union. Washburn declared Bailey to have been "the immediate founder" of the new party."[36]

BAILEY'S EXPERIENCE IN Cincinnati, his engagement in antislavery politics at the national level, and his hopes to attract white southerners to the antislavery movement influenced his views and actions regarding slavery and race. Although he had become an immediate abolitionist in 1834, his life on the border between the free and slave states set him on a different, more conservative course than his counterparts in New England and New York. As more radical abolitionists advocated either concentration on northern public opinion and disunion or direct intervention in the South to help slaves escape, Bailey insisted that the only way to peaceful emancipation lay in persuading white southerners voluntarily to embrace emancipation. In Washington his views on emancipation and racial issues grew even more conservative.

In comparison to many white antislavery politicians, Bailey had an admirable record on black rights. Since the 1830s he advocated abolition *and* eliminating prejudicial legislation affecting the free black population. During the early 1840s he joined other Ohio Liberty abolitionists in calling for the repeal of that state's discriminatory Black Laws. In 1841 he declared that these laws "violated the rights of humanity" by discriminating against African Americans in the courts and schools and by punishing white Ohioans who treated a fugitive slave "as a fellow man free and equal to themselves."

---

[36]Bailey to James S. Pike, May 21, 1854, Pike Papers, Calais Free Library, Calais, Maine; Israel Washburn, "Gamaliel Bailey," *Universalist Quarterly* 5 (1868):298, 300–301; Henry Wilson, *History of the Rise and Fall of the Slave Power in America*, 2 vols., 3d ed. (Boston, 1876), 2:410–11; William E. Gienapp, *Origins of the Republican Party 1852–1856* (New York, 1986), pp. 78–79; Harrold, *Bailey*, pp. 158–60.

In most respects his removal to Washington changed none of this. In 1848 he wrote, "Common Sense and Christianity recognize but one Humanity; with various aspects, but identical Rights—a Humanity, one in Origin, Duty, and Destiny; and God, who is the father of all men, frowns upon that insensate pride which leads one portion of this great Family to deny the rights of Brotherhood to the rest." In 1856 he reaffirmed his belief that the Declaration of Independence applied to all men and endorsed "laws and usages tending to equalize the condition of all men."[37]

Throughout the late 1840s and the decade of the 1850s, Bailey followed these principles in making the *National Era* a proponent of better treatment for the District of Columbia's free black population. He often described an industrious local black population struggling to improve its condition amid hostile surroundings. He protested against an unjust local legal system that harshly punished African Americans for trivial offenses while not protecting them from white criminals. He opposed race-specific curfews, taxes, and residence requirements. He continued to refute racist contentions that the poverty of most free African Americans indicated an innate inferiority. "It ought not be deemed surprising, he wrote in 1854, that men and women who have toiled for others all their lives should find themselves destitute on emerging from their condition of thralldom." In 1856 he wrote, "Society owes it to itself, to its own peace, safety, and comfort, to promote the elevation of its humblest members," and he acted on that assumption by actively supporting Myrtella Miner's Washington School for Negro Girls."[38] In 1857 Bailey raised the money to fund Montgomery Blair's presentation of Dred Scott's case before the Supreme Court. He got each Republican member of Congress to pay two dollars and contributed four himself. When the Court ruled against Scott and black citizenship, Bailey insisted that African Americans were citizens entitled to the same protection as white citizens.[39]

But, during his years in Washington, some of Bailey's views and actions raised questions about the depth of his commitment to black equality in the

---

[37] *Philanthropist* (Cincinnati), Sept. 1, Oct. 31, 1841; *National Era,* Jan. 13, 1848, Jan. 24, 1856.

[38] *National Era,* May 18, Nov. 9, 1848, Aug. 2, 1849, June 20, Dec. 12, 26, 1850, Feb. 13, June 16, Oct. 23, 1851, Jan. 27, Apr. 28, 1853, Aug. 24, 1854, May 24, 1855, Mar. 27, Aug. 7, 1856, May 14, July 9, 1857, Dec. 30, 1858; Harrold, *Subversives,* pp. 185–86.

[39] Bailey to William H. Seward, May 8, 1857 (circular), Seward Papers, University of Rochester; Bailey to Lyman Trumbull, May 12, 1857, Trumbull Papers, Library of Congress; William E. Smith, *Francis Preston Blair Family in Politics* (New York, 1933), pp. 385–86; *National Era,* Mar. 12–26, Apr. 2, June 4, 1857.

United States. Shortly after he arrived he stopped using the term "abolitionist" in favor of the less precise "antislavery." In December 1848 he disagreed
with his friend Joshua R. Giddings, who represented Ohio's Western Reserve in Congress, over Giddings's bill for uncompensated emancipation in
the District of Columbia. Bailey contended that the bill—which had no
chance to pass—would encourage local masters to sell their slaves south,
strengthen Calhoun's effort to form a southern caucus, and raise a fierce
hostility that a bill providing for "liberal" compensation would not. In response, Giddings admonished Bailey for having "done wrong," and Lewis
Tappan expressed concern that he had adopted a "principle at variance
with the formulative principle" of the American and Foreign Anti-Slavery
Society.[40] In addition, Bailey never published black writers, and the only
African Americans who attended his social gatherings were his family's black
servants. In 1856, at a time when the *National Era* faced financial difficulties,
Bailey rejected Tappan's suggestion that he take on Frederick Douglass as
associate editor. The same year that Bailey objected to the Dred Scott decision, he predicted that African Americans would require a long period of
training to undo the "mischief wrought by slavery," and he had earlier implied that they might exist as an unequal caste for centuries.[41] Gradually he
came to agree with many Border-South opponents of slavery that free African
Americans should be encouraged to leave the United States.

Bailey was not exceptional in his despondency concerning the future
of African Americans in the United States. He shared with other white
Americans—including white abolitionists—a belief that black people and
white people were naturally destined to inhabit different climatic zones. Also,
during the late 1840s and early 1850s, several more radical abolitionists believed white prejudice would never allow African Americans to achieve equal
rights without the establishment of a black emigrant community in Africa
or Latin America. Henry Highland Garnet and Martin R. Delany best rep-

---

[40]James Brewer Stewart, *Joshua R. Giddings and the Tactics of Radical Politics* (Cleveland,
1970), pp. 168–69; Giddings, diary entries, Dec. 26, 27, [1848], Giddings Papers; Lewis
Tappan to F. Julius LeMoyne, Feb. 8, 1849, in "Letters of Dr. F. J. LeMoyne," *Journal of Negro
History* 18(1933):454.

[41]Tappan to Bailey, Dec. 18, 31, 1856, letter book copies, Tappan Papers; Bailey to
Seward, [Sept. 28, 1858], Seward Papers; *National Era*, Mar. 22, 1849, June 18, 1857. See also
George M. Fredrickson, *Black Image in the White Mind: The Debate on Afro-American Character and
Destiny 1817–1914* (New York, 1971), pp. 130–64; Eric Foner, *Free Soil, Free Labor, Free Men: The
Ideology of the Republican Party before the Civil War* (New York, 1970), pp. 261–330.

resented this point of view among black abolitionists; and James G. Birney, among white abolitionists.[42] Like these individuals, Bailey continued to oppose the American Colonization Society as proslavery. He rejected forcing free African Americans to leave the United States. But for years he suggested that free black people voluntarily undertake colonization efforts in Latin America. In 1858 he supported the plan for black colonization of Central America that Missouri representative Francis P. Blair, Jr., presented to the House of Representatives. Pointing out that such abolitionists as Gerrit Smith and Theodore Parker supported the plan, Bailey argued that it was essentially antislavery. Manifest Destiny, Bailey declared in early 1859, determined that the United States would control Central America. Because of that region's climate, he contended, the only question was whether African Americans who went there to work would be free or enslaved. Blair's plan therefore would prevent the spread of slavery, which Bailey—forced to choose —favored over consistent advocacy of black rights in the United States.[43]

LARGELY BECAUSE OF where he lived and worked—Baltimore, Cincinnati, and Washington—Bailey differed substantially in intellectual orientation and political tactics from prominent abolitionists who lived far to his north. What he held to be necessary to self-preservation and introducing antislavery principles to a white southern audience, they regarded as cowardly and racist. Among Bailey's stronger critics were radical political abolitionists centered in western New York and those—such as Frederick Douglass—who by the late 1840s tended toward the New Yorkers' point of view. William Lloyd Garrison and many of his associates, who distrusted Bailey's mild language, his politics, and especially his efforts in the South, joined in by the time he reached Washington.

In remarks that angered radical political abolitionist leader Gerrit Smith, Bailey had in October 1841—a few weeks after a mob had destroyed his *Philanthropist* press—criticized the efforts of three young white men from Illinois who had gone into Missouri to help slaves escape. "It is impossible

[42] *Philanthropist* (Cincinnati), Sept. 22, 1841; *National Era,* Jan. 28, 1847, Mar. 22, 1849, Mar. 13, 1851, Oct. 27, 1853, June 10, Sept. 23, 1858; Sewell, *Ballots,* p. 186; Benjamin Quarles, *Black Abolitionists* (New York, 1969), pp. 215–18; Fladeland, *Birney,* p. 280; James Oliver Horton and Lois E. Horton, *In Hope of Liberty: Culture, Community and Protest among Northern Free Blacks, 1700–1860* (New York, 1997), pp. 260–63.
[43] *National Era,* Jan. 21, 1848, Mar. 13, Apr. 17, 24, 1851, Apr. 1, May 13, June 10, 1858.

that aggression like this on the citizens of other states should effect the abolition of slavery, while it could not fail to involve the anti-slavery cause in
unnecessary odium," Bailey declared. A few months later, Bailey objected to
Smith urging abolitionists to go south to help slaves escape and calling on
slaves to steal if necessary to escape. In response, Smith charged that Bailey
and other Cincinnati abolitionists were callous and selfish, concerned only
with protecting themselves and other white people from slavery's influences.[44]

As the *National Era* got under way, Bailey's radical political abolitionist
and Garrisonian critics stressed that his moderation sacrificed the moral
righteousness and sympathy for the slave that underlay the antislavery cause.
New York abolitionist Beriah Green dismissed Bailey's tact, maintaining
that "in the great conflict . . . in which the Era is professedly engaged, a little
bravery . . . may be as much to the purpose as a good deal of discretion." The
Anti-Slavery Bugle—a Garrisonian newspaper published in Salem, Ohio—
observed that the conduct of the *National Era* was "*exceedingly judicious*" and
would not be "indicted for incendiarism, fanaticism, and we almost said
abolitionism." Garrison's *Liberator*—published in Boston—added that "a genuine anti-slavery journal would not be tolerated twenty four hours in that
District." Garrison charged that Bailey was "cautious to craftiness" and was
never "hurried into any excess of speech or language by generous impulses.
. . . Though ostensibly engaged in one of the most exciting reforms . . . he
manages so discretely, utters himself so unoffensively, and studies to behave
so gentlemanly, that he creates no alarms . . . and is regarded . . . with stolid
indifference." In 1851 Frederick Douglass condemned the *National Era* in
even more graphic terms. "It is," he told Gerrit Smith, "most attractive and
fair seeming to the eye, but it is cold and lifeless as marble. Were it but half
as faithful as it is beautiful, it would shake this guilty land. But alas! It is dead.
No living heart throbs beneath its pure white ruffles. It is powerless for Good,
and only remains to taint the anti-slavery atmosphere."[45]

During the riotous time following the *Pearl* escape attempt, Bailey further
angered his northern abolitionist critics by denying that he would "support

---

[44]*Philanthropist* (Cincinnati), Oct. 13, 1841, Feb. 9, Apr. 6, Aug. 27, 1842; [Gerrit Smith],
"Address . . . to the Slaves in the U. States of America," in *Liberator*, Feb. 11, 1842; Smith to
Bailey, Sept. 13, 1842, in *Philanthropist* (Cincinnati), Oct. 15, 1842; Harrold, *Rise of Aggressive
Abolitionism*, p. 114.

[45]Green to James G. Birney, Aug. 2, 1847, in *Birney Letters*, 2:1078; *Anti-Slavery Bugle*, Jan. 29,
1847; *Liberator*, June 25, July 16, 1847; Douglass to Smith, May 1, 1851, in Philip S. Foner, *Life
and Writings of Frederick Douglass* (New York, 1950–55), 2:151–52.

illegal or unconstitutional measures to end slavery" and would not engage in "a clandestine policy." Radical political abolitionists denounced him for implying that the white men who had aided the *Pearl* fugitives had done wrong. They condemned his "respect for slave laws," his lack of "heart," and his failure to recognize "the negro . . . [as] fully a man, and fully possessed of the rights of man." Among Garrisonians, Wendell Phillips derided Bailey as an "apostate and reprobate." Phillips said the *National Era* was a "nuisance." Bailey responded to his northern abolitionist critics by reminding them that he took a stand as far south as he dared, while they remained safely in the far North. He ridiculed Garrison as a "self-righteous reformer" who regarded Christ's tolerance and persuasiveness as "mere 'milk and water,'" who adored truth "but never . . . hesitates to misrepresent and caricature an adversary," who abjured violence "but, with a tongue set on fire by hell, scathes and devours what ever crosses his path."[46]

Most abolitionists—especially those who like him were headed into mass antislavery politics—supported Bailey. Lewis Tappan—who later changed his mind—told Gerrit Smith that "had Garrison etc. who revile him, or you who censure him, been there and conducted an anti-slavery paper with more ultra views, the paper would have been destroyed and the cause injured." Henry B. Stanton, who had a well-deserved reputation for facing down mobs, branded Bailey's critics cowards who found it easy to boast "of what wonderful feats of skill and bravery" they would perform if only *they* were in Washington. Quaker abolitionist Samuel M. Janney, a Virginia resident, told a Garrisonian journalist, "I take the N. Era which is much approved by the anti-slavery friends here & the wholesome truths it contains will, I hope, do much good. . . . Why not let Doct Bailey alone to labour in the field he has chosen? It is a locality in which your society *cannot labour* with your present views."[47]

Proslavery journalists agreed that Bailey and the *National Era* constituted a threat to the peculiar institution. In Alabama the *Montgomery Times* warned slaveholders in 1853, "This is one of the ablest papers in the Government. . . . [It] is furnishing the axe which is to cleave your heads." In 1852 the *New York Herald* advised, "Southern editors who are so frequently shocked by

---

[46]*National Era*, May 20, July 1, 22, 1847, Apr. 20, May 18, 1848; *Proceedings of the National Liberty Convention, Held at Buffalo, New York, June 14th and 15th, 1848*, pp. 8, 46, 47, in Goodell Anti-Slavery Collection, Oberlin College; *Liberator*, July 16, 1847.

[47]Tappan to Smith, July 5, 1848, Smith Papers; *Liberty Press*, quoted in *Emancipator*, June 14, 1848; Janney to Sydney Howard Gay, July 12, 1847, Gay Papers, Columbia University.

[Horace] Greeley, Douglass, Abby Kelley, Garrison and Lucretia Mott would do well to turn their attention to the more important subject of the success and influence of the central abolition organ in Washington." In 1850 fifty southern politicians led by Robert Toombs of Georgia and Andrew P. Butler of South Carolina cooperated in establishing the *Southern Press* in Washington as proslavery journal to counter the *National Era*'s impact on the Upper South.[48]

Bailey's influence peaked in late 1855 and early 1856 as he led in planning a convention in Pittsburgh that created a national Republican organization. By mid-1856 it had declined as practical politicians regarded his moderate abolitionism as too extreme. The *National Era*'s circulation also suffered as it came into direct competition with the weekly editions of such large Republican journals as the *New York Tribune*, the *New York Times*, and the *Chicago Tribune*. To a degree the success of Bailey's advocacy of antislavery union in a mass political party had doomed the *National Era*, and the Panic of 1857 caused further difficulties. He had always been a dyspeptic worrier despite his cheerful public demeanor, and as his political and financial standing declined so did his fragile health, which in late 1858 began a precipitous decline —probably due to stomach cancer. He died in June 1859, during a voyage to Europe futilely undertaken in hope that it would provide a remedy. The *National Era* outlived Bailey by less than a year as Margaret Bailey's effort to keep it going collapsed in March 1860.[49] Republicans and most abolitionists lamented Bailey's death and noted his journalistic, literary, and political contributions to the antislavery cause. But the rush of events leading up to the Civil War and later Margaret Bailey's failure to complete a biography of her husband obscured his role. His body lies in an unmarked grave in Oak Hill Cemetery in Georgetown.[50]

Since this essay questions the depth of Bailey's commitment to black rights, it is essential to mention in closing that members of Washington's African American community joined in mourning his death. They remembered him for years afterward, suggesting that there was more to the relationship than surviving records reveal. Shortly after he died two young black women who

---

[48]*Montgomery Times*, quoted in *National Era*, Jan. 6, 1853; *New York Herald*, quoted in *National Era*, Feb. 26, 1852; *Southern Press*, July 19, 22, 1850; *National Era*, June 20, 1850; Nye, *Fettered Freedom*, p. 96.

[49]William H. Seward to wife, June 26, 1856, in Seward, *Seward*, 2:279; Gienapp, *Origins of the Republican Party*, pp. 343–44; Harrold, *Bailey*, pp. 167–200, 210–12.

[50]Harrold, *Bailey*, pp. 212–15.

attended the biracial church he helped establish in the city privately expressed their grief. One of them wrote, "The death of Dr. Bailey is much regretted in this city, we believed him to be a true friend of our people."[51]

Over a decade later, the January 20, 1870, issue of the *New Era*, a black journal soon to be renamed the *New National Era*, remembered Bailey. J. Sella Martin, a former slave, and since 1868 the pastor of Washington's Fifteenth Street Presbyterian Church, served as the paper's editor, and Frederick Douglass served as corresponding editor. Under the heading "THE OLD 'ERA,'" Martin wrote, "That was a knightly spirit in Gamaliel Bailey to come to the Capital during the old *regime*, within [range] of the bondman's cry, that he might translate the despairing wail into the language of humanity, through the columns of the *National Era*. . . . The editor carried with him a martyr's heart in sustaining the bridges of his paper against all odds for so many years. How glorious was the work which he did! We all remember how Mr. Bailey carried his life in his hand[s] for years: here under what was called ironically we suppose the protecting might of the Capital." Bailey and his helpers, Martin recalled, "spoke for us when we were dumb, and now we use our [free voice] to honor their memories and to chronicle their work. . . . By the vindication of their doctrine and the fulfillment of their prophecies—that we are all equal before God and that the negro would himself some day prove it—we may make the NEW ERA as glorious in its achievements as those saints of the *Old Era* were luminant in self-sacrifice."[52]

GAMALIEL BAILEY'S CAREER as a journalist and lobbyist illuminates an intersection between immediate abolitionism and mass antislavery politics that is obscured in studies that concentrate on one aspect or the other of the struggle against slavery in antebellum America. Historians often emphasize the differences between moral reformers and practical politicians. Bailey's work in Washington bridges that gap. All abolitionists hoped to have a political impact and influence the South. Radical political antislavery leader Gerrit Smith served a term in Congress. Garrison and Douglass encouraged the formation of the Free-Soil and Republican parties, even as they criticized each party's shortcoming in regard to abolition and black rights. Bailey's location on the border between the free and slave states led him to conceive

---

[51] Bettie [Browne] to Emily Howland, July 13, 1859 (quotation) and Emma V. Brown to Howland, July 14, 1859, in Emily Howland Papers, Cornell University, Ithaca, N.Y.

[52] *New Era* (Washington, D.C.), Jan. 20, 1870.

a political antislavery strategy that had great potential appeal among white Americans but forced him to compromise basic abolitionist principles. His hope to transform white southern opinion, which he shared with other antislavery activists in the border region, never achieved success. But his skill as a journalist and lobbyist allowed him to influence the formation of a political party, however imperfect, that through war and politics ended slavery in 1865 and laid a constitutional basis for black rights established over a century later.

Jonathan Earle

Saturday Nights at the Baileys'

Building an Antislavery Movement in Congress, 1838–1854

T HE COLD WINTER of 1850 caused residents of the nation's capital to
focus on indoor activities for amusement. In the numerous saloons,
boardinghouse messes, and theaters that lined the streets near the Capitol,
the favorite topic of conversation was the massive omnibus compromise bill
wending its way through Congress. For the architect of the omnibus bill,
seventy-three-year-old Henry Clay, high-stakes poker and smoky games of
whist were favorite pastimes during the long, cold nights during which the
compromise was hammered out. Inside a spacious house on C Street, however, a very different type of gathering took place each Saturday night, every
bit as political as one of Clay's compromise sessions.

It was not always obvious: each weekly gathering on C Street was attended
by roughly equal numbers of men and women whose activities were not
segregated by sex. No alcohol was served, and there was no gambling on the
premises. Indeed, charades, epigram-writing, "hurly-burly," and blind-man's
bluff each vied for the raciest form of entertainment. On one particularly
risqué evening, Ohio Representative Joshua Giddings, the silver-haired dean

The author wishes to thank Paul Finkelman and Donald R. Kennon for convening an
exhilarating symposium on slavery and Congress in the spring of 2006, and for their patience and wisdom. Thanks also to Michael Holt and, especially, Stanley Harrold, whose
Gamaliel Bailey and Antislavery Union (Kent, Ohio, 1986) and more recent *Subversives: Antislavery
Community in Washington D.C.* (Baton Rouge, 2003) significantly influenced the arguments in
this essay.

of the tiny antislavery minority in Congress, collided while blindfolded with
a comely twenty-seven-year-old governess and writer named Sara Jane Clarke,
and the two collapsed to the floor in a tangled mess of limbs and mussed
clothes. To one of the other guests in attendance that evening, the collision
was part of a larger, brilliant strategy hit upon by the evenings' host to bind
together and lift the spirits of the city's beleaguered antislavery residents: in
every game of blind-man's bluff the guest saw "the plotting . . . heart and
policy of the great editor [Gamaliel] Bailey" and his wife, Margaret.[1]

The Baileys *were*, in fact, engaged in an elaborate plot during the early
1850s that went far beyond the various reform-minded publications the
couple edited at the time: they conceived of their parlor as the epicenter and
nurturing ground for a movement, within the capital, to eradicate slavery.
According to Clarke, the literary governess who wrote for Gamaliel Bailey's
National Era and other publications under the pseudonym Grace Greenwood,
the gatherings were much like a French salon, "except that it was more cosmopolitan, and had a purer moral atmosphere." The Baileys extended a
standing invitation to "all men and women inclined toward the antislavery
faith . . . and even such honest supporters of the 'institution' as were fearless
or curious enough to enter [their] hospitable house." Most welcome, Clarke
recalled years later, were U.S. senators, congressmen, and "even such honest
supporters of [slavery] as were fearless or curious enough to enter."[2]

Indiana Free-Soiler George W. Julian first attended the Baileys' gatherings as a freshman congressman, during a lonely period of separation from
his wife, Ann Elizabeth Julian. His letters to her are full of vivid descriptions
of the "glorious," "rollicking" evenings at the house and of the games—including fortune-telling and another where guests took turns donning a blind-
fold, turning around three times, and then attempting to blow out a candle.
"I have not laughed so much in months," Julian wrote home. Yet four decades later, Julian passed over the play and focused instead on the political
significance: "Those gatherings were not by any means entirely social. They
had a political value and significance. They strengthened the faith and stimulated the courage of the anti-slavery minority, while Dr. Bailey took care to
invite sundry men who were not committed to the Free-Soil gospel, but who

---

[1]Josiah B. Grinnell, *Men and Events of Forty Years: Autobiographical Reminiscences of an Active Career from 1850 to 1890* (Boston, 1891), p. 60; Harrold, *Gamaliel Bailey*, p. 134.

[2]Grace Greenwood, "An American Salon," *Cosmopolitan* 8 (1890):443; Grace Julian Clark, "Home Letters of George W. Julian," *Indiana Magazine of History* 29 (1933):156.

were tending in that direction, and such were evidently helped forward by the influence of these meetings."[3]

What the Baileys clearly realized was the importance sociability plays in building and sustaining a politically unpopular movement, especially in a hostile atmosphere like the nation's capital at midcentury. It is a realization shared by many in government today: witness the ecumenical prayer breakfasts on Capitol Hill or the Opus Dei house, where members affiliated with the lay-Catholic organization live together while Congress is in session. Modern Congress-watchers have also blamed the recent increase of partisanship and mean-spiritedness on the relative *absence* of sociability between representatives known as "Tuesday to Thursday" members for their schedules in Washington.[4]

Hatching an antislavery movement within the capital took considerable effort and patience, and lagged far behind the crusade in the northern states. Indeed, it was not until the issues like a potential Mexican cession, the Wilmot Proviso, and the Free-Soil election—fifteen years or more after Nat Turner's rebellion and the founding of the *Liberator*—that a critical mass of antislavery congressmen and their allies made a permanent movement consciousness possible. The founding of the antislavery journal *National Era* in Washington and the relocation of the Baileys to the city to edit it was also a significant factor in building a true movement culture there—by which I mean the shared values, behaviors, language, traditions, symbols, and other forms of group definition by which a social movement marks itself as unique.[5]

In this essay I will describe the coming together of the small antislavery vanguard in Washington in the late 1840s and how its members enlarged their circle and increasingly turned the attention of the federal government to the slavery issue. I will argue that the formation of new political alliances (such as the Free-Soil party), combined with the conscious facilitating of a movement culture—in Washington boardinghouses, the lobbies of the Capitol, and the parlors at the Baileys'—took place during the long buildup to the

---

[3]George Julian to Elizabeth Julian, Jan. 22, 1851, in Clark, "Home Letters of George W. Julian," p. 157; George Julian quoted in Greenwood, "An American Salon," p. 447.

[4]Juliet Eilperin, *Fight Club Politics: How Partisanship Is Poisoning the House of Representatives* (Lanham, Md., 2006). "Tuesday to Thursday" members spend only three days a week in Washington, returning to their districts on the weekend.

[5]Social scientists write of tangible markers of movement culture, including a special way of speaking (a shared slang or movement-specific slogans), rituals or ritualized behavior, a uniform of stylized clothing, a symbol, movement folklore, and identification with tradition.

fateful Compromise of 1850. Although the circle of antislavery partisans were unable to derail the compromise, they did help to cement a new *political* antislavery ideology and began a movement within Congress that ended only with the adoption of the Thirteenth Amendment fifteen years later.

The 1830s: No "Movement Culture"

Antislavery talk in Congress was nothing new in the 1840s and 1850s. As Sean Wilentz has recently shown, hardly a year went by after the federal compromises of 1787 without some discussion that touched on the matter of slavery. The First Congress, for example, argued over whether to include a special tariff on imported slaves, and whether to accept petitions for regulating the "debasing" and "abominable" slave trade and for gradual emancipation. Both proposals failed.[6] Other efforts to ban slavery in the newly acquired Louisiana Territory and for gradual emancipation in the District of Columbia similarly went down to defeat, and even the formal abolition of the transatlantic slave trade in 1807 was accomplished only over the strong objections of both Federalists and Republicans from the Deep South.

In 1819 New York Congressman James Tallmadge caught his colleagues off guard when he proposed an amendment to Missouri's application for statehood. When Tallmadge proposed prohibiting "the further introduction of slavery" into Missouri and provided that slaves born in Missouri after it became a state "shall be free, but may be held to service until the age of twenty-five years" he set in motion what Leonard Richards memorably called a "congressional donnybrook" that lasted almost two years.[7] Rufus King, who back in 1787 had argued strenuously against the Constitution's three-fifths clause and, at sixty-four, was the last of the original Federalists still in national politics, eloquently supported Tallmadge's amendment in the Senate. And a coterie of Republican "restrictionists" in the House banded together to enunciate for the first time antislavery *Jeffersonian* readings of politics and

---

[6]*Annals of Congress*, 1st Cong., 2d sess., 1790, pp. 1224–25; Sean Wilentz, *The Rise of American Democracy* (New York, 2005), pp. 218–19; Richard Newman, "Prelude to the Gag Rule: Southern Reaction to Antislavery Petitions in the First Federal Congress," *Journal of the Early Republic* 16 (1996):571–99.

[7]*Annals of Congress*, 15th Cong., 2d sess., 1818–19, p. 1170; Leonard Richards, *The Slave Power* (Baton Rouge, 2000), p. 53.

the Constitution that presaged later arguments in the platforms of the Liberty, Free-Soil, and Republican parties.[8]

The compromise that resulted from the Missouri Crisis was a carefully laid one, and a new generation of politicians (led by the canny New York Senator Martin Van Buren) worked to ensure that the destabilizing slavery issue would be kept largely at the margins of federal lawmaking for the next quarter century. Yet keeping slavery out of politics became increasingly difficult to accomplish after the birth of the radical, "immediatist" abolition movement in 1831. Four years later, the American Anti-Slavery Society began to bombard the country with free and incendiary pamphlets that starkly portrayed the violence, lustfulness, and brutality of southern slaveholders—and Congress with hundreds of thousands of petitions calling for an end to slavery in the nation's capital.

Although one scholar has written that "the 'people' were [in Congress] . . . in the form of signatures scribbled on thousands of petitions, with which they inundated Congress," the truth was "the people" were muzzled by the series of gag rules passed on the first day of each congressional session between 1836 and 1844.[9] During these years several brave and outspoken representatives fought the slaveholders and their allies, often (as in the case of former President John Quincy Adams and the gag rule) with some success. But in each case the antislavery side's numbers were too small and their attempts to foment a viable movement in the capital thwarted. I will briefly discuss one little-known example here and try to account for the failure of one member of Congress's stand against slavery and slaveholders to catch fire during the dark days of the gag.

Thomas Morris, a Van Burenite senator from southern Ohio, had shown no indication that he supported abolitionism or the American Anti-Slavery Society's petition drive when he presented a routine petition for abolition in the District of Columbia forwarded to him by the ladies of his hometown

---

[8]Jonathan Earle, *Jacksonian Antislavery and the Politics of Free Soil* (Chapel Hill, 2004); Wilentz, *The Rise of American Democracy*, p. 225. Strict construction of the Constitution and preservation of individual rights against powerful aristocratic forces, they argued, demanded slavery's restriction.

[9]Before Representative Henry Pinckney of South Carolina proposed that all antislavery petitions be referred to a select committee (where they would be "laid on the table" with "no further action whatever") in February 1836 chaos often reigned on the House floor during the session's opening days, as anti- and proslavery congressmen used dueling parliamentary maneuvers. See Richards, *The Slave Power*, pp. 131–36.

near Cincinnati. John C. Calhoun, who occupied the desk next to Morris's in the Senate chamber, quickly rose to his feet and attacked the petitioners as "fanatics" and accused Morris of fomenting rebellion in the South, since presenting abolitionist petitions would "compel the Southern press to discuss slavery in the very presence of Slaves, who would be induced to believe that there was a powerful party in the North ready to assist them." Morris's response to Calhoun took other senators by surprise in that it violated an unspoken gentlemen's agreement to refrain from open debate on the slavery issue—in other words, slavery was excluded from gentlemen's talk. (I have found no evidence that Morris consulted any other member of Congress—or even any other member of his family—before answering Calhoun's attack). The Ohioan angrily retorted that whether Calhoun liked it or not, the Constitution granted Congress the authority to abolish slavery in the District of Columbia if it so chose; he also objected to Calhoun's call to gag the people of his district: "If you are to tell the people that they are only to petition on this or that subject, or in this or that manner," he told Calhoun, "the right of petition is but a mockery."[10]

These comments were all the more unusual having come from a heretofore loyal, hard-money Democrat like Morris. There are hints that Morris felt that Calhoun in particular and what he called the "Southern majority" in general carried too much influence in national affairs, and that Calhoun's call to ban his constituents' antislavery petitions struck him as "haughty and aristocratic."[11]

The next year Morris shocked the Democratic party in Ohio by announcing for the first time that he was "opposed to slavery in all its forms, and against its further extension in our country." As had become usual practice for "coming out of the closet" on slavery, party officials summarily revoked Morris's Senate seat (replacing him, interestingly enough, with Benjamin Tappan, who had little in common politically with his famous abolitionist brothers Lewis and Arthur). Emancipated by what he called his "unceremonious lopping off," Morris delivered a speech where he coined a potent new

---

[10] *Congressional Globe*, 24th Cong., 1st sess., 1835–36, p. 77. Morris gave no reason for his sudden support for abolitionists' petition rights. He did, however, complain repeatedly to his son that the Senate was "the aristocratic branch of government" and expressed disappointment in the "appearance and management of the great men." Morris to Jonathan D. Morris, Dec. 22, 1833, in Benjamin Franklin Morris, ed., *The Life of Thomas Morris: Pioneer and Long a Legislator of Ohio, and U.S. Senator from 1833 to 1839* (Cincinnati, 1856), pp. 348–49.

[11] Thomas Morris to Jonathan D. Morris, Nov. 30, Dec. 17, 22, 1833, in Morris, *The Life of Thomas Morris*, pp. 345–49.

phrase picked up by Free-Soilers and Republicans in later decades: "The slave power of the South, and the banking power of the North, are now uniting to rule this country," he said in February 1839. And while he became a sort of folk hero to the men who formed the Liberty (and later, Free-Soil) party, no movement coalesced around Morris in the capital. No dinners were held in his honor. He just packed his things at the end of the short session and went home.[12]

JUST DAYS INTO his forced retirement in the spring of 1839, Morris spoke at a public meeting in Cincinnati's courthouse to defend his course in Congress and denounce the state's new fugitive slave law. Gamaliel Bailey covered the meeting exhaustively and printed Morris's speech in his Cincinnati-based newspaper, the *Philanthropist*, even though "a majority of the Abolitionists in the city knew nothing of the meeting till it was over." What elicited Bailey's interest was not the substance of Morris's comments (attacks on the Servile Bill and speeches vindicating abolitionism were common fare in the *Philanthropist*). What was different about the courthouse meeting was its audience: "be it remembered," Bailey wrote, "Abolitionists were but a small portion of the meeting. The great applause came chiefly from the citizens uncommitted to Abolition—most of them Democrats."[13]

Bailey saw a new future for the antislavery movement that day, and he quickly ceased to be what he called a "one-idead" abolitionist. For Bailey, this meant broadening the antislavery appeal and working to break bread with potential allies in both major parties (although, interestingly, his own views lurched toward the Democratic side on most issues other than slavery).[14] This "political" turn made Bailey a pariah among many immediatists and caused much suspicion of him within Liberty party ranks. After the introduction of the Wilmot Proviso in August 1846 (when he again suggested that a broader *political* antislavery coalition could become a reality), Bailey agreed to edit the American and Foreign Anti-Slavery Society's new national

---

[12] *Congressional Globe*, 25th Cong., 3d sess., 1838–39, app., p. 167.

[13] *Philanthropist* (Cincinnati), May 15, 1839; Earle, *Jacksonian Antislavery*, pp. 146–47.

[14] The Jacksonians' philosophy, Bailey wrote, provided better guarantees for "individual liberty," while the Whigs were the "party of the capitalists" and the "anti-democratic party." Bailey's strong identification with Western interests and his experience as a Methodist Protestant, according to his biographer, "inclined him to this viewpoint." Bailey to Joshua Giddings, Jan. 11, 1841, Giddings-Julian Papers, Library of Congress, Manuscript Division, Washington, D.C.; see also *Philanthropist* (Cincinnati), July 21, 1840; Harrold, *Gamaliel Bailey*, pp. 98–101.

newspaper in Washington. The wealthy New York merchant Lewis Tappan agreed to purchase the *Philanthropist*'s subscription list at a price that allowed Bailey to pay off his debts, and Margaret Bailey jumped at the chance to move from the run-down section of Cincinnati where the family had relocated due to the declining financial situation. She also planned to resume her writing career and hire a governess to help raise her children in the capital.[15]

PERHAPS A WORD or two on Gamaliel Bailey's unusual antislavery journey to Washington is in order here. Bailey came to the antislavery movement from a strikingly different background than, say, the former slaveholder James Birney, the Whiggish Joshua Giddings, or the evangelical Theodore Weld. He was born in 1807 and grew up in southern New Jersey, a world away from New England and its swath of western migration. And unlike most abolitionist leaders, who came from Congregationalist, Unitarian, Quaker or Baptist backgrounds, Bailey was raised a Methodist. In the lowest part of the Lower North, Bailey's Methodist Protestant Church, headquartered in Baltimore, had strong southern ties.

Like his father, Bailey trained to be a physician. He worked as a ship's surgeon aboard a China trader in 1830, but the life of the sea did not agree with the young doctor. Much of Bailey's time onboard was spent tending to the ship's numerous cholera victims. An epidemic raged through Canton, dotting the harbor with floating corpses and filling Bailey with horror. The episode also precipitated for the sensitive medic a religious experience: he returned home in the summer of 1830 committed to act upon his newfound faith.

Bailey gladly traded saw and scalpel for the journalist's pen in 1831 when a schism within the Methodist Episcopal church led to the founding of the *Methodist Protestant* in Baltimore and Bailey was offered a job at the paper. He quickly rose to become its editor.[16] Bailey became an abolitionist after mov-

---

[15]Joel Goldfarb, "The Life of Gamaliel Bailey Prior to the Founding of the *National Era:* The Orientation of a Practical Abolitionist," Ph.D. diss., University of California, 1958, p. 390.

[16]The new Methodist Protestant Church was founded by Methodist Episcopal dissenters (mostly laymen and itinerant preachers like Bailey's father) who wanted representation in the church's annual and general conferences. The new church removed all distinctions between itinerant and local preachers, gave equal representation to lay members, and abolished all hierarchical offices. See Donald G. Mathews, *Slavery and Methodism: A Chapter in American Morality* (Princeton, 1965), pp. vii, 207; Harrold, *Gamaliel Bailey*, p. 5.

ing to Cincinnati and lecturing on physiology at Lane Theological Seminary, where he participated in Theodore Dwight Weld's famous debate weighing the merits of colonization versus immediatism. By September of 1834 he was almost entirely responsible for the *Philanthropist,* one of the most important antislavery newspapers in the West. He had also married Margaret Shands, a minister's daughter from an aristocratic Virginia family with whom he shared a marriage "on terms of perfect equality."[17]

Bailey was in a unique position among abolitionists by the late 1830s. Far from the roiling controversies in the East between Garrison and the Tappans (which led to the breakup of the American Antislavery Society), he was free to develop a "third way" of political action.[18] In the *Philanthropist* and in meetings of the Ohio Anti-Slavery Society (where he was secretary) Bailey made Thomas Morris's concept of the slave power conspiracy a political centerpiece. After Liberty party candidate James Birney's miserable showing in the 1840 election (he won only 6,225 votes nationwide, or .002 percent), Bailey theorized that any future success depended on luring support from the thousands of antislavery voters who had cast their ballots for Van Buren and Harrison. The next year he announced two other initiatives that placed him apart from other abolitionists: a determination to support non-abolitionist candidates and an avowal not to act politically to abolish slavery in the South.[19] Many prominent abolitionists (including Gerrit Smith and Birney) feared that Bailey's diplomacy was a mask for weakness and coward-ice and pushed Joshua Leavitt for the job of editing the new national paper in Washington, but Tappan chose Bailey, who he wrote was "never ultra or vulgar or course"—valuable traits for an abolitionist editor on slave soil. Bailey may not have been an ideological purist, the sort who was unwilling to talk to those who did not precisely share his views, but he had his own

---

[17]Mary Abigail Dodge, quoted in Harrold, *Gamaliel Bailey,* p. 13.

[18]On the split in the AAS, see James B. Stewart, *Holy Warriors* (New York, 1976), pp. 88–96. Garrisonians, of course, opposed all political action by abolitionists, relying solely on moral suasion to transform public opinion. The other wing, led by Joshua Leavitt and Lewis Tappan, favored combating the single issue of slavery in the political realm. This latter group also disagreed among themselves on whether to accomplish this end through third-party action or within the Whig party.

[19]Bailey's antislavery was profoundly influenced by the politics and society of southern Ohio and, specifically, Cincinnati, the West's most important city and a cultural crossroads between north, south, east, and west. It was home to large populations of both pro- and antislavery voters and another world from the Yankee-settled Western Reserve bordering Lake Erie, a center of antislavery Whiggery. See Earle, *Jacksonian Antislavery,* pp. 144–54.

plans for building and expanding the movement, and they were from within the walls of the slave power.[20]

WHEN GAMALIEL AND Margaret Bailey arrived in Washington in 1847 with their six children and his parents in tow, they could not have felt particularly welcome. As has been well documented, most Washingtonians were firmly committed to slavery and opposed to granting even modest rights to the city's large population of free blacks. Abolitionists were derided as fanatics. The Baileys knew that they could be mobbed at any moment but believed it was their mission to influence Washington and the South generally. Stanley Harrold notes that in his first months in the capital Bailey made a point NOT to demand abolition there, instead concentrating on finding a legal way to end the slave trade—a "moderation" that was not meant to ingratiate himself with slaveholders but to "assuage local interests."[21] He presented letters of introduction and friendship to notable conservative opinion-makers like Joseph Gales and William Seaton (of the *National Intelligencer*), and even Thomas Ritchie, whose Democratic *Union* was the mouthpiece of the expansionist Polk administration.

Bailey was quickly forced to put his powers of sociability and persuasion to use in the spring of 1848 when a series of anti-abolitionist mobs threatened the *National Era* and the personal safety of his entire family. That April naval authorities boarded the schooner *Pearl* in the Potomac and found seventy fugitive slaves aboard, attempting to sail to freedom. Even though the white captain and first mate were taken into custody and court proceedings later proved the plot had been hatched by free blacks and not the city's white abolitionists, a mob turned its anger on the *National Era* and its proprietor. After three days of unrest (during which authorities asked Bailey to leave town with his press to avoid violence), a mob gathered outside the Baileys' home on E Street, conveniently located next door to the editor William Seaton, who was also the city's mayor. Bailey, with Margaret at his side, responded to the threat of tar and feathers with a reasoned appeal to patriotism and the rights of property. "Men who came to curse remained to cheer," wrote Greenwood, and "the crowd, with but one dissenting voice, moved

---

[20]Harrold, *Gamaliel Bailey*, p. 83.
[21]Ibid., p. 88.

an adjournment and quietly dispersed—some actually calling back 'Goodnight, doctor!!'"[22]

Safe for the moment, Bailey expended considerable effort making the *National Era* into a strikingly good journal. Bailey's own editorials were pithy, informative, and relatively short. He did not bloviate. John Greenleaf Whittier submitted more than one hundred original poems and three hundred prose contributions and other "back of the book" literary contributions, including works by Lydia Maria Child, Robert Dale Owen, Harriet Martineau, William Brisbane, Oliver Wendell Holmes, and Grace Greenwood. He published and encouraged southern writers and commentators like Joseph E. Snodgrass and Daniel R. Goodloe, both to report on actual antislavery (or antislaveholder) activity in the Upper South and to give the impression the movement was growing there. And, of course, Bailey earned his greatest fame publishing serially (and underwriting) Harriet Beecher Stowe's "Uncle Tom's Cabin; or, The Man that Was a Thing." The first installment appeared June 5, 1851, with a welcome change in the subtitle to "Life among the Lowly," and became a runaway sensation. Soon after the final piece ran in April 1852, Stowe became the author of the nineteenth century's bestselling book. Ironically, though, Bailey himself was not particularly interested in the story during its early run in his newspaper; Margaret Bailey and Salmon Chase helped convince him to cough up an additional two hundred dollars to keep the serials coming. Through his own talents and the help of family and friends, the *National Era* remained one of the more readable papers of the time.[23]

LITERARY INTERESTS ASIDE, Bailey believed his chief mission in Washington was to unite the political antislavery movement behind a firm opposition to territorial compromise. After the initial (and purely sectional) votes on the Wilmot Proviso during the Twenty-ninth Congress, it was clear to political observers like Bailey, Salmon Chase, and Van Burenites like Preston King

---

[22]*National Era*, Apr. 27, 1848; Greenwood, "An American Salon," p. 439. Bailey's decision to say little about the incident, and about Drayton and Sayres's actions on the boat, drew harsh criticism from abolitionists. Elizur Wright and Frederick Douglass angrily attacked him for suggesting the two were wrong for helping the slaves to escape, and Wendell Phillips called him an "apostate and reprobate." Harrold, *Gamaliel Bailey*, p. 127.

[23]*National Era*, May 8, June 5, 1851; E. Bruce Kirkham, *The Building of Uncle Tom's Cabin* (Knoxville, 1977), pp. 141–44; Harrold, *Gamaliel Bailey*, pp. 142–43.

and John P. Hale that slavery restriction was an issue under which anti-slavery forces (whether Liberty, Whig, or Democratic) could bind together. Bailey worked through the *National Era* and in his capacity as the semiofficial antislavery lobbyist at the Capitol was able to unearth documents and fashion convincing arguments for congressmen to use. He became a fixture on the Hill and spent considerable energy working with the usual suspects (Joshua Giddings, John G. Palfrey, and Hale) and various "conservative" antislavery prospects like John Quincy Adams, Thomas Corwin, William Wick, and Thomas Hart Benton. During 1847 Bailey began to caucus informally with the small antislavery delegation; he also made a promise (which he kept) to oppose every compromise measure that permitted slavery to expand into new territories. With more antislavery congressmen arriving with each session (even if at the rate of a trickle), Bailey was optimistic in a letter to Chase: "[with] Palfrey, Giddings, Tuck, [James] Wilson, Caleb Smith & Hale in Congress, and you and I out, acting and advising with [them], depend on it, something may be done . . . [Still], Democratic knees will need strengthening—Whig brains enlightenment."[24]

Conveniently for Bailey (and for the Free-Soil cause), most antislavery members of Congress already lived near, and often with, each other. Wilmot, for example, roomed with several Barnburner Democrats at Masi's boardinghouse in Pennsylvania Avenue; when George Julian arrived in Washington as a Free-Soiler in December 1849, he found lodging at Mrs. Sprigg's boardinghouse on the north side of the public grounds facing the Capitol—the longtime residences of Joshua Giddings and Charles Allen.[25] In addition to Julian, ten other Free-Soilers were elected to Congress, and Bailey knew that they would need to pull together to avert a sectional compromise that, for the sake of union, permitted slavery to enter the territories.[26]

It was in this climate that the Baileys turned their frequent gatherings into standing weekly invitations. Each realized how lonely and disheartening it could be for northern congressmen, far from their families, isolated in a hostile and parochial southern town. To supplement the weekly soirees, Bailey founded the Washington Free-Soil Association (WFSA), run first by

[24]Bailey to Chase, Sept. 14, 1847, Chase Papers, Library of Congress, Manuscript Division, Washington, D.C.

[25]Earle, *Jacksonian Antislavery*, pp. 1–4; Clarke, "Home Letters of George W. Julian," p. 130.

[26]Like many Free-Soilers, Bailey believed slavery had to expand in order to survive. See Harrold, *Gamaliel Bailey*, p. 130; Earle, *Jacksonian Antislavery*, pp. 123–44.

his editorial assistant Andrew Gangwere, a protégé of Salmon Chase's, and later Lewis Clephane. The WFSA maintained a comfortable reading room on Capitol Hill and published moderate antislavery tracts in conjunction with the *Era*. Bailey even attempted to found an antislavery church in the capital to serve congressmen like Hale, Palfrey, and Julian and "spread the antislavery gospel" among the population; I have been unable to find out anything more about how these plans developed.[27]

Far and away the most successful of the Baileys' strategies in Washington, though, was their weekly gathering for Free-Soilers and any conceivable ally that could be cajoled into joining in for an evening's entertainment. For in the Baileys' parlor, feelings of isolation and ostracism melted into fellowship and inclusion. "We knew that we had been 'sent to Coventry,'" recalled Clarke (using a phrase from the English Civil War that referenced being shunned by fellow citizens and friends), "and set about making 'Coventry' a jolly sort of place." Senators Hale and Chase led the delegations, and their colleagues from the upper house Corwin and Seward joined often (though not as often as their wives, according to Conway). Other regulars during the session included, using Grace Greenway's nicknames (in her moniker-giving she resembled former President George W. Bush): "Father Giddings," "Proviso Wilmot," Hannibal Hamlin (apparently a fine dancer), and Julian, who "blushed like a girl when one of his speeches was commended."[28] There were as many women present as men, and all guests discussed the politics of the day. "There are those living," Clarke wrote fifty years later, "who still remember, with a glow of pleasure, the merry yet intellectual young ladies who did so much to render the Bailey *salon* so charming: poetic Annie Phillips, ethereal Eva Ball, graceful Nellie Tarr, witty Lizzie Ellicot . . . and of course Mrs. Stowe." Wordplay joined the charades and trust-building games, especially on stormy evenings "after the grave strangers" had left. From one game of epigram-writing, one example remains, from Chase's pen (about Margaret Bailey):

---

[27]Two antislavery ministers, Moncure Conway of Virginia and Joshua Grinnell of Vermont (and later Iowa), were part of Bailey's plans for the antislavery congregation in Washington. Conway, *Autobiography, Memories and Experiences* (New York, 1904), p. 186; Grinnell, *Men and Events*, pp. 51–55.

[28]Greenwood, "An American Salon," pp. 442–43; Conway, *Autobiography*, p. 186. It is entirely possible that it may have been the handsome appearance of Clarke, and not just modesty about his speeches, that led the young congressman (whose wife was away) to become flustered.

When Margaret Shands was young and fair,
She sung "Love in a Cottage," gaily;
But later years brought graver cares,
She now is a prisoner of "Old Bailey."

Hamlin recalled years later how important the evenings were for the Free-Soil cause—and I'm going to agree with him: "Those meetings . . . served to unite and strengthen all who participated in them and to extend their sphere of useful activity. They cheered the resolute and determined in opinion the timid."[29]

The Saturday night salon at the Baileys' was not enough to halt the Compromise of 1850. Stephen Douglas deftly guided each of the separate compromise measures through Congress after Henry Clay's omnibus bill failed to win support of a majority in the Senate, and an exhausted American public decided to give the measures a try. The four years between the Compromise's passage in September 1850 and Douglas's next trick, the Kansas-Nebraska Act, in 1854 were extremely bleak for the antislavery movement. Newspapers folded, schismatics returned to their respective parties, Free-Soil organizations had trouble drawing people to their formerly robust meetings. It was during these years that Bailey had his greatest effect on the antislavery movement, keeping it alive in Congress with the small-yet-stalwart Free-Soil caucus, keeping spirits up with entertainments at the House, and railing continually against the Fugitive Slave Act in the pages of the *Era*. He also moved, with Chase and other members of the salon, to create a "Union of the liberal men of all parties, for Freedom against any party whose principle of cohesion, is Servility to the Slave Power."[30] Even as most newspapers trumpeted the Compromise as a fair and honest "solution" to the vexing slavery issue, Bailey vowed still more agitation: "Between the antagonistic elements of Freedom and Slavery, a hollow truce may be occasionally patched up by adroit politicians," he wrote. "But there can be no solid, permanent peace." With that he gathered up his things, returned home, and began planning for the next evening's soiree at chez Bailey—and for the next political crisis that would make his broad-based antislavery alliance a reality.[31]

---

[29]Hamlin to Clarke, in Greenwood, "An American Salon," p. 447; Harrold, *Gamaliel Bailey*, p. 134.

[30]*National Era*, Feb. 20, 1851.

[31]*National Era*, Dec. 5, 1850.

Susan Zaeske

"A nest of rattlesnakes let loose among them"

Congressional Debates over Women's Antislavery Petitions,
1835–1845

"JUST THE MOST exciting incident that occurs in the Houses of Congress
is the presentation of petitions for the abolition of Slavery in this District," reported a Capitol observer during the first days of 1837. It was during this, the second session of the Twenty-fourth Congress, that abolitionists
loaded the desks of their representatives with memorials signed by thousands of constituents. The effect was "electrical" when time after time a few
members to whom the memorials had been entrusted rose to state the content of the petitions. Already at the last session of Congress the growing
number of antislavery petitions had thrown the House of Representatives
into such commotion that southern members proposed and northern
members acquiesced to the passage of a rule that immediately tabled the
bothersome papers. But no gag rule had been instituted at this new session
and the antislavery petitions burst upon the floor. "If a nest of rattlesnakes
were suddenly let loose among them, the members could manifest but
little more 'agitation'—except perhaps, that they retain their seats a *little*
better," the observer wrote. "The Southern hotspurs are almost ready to
dance with rage at the attack, as they called it, upon their peculiar domestic institutions."[1]

The author wishes to thank Paul Finkelman for the invitation to participate in the symposium and Mary Louise Roberts for her insightful suggestions on multiple drafts of this
essay.
[1] *Emancipator,* Jan. 19, 1837.

A nest of rattlesnakes had been let loose in the House. Southern congress-men could not have been more angry, antislavery activists could not have been more pleased. Petitions for the abolition of slavery, with their venom-ous attacks on the peculiar institution, inflamed the jealous pride of south-ern members entangling them in debates over slavery, an issue that American statesmen of all sorts had studiously avoided during the first fifty years of the young republic. Thus, the debate sparked by the antislavery petitions was one of the most important in the history of the Congress and the nation. William Freehling has deemed this debate "the Pearl Harbor of the slavery controversy." And William Lee Miller has identified this battle over the right to petition against slavery "the first explicit and extended struggle between American slavery and what would be called, in a later century, the American Creed." "It was," writes Miller, "the articulate beginning of a national fork-in-the-road choice between inherited despotism and developing democracy. Or between tragic evil and human ideals."[2]

Yet, the congressional debates over the reception of antislavery petitions were monumental in another respect that has gone largely unremarked. Be-cause tens of thousands of women signed antislavery petitions, the debates over the reception of female antislavery petitions provoked what was per-haps the first sustained discussion of women's political rights and their status as citizens in the history of the U.S. Congress. To be sure, during the Revo-lutionary period the rights of women had been deliberated in private cor-respondence and, during the post-Revolutionary period, in ladies magazines. But, as Rosemarie Zagarri has observed, these discussions "did not occur within official political institutions."[3] And while the Supreme Court consid-ered women's citizenship rights in *Martin v. Massachusetts* (1805) and state con-stitutional conventions contemplated extending the franchise to women, no sustained consideration of women's political rights took place in Congress until the debate over female antislavery petitions.[1]

The debates in Congress, in fact, constituted a significant moment in the ongoing negotiation of women's citizenship. By signing petitions, antislavery women struggled to gain access to the political space of the House of Rep-

[2]William Lee Miller, *Arguing about Slavery: The Great Battle in the United States Congress* (New York, 1996), p. 24.

[3]Rosemarie Zagarri, "The Rights of Man and Woman in Post-Revolutionary America," *William and Mary Quarterly*, 3d ser., 55 (1998):203.

[1]Linda K. Kerber, "The Paradox of Women's Citizenship in the Early Republic: The Case of *Martin v. Massachusetts,*" *American Historical Review* (1992):349–78.

resentatives where their representatives could hear their requests and where they could attempt to influence national policy. In the texts of their petitions, women opposed slavery and justified entering the halls of the Capitol with a series of moral complaints against slaveholders and increasingly bold claims to the rights of American citizenship. In the course of doing so, they offended the sensibilities of southern members, who perceived the northern women as questioning the honor of southern elites while uncouthly violating norms governing female conduct. When angered slaveholding members rose to defend the South and silence the northern women, they employed an oratorical style rooted in the culture of honor that replicated aspects of dueling. Fully understanding that the debate revolved around not only constitutional but cultural differences, the most outspoken defender of the women's abolition petitions, Representative John Quincy Adams, replied by parodying the rhetorical style of southern members as he defended northern women's right to petition. Adams, moreover, went so far as to question the longstanding denial to women of the right to vote. The House debate over women's antislavery petitions, then, amounted to a battle over women's constitutional rights as citizens waged in a language of gender and sexuality.

THAT "NEST OF RATTLESNAKES" that scared representatives out of their seats in January 1837, rather than springing without warning, hatched from the growing pile of northern women's antislavery petitions. Although since the colonial period American women had limited their petitioning to individual requests regarding personal issues, in the early 1830s black and white women began to make use of organized mass petitioning, as white men had decades earlier, to agitate public opinion in order to achieve their political goals.[5] This change in women's petitioning practices coincided with the "Second Great Awakening," which motivated large numbers of women to band together in associations devoted to reforming society. At the radical end of the spectrum of these organizations were female antislavery societies, which initially focused on boycotting products of slave labor, educating free blacks, and raising money for the antislavery cause. Inspired by British female abolitionists who in 1833 alone won almost 299,000 women's signatures to a memorial abolishing slavery in the British dominions, the following year

---

[5]For a history of women's petitioning in the American colonies and the United States before 1834, see Susan Zaeske, *Signatures of Citizenship: Petitioning, Antislavery and Women's Political Identity* (Chapel Hill, 2003), chap. 1.

100   *Susan Zaeske*

American women began to petition Congress to abolish slavery in the District of Columbia. In 1834 women sent a dozen antislavery petitions to Congress, and in 1835 they sent nine—a noticeable increase, but hardly enough to alarm apologists of slavery.

When the first session of the Twenty-fourth Congress convened on December 7, 1835, representatives were greeted by eighty-four female antislavery petitions signed by some 15,000 women. This influx of women's petitions bolstered the number sent by men and culminated in a ninefold increase in antislavery petitions compared to the previous session.[6] Senator John C. Calhoun complained that the petitions came, not as in the past, "singly and far apart, from the quiet routine of the Society of Friends or the obscure vanity of some philanthropist club," but "from soured and agitated communities."[7] Calhoun's lamentations did little to slow the tide of petitions, for when Congress convened in special session in September 1837, it was deluged with petitions against the annexation of Texas signed by 200,000 Americans, about 77,400 of them women. And when the regular session of Congress convened on December 4, 1837, members were overwhelmed with antislavery petitions signed by more than 414,000 Americans, about 201,000 of them women.[8] Over the next few years, hundreds of thousands of women petitioned Congress to end slavery in the district and the territories. Their efforts peaked from 1837 to 1839 and declined after 1840, though huge numbers of women lent their names to memorials demanding repeal of the Fugitive Slave Act and, in the 1860s, passage of the Thirteenth Amendment.[9]

As women crossed into new terrain by petitioning their political representatives in hopes of influencing debate on a national issue, their petitions initially employed a rhetoric not of newly found political authority but of humility and disavowal. During the first period of women's antislavery peti-

[6]Miller, *Arguing about Slavery*, p. 111. The figures on the increase in women's petitions come from the Our Mothers Before Us Database and were confirmed in personal correspondence with Sarah Boyle, National Archives, Nov. 5, 1996.

[7]Calhoun quoted in Miller, *Arguing about Slavery*, p. 30.

[8]Miller, *Arguing about Slavery*, pp. 277–79; "Correspondence between the Hon. F. H. Elmore, One of the South Carolina Delegation to Congress, and James G. Birney, One of the Secretaries of the American Anti-Slavery Society," *Antislavery Examiner*, no.8 (New York, 1838), p. 65. Gilbert Hobbs Barnes, *The Antislavery Impulse* (New York, 1933), p. 266 n. 39. The 1837–38 total comes from Russel B. Nye, *Fettered Freedom: Civil Liberties and the Slavery Controversy, 1830–1860* (East Lansing, Mich., 1963), p. 37. The 34,000 figure for the number of signatures sent to Congress in 1835–36 comes from Barnes, *Antislavery Impulse*, p. 131.

[9]Zaeske, *Signatures of Citizenship*, p. 146.

tioning from 1831 to 1836, the text of their petitions depicted women as assuming a humble stance and politely seeking the attention of representatives rather than making political demands on male authorities. The tone of the petition submitted by 800 women of New York is illustrative. "That while we would not obtrude on your honorable body, the expression of our opinions on questions of mere pecuniary expediency or political economy," they said, "we yet conceive that there are occasions when the voice of female remonstrance and entreaty may be heard in the councils of a great nation."[10] Perhaps the most deferential of all female antislavery petitions was the "Fathers and Rulers of Our Country" form, which was signed by women from almost every northern state and was the most popular petition form employed by abolitionists before 1837. Unlike antislavery petitions signed exclusively by men, which were addressed "To the Honorable Senate and House," the "Fathers and Rulers" form replaced that appellation with "To the Fathers and Rulers of Our Country." Such phrasing elevated the recipients from political representatives to even more powerful figures and diminished the petitioners from constituents to dependents. The text of the petition continued in this supplicatory vein, stating in its first line, "Suffer us, we pray you, with the sympathies which we are constrained to feel as wives, as mothers, and as daughters, to plead with you in behalf of a long oppressed and deeply injured class of native Americans." Rather than directly stating why they approached their representatives, the women petitioners begged and prayed to be heard. After fawning, they switched to flattering: "We should poorly estimate the virtues which ought ever to distinguish your honorable body could we anticipate any other than a favorable hearing when our appeal is to men, to philanthropists, to patriots, to the legislators and guardians of a Christian people."[11]

While in many respects the rhetoric of the early women's petitions was deferential, in other ways it claimed new space and new political power for northern women. Although on the surface the "Fathers and Rulers" form appears exceedingly deferential, in fact, the narrative embedded in the petition identified the actors as "Fathers," "mothers," "wives," and "daughters," and in so doing refigured the scene of its reception from that of the floor of the U.S. Congress, a male-dominated political space, to a domestic space,

---

[10]Ibid., p. 54.
[11]Ibid., pp. 55–59.

where women possessed greater power, especially greater moral power. Narratives of other petitions sent by women attempted to create the sense of women being physically present to plead with their representatives. An 1836 petition from the "females of Winthrop, Maine," for example, stated that the signers "approach your honorable body as humble supplicants," and the "Fathers and Rulers" petition urged legislators to "lend their ear to our appeals," as if representatives were listening to requests uttered by female petitions appearing before them rather than reading women's petitions sent from afar. In addition to the petition narratives, the lists of signatures implied the presence of women not just individually but as a collective, a congregation. The signatures functioned as lasting inscriptions of the existence of groups of women who had coalesced in deeds and ultimately in words. The narratives and signatures, then, not only presented women's opinions about slavery, but also asserted that women were present individually and collectively in the supreme American political space—the U.S. Congress.[12]

As northern women grew more accustomed to petitioning even while their right to do so was questioned, their petitions more boldly asserted their right to engage in political deliberation. Passage of the gag rule in 1836 led abolitionist women to redouble their petitioning efforts and to more strongly assert their right to petition. Female antislavery rhetoric at this point went beyond claiming that women possessed a moral duty to petition to asserting that women were citizens and, as such, possessed a constitutional right to petition. For example, *An Address of the Female Anti-Slavery Society of Philadelphia*, published in response to passage of the gag rule with a form of petition to Congress attached, demanded: "Will you say that woman's duties lie within the hallowed precincts of the home, not the field of controversy, or the halls of Congress?" The address accused congressmen of corrupting the deliberative process by letting "loose storms of passion . . . instead of listening to the voice of woman's entreaty for the rescue" of the slave. Congressmen, the Philadelphians complained, "would fain rob her of the right of petition, and the privileges of a citizen, in order to close her lips for ever in behalf of her outraged sisters." In the course of calling women to petition, again and again the Philadelphia address asserted in no uncertain terms that women

---

[12]Susan Zaeske, "Signatures of Citizenship: The Rhetoric of Women's Antislavery Petitions," *Quarterly Journal of Speech* 88, no. 2 (2002):156.

were citizens and must fulfill the duties incumbent upon citizens, stating: "As Northern citizens *we* are bound, dear sisters, to put forth all *our* energies in this mighty work. Yes, although we are *women, we* are still citizens, and it is to *us,* that the captive wives and mothers, sisters and daughters of the South have a particular right to look for help in this day of approaching emancipation."[13] This petition, and others, obfuscated the referent of "captive wives and mothers, sisters and daughters of the South." This ambiguity left open the possibility that the petitioners were decrying the treatment of slave women as well as elite women, whom, they implied, were held captive to their husbands' immorality.

While female antislavery petitions necessarily defended the right of women to engage in political deliberation, their primary goal, ostensibly at least, was to publicly protest American slavery. To fulfill this duty, women petitioners directly condemned slavery and slaveholders as sinful. "As Christians," stated the women of Washington County, Vermont, "we mourn the toleration of this system, and deprecate the continuance of such flagrant violations of the pure and benignant precepts of our Holy Lawgiver, whose divine injunction is, 'Whatsoever ye would that men should do to you, do ye even so to them.'"[14] Likewise, the Ladies of Dousa, New Hampshire, and those of Massachusetts claimed that they "consider[ed] the toleration of slavery in the District of Columbia as a direct violation of the precepts of the Gospel, and shamefully inconsistent with the principles promulgated in the Declaration of Independence."[15]

In addition to decrying the sinfulness of slavery, women's petitions warned that slavery corroded the moral health of the republic, which would eventually provoke God to punish the nation. The female inhabitants of South Reading, Massachusetts, warned that for the U.S. Congress, "the Representatives of a free, republican and Christian people," to declare "their consent to and approval of the extension of the evils of slavery in our land would be

---

[13]Zaeske, *Signatures of Citizenship,* p. 77.

[14]Petition of the Females of Washington County, Vermont, for the Abolition of Slavery in the District of Columbia and Various States, 1836, HR24-G22.4, National Archives Box 14 of Library of Congress Box 75.

[15]Petition of the Ladies of Dousa, New Hampshire for Abolition of Slavery in the District of Columbia, 1836, HR 24-G22.4, National Archives Box 14 of Library of Congress Box 75; Petition of the Ladies of Massachusetts for Abolition of Slavery in the District of Columbia, December 18, 1835, to June 6, 1836, HR24A-H1.3, TABLED.

a blot on our national character that could never be effaced, and which would invoke the judgments of Heaven."[16] Expressions of concern for the health of the country implied that women's interest in preserving the national character extended beyond raising children to being good citizens to monitoring the morality of federal policy. Elevating the female petitioners to the position of concerned republican citizens, these statements indirectly though unquestionably rebuked slaveholding members for harming the reputation of the nation and invoking divine wrath upon it. In that way, the petitions implied that female signers were better citizens than slaveholding southern representatives.

While indictments of slaveholders as sinful and harmful to the republic undoubtedly insulted southern members, far more inflammatory were petitioners' accusations of miscegenation. Female antislavery petitions dwelled on the suffering of the female slave and repeatedly condemned slaveholders for their brutal, lascivious behavior toward female slaves. The "Fathers and Rulers" petition, for instance, explained, "We should be less than women, if the nameless and unnumbered wrongs of which the slaves of our sex are made defenseless victims, did not fill us with horror and constrain us, in earnestness and agony of spirit to pray for their deliverances."[17] Descriptions of the horrors of slavery in women's petitions stressed the particular afflictions suffered by female slaves. Time and again they represented the slave woman as sexually and spiritually vulnerable, "degraded," "brutified," "the victims of insatiable avarice," "wronged," and "denied of male relatives to offer them protection." Slavery denied "the weak and innocent" legal protection and "sundered all the sacred ties of domestic life . . . for the gratification of avarice," complained an 1835 petition sent by women of New York State.[18] Another petition decried how under slavery "the soul formed for companionship with angels, is despoiled and brutified, and consigned to

[16]Petition of the Female Inhabitants of South Reading, Massachusetts, Against the Admission of the Territory of Arkansas to the Union as a Slaveholding State, June 6, 1836, HR24A-H1.4, National Archives Box 3 of Library of Congress Box 46.

[17]"Fathers and Rulers of Our Country Petition Form," Nov. 1834, in Gilbert H. Barnes and Dwight L. Dumond, eds., *Letters of Theodore Weld, Angelina Grimké Weld and Sarah Grimké, 1822–1844,* 2 vols. (New York, 1934), 1:175–76.

[18]Petition of the Ladies of Marshfield for Abolition of Slavery in the District of Columbia, December 18, 1835, to June 6, 1836, HR24A-H1.3, Slavery in the District of Columbia, TABLED; Petition of the Ladies of Glastenbury for Abolition of Slavery in the District of Columbia, 1836, HR24A-H1.3, National Archives Box 3 of Library of Congress Box 47.

ignorance, pollution, and ruin."[19] Allusions to the "gratification of avarice" appeared in many of the petitions sent by women and were a thinly veiled accusations that slaveholders were sexually exploiting women who possessed no means to defend themselves.

Another particularly provocative complaint leveled by female antislavery petitions was that slaveholders failed to safeguard womanhood. The petition of Rebecca Buffum and twenty-seven "female citizens" of Cincinnati sent to Congress on December 22, 1842, began by reminding representatives that women have been "taught to regard our male fellow Citizens, as our national protectors." It then proceeded to chastise Congress for making laws that protect men and "dumb animals" while they have left "their Mothers, Wives, Sisters, Daughters" completely unprotected from "the ruthless invader," the slave hunter. Echoing antislavery rhetoric that preyed upon anxieties that the slave power sought to destroy northerners' rights, the petition explained that the Fugitive Slave Act authorized any man who called himself a slaveholder to "seize us without warrant, and to carry us to the land of manacles, whips, and despair." In such cases, they complained, women would be denied the right of a jury trial, though such a right is guaranteed when a man lays claims to a pig. Yet the petition's most insolent request was reserved for its conclusion, where the female citizens asked that if Congress were unable to fully protect women against claims of slaveholders, would it at least grant women the "same protection, which by the laws of the land you now have, for your dumb animals."[20]

Taken as a whole, female antislavery petitions sent to Congress from 1835 to 1845 asserted an expanded role for women in public deliberation of a national political issue. The petitions, moreover, condemned slaveholders as cruel, lascivious, unchristian, and unrepublican, implying that northern women were morally superior. Slaveholders, southern congressmen among them, were judged against the criteria of northern virtues as morally unfit to call themselves true republicans and heirs to the legacy of the American Revolution. Consequently, women petitioners asserted that given their devotion to the moral health of the republic while slaveholders despoiled it,

---

[19]"The Fathers and Rulers of Our Country Petition Form," in Barnes and Dumond, *Letters of Theodore Weld*, 1:175–76; Petition of 600 Ladies of Utica, Oneida, County, New York, for abolition of slavery and the slave trade in the District of Columbia, Mar. 21, 1836, National Archives Box 3 of Library of Congress Box 47.

[20]Zaeske, *Signatures of Citizenship*, p. 158.

they possessed a truer claim to American citizenship than even slaveholding members of Congress. It is not surprising, then, that the women's petitions provoked violent responses from southern members, who rose to defend their individual honor and the honor of the south as well as to bulwark male political dominance.

"The South arose as one man"

Bristling from repeated insults hurled by the petitions, James W. Bouldin of Virginia complained that northerners "took a swaggering stand over the South, and proposed a kind of guardianship over [our] morals."[21] Bouldin's reaction to the petitions is particularly revealing, for he expressed the abiding sentiment that the petitions had provoked a challenge not between the petitioners and slaveholders, but between the North and the South. He perceived the situation not as a debate over interpretation of the First Amendment right of petition, but rather as a moral attack on the South. This attack, as Bouldin understood it, was more than verbal—northerners had taken "a swaggering," in-your-face, physical stance over the South. The impression that the antislavery petitions had sparked something more than a rational response was intuited by a correspondent from the *New York Commercial Advertiser*. The petitions, he reported, "struck the sensitive nerve which pervades and vibrates throughout the entire South." This "sensitive nerve" the reporter described as "the absorbing, controlling and vital principle which animates the whole South—electrifies the South—*unites* the South—in their morals, habits, feelings, religion, politics—nullification—PRESIDENTIAL CANDIDATES." As the petitions poked the sensitive southern nerve, "it thrilled and twinged, like the agonies of a decayed tooth." According to the reporter, northern representatives looked surprised and alarmed as "the South arose as one man."[22]

Surprised though they may have been, all were aware of the general sense of discomfiture that hung over the daily interaction of northern and southern congressmen. This uneasiness in the halls and chambers of the nation's Capitol was described by John Quincy Adams, a former president serving in

---

[21] *Register of Debates*, 24th Cong., 1st sess., 1835, pp. 2002–4.
[22] *New York Commercial Advertiser*, correspondence from Washington dated Feb. 16, 1835, quoted in the *Liberator*, Mar. 7, 1835.

the House, when in 1837 he visited the eminent Boston theologian Dr. William Ellery Channing. "There was," said Adams, "so marked a difference between the manners of the South and of the North that their members could never be very intimate personally together." Given Adams's experience in the presidential race a decade earlier, it is hardly surprising that Adams should come to such a conclusion. For it was the bitter 1828 presidential race between Adams of Massachusetts and Andrew Jackson of Tennessee that embodied the deepening conflict between the political cultures of the North and South. This election, as Norma Basch has so convincingly demonstrated, centered on "an intense and gendered political controversy" that is strikingly evident in the discourse produced by both candidates. The campaign pitted against one another on the national political stage not only two men, but two conflicting codes of gender and sexual conduct. A glance at the cultural dynamics of that campaign lends understanding to the tensions pervading the House debates over women's antislavery petitions.

The ethos Jackson cultivated throughout the 1828 campaign epitomized the southern ethic of honor and appealed to large aggregations of the male populace. As a major general in the Tennessee militia, Jackson had defeated the Creeks at the Battle of Horseshoe Bend in 1814 and a year later led U.S. Army troops to successfully defend the city of New Orleans. With a reputation as a fierce Indian fighter and the "Hero of New Orleans," Jackson had achieved unquestionable valor, a character trait essential for any man of honor. Jackson, moreover, was viewed as possessing a ferocious will that rendered him ready to defend his family and community against assault. Indeed, Jackson was perceived as just as willing to fight on the battlefield as on the ultimate field of honor—the dueling ground. Jackson had actually fought numerous duels in his lifetime and on one occasion killed a man. In fact, Jackson was the only elected president to have fought duels.[23]

The character that Adams cultivated during the 1828 campaign could hardly have been more different. While Jackson, the rugged frontiersman and soldier, was known as "Old Hickory," Adams, the urbane statesman and aristocrat, was hailed as the "Sage of Quincy." Rather than enacting the code of honor cherished by elite southerners, Adams embodied the humane sensibilities shared by the emerging middle-class of industrializing New England. In sharp contrast to Jackson, Adams exerted his energies not on the

---

[23]Bertram Wyatt-Brown, "Andrew Jackson's Honor," *Journal of the Early Republic* 17 (1997):3, 8, 17–18.

battle-field but in fields of knowledge such as constitutional law, rhetoric, philosophy, and history. Indeed, like his northeastern constituents, Adams renounced violence in all its forms, in its place privileging restraint. A fervent opponent of dueling, Adams dismissed the custom as a barbarous appendage of slavery and its code of honor. Sharing Adams's disdain for violence, during the 1828 campaign his supporters circulated a pamphlet that accused Jackson of having "killed, slashed, and clawed various American citizens" on fourteen occasions. For Adams and the emerging middle-class of New England, then, manhood was not predicated on willingness to face an opponent in the dueling ring to establish "honor," but rather it was based on one's ability to achieve "respectability." A man could attain respect by demonstrating restraint, reliability, and a commitment to domestic and civic virtue. These traits could be displayed by temperate behavior rather than indulgence in substances such as alcohol and tobacco associated in the South with masculinity.[24] As for Adams, he was a man so restrained in his emotions that even his youngest son, Charles, called his poker-faced father "Iron Mask." Like the New England Puritans, Adams neither drank nor smoked but was an early riser who every morning while in Washington took a chilly dive into the Potomac.[25]

The moral codes of either section dictated proper behavior not only for men, but also for women. Codes of gentlemanliness were intrinsically linked to strictures governing the behavior of women. When Jackson killed a man in cold blood during a duel, for example, he did so because the man had dared question the sexual purity of his wife, Rachel. The only proper response for a man of honor to preserve the reputation of his wife was to fight a duel. So important was a lady's reputed purity in the culture of southern elites that after Rachel discovered literature from the 1828 presidential campaign that accused her of adultery and bigamy, it is said that she became hysterical, suffered a severe heart attack, and died.[26]

Besides sexual honor, another virtue required of the southern woman was to be politically aware but never "to mingle in discussion."[27] T. R. Dew of the College of William and Mary, for example, instructed that a lady

---

[24]Bertram Wyatt-Brown, *Honor and Violence in the Old South* (New York, 1986), p. 19.

[25]Leonard L. Richards, *The Life and Times of Congressman John Quincy Adams* (New York, 1986), p. 4.

[26]Wyatt-Brown, "Jackson's Honor," pp. 10, 33.

[27]Bertram Wyatt-Brown, *Southern Honor: Ethics and Behavior in the Old South* (Oxford, 1982), p. 50.

ought never to "give utterance to her passions like man," but to display a "contentment and ease which may impose upon an inquisitive and scrutinizing world." Alabama planter Bolling Hall tutored his daughter on the ideal demeanor of a lady, advising, "If you learn to restrain every thought, action and word by virtue and religion, you will become an ornament."[28]

With northern conceptions of manhood differing strikingly from those of elite southerners, it is not surprising that notions of womanhood also differed significantly. Adams, who ironically was married to a southern-born woman, witnessed firsthand clashes between northern and southern notions of ideal female conduct. His wife, Louisa, had been raised in Europe by an English mother and a father from Maryland who deeply distrusted Yankees. In her memoirs Louisa stated that having been raised in luxury, she never "dreamt of anything beyond the hour." Such short-sightedness did little to ingratiate Louisa with her northern in-laws, especially the venerable New England–bred Abigail Adams. They viewed her as weak and flighty and had little tolerance for her moods and fainting fits. Louisa disagreed vehemently with the Adamses over philosophies of child rearing, she espousing a policy of indulgence and the Adams family a policy of sternness. The conflict between the northern woman on the one hand and the southern woman on the other was aptly characterized by a John Quincy Adams biographer who wrote: "Sickly and delicate, [Louisa] lacked the mental toughness, the resourcefulness, the strict standards of thrift, and the zest for life that made her mother-in-law, Abigail Adams, the measure of womanly excellence in New England."[29] While the difference in character between the Adams women is but an individual case, starting in the mid-1820s and continuing through the 1830s, northern female novelists such as Catharine Sedgwick, Sarah Hale, and Eliza Follen published widely successful novels that portrayed southern women as luxury-loving, self-absorbed, and lazy. The characters of northern women, by contrast, were hard-working, efficient, and concerned with the world around them.[30]

When in 1828 Jackson won both the popular and the electoral vote to be elected president, his victory demonstrated not only the appeal of his character but also the strength of the South. Predictably, Jackson lost in Adams's

---

[28]Wyatt-Brown, *Honor and Violence*, pp. vii–viii, 53, 86.

[29]Richards, *Congressman John Quincy Adams*, pp. 16–17.

[30]Anne Lewis Osler, "That Damned Mob: Northern and Southern Women Writers and the Coming of the American Civil War," Ph.D. diss., University of Wisconsin–Madison, 1995.

home territory of New England, but the war hero won half the popular vote in the North as a whole. Jackson was propelled into office by his immense popularity in the slave states, where he won almost 73 percent of the vote and dominated in the Deep South with over 80 percent of the vote in Alabama and Mississippi, and almost 100 percent in Georgia. Incensed, Adams blamed his loss on the power of slavery and considered Jackson's election a danger to democracy and a victory for the South. Moved beyond anger, Adams sought revenge on Jackson and on the South. Thus, the former president allowed his constituents to elect him to the House of Representatives in 1830.[31]

In the House, Adams would encounter not Jackson in the flesh, but rather those who were of the same mind as the president. For, like Jackson, most representatives from the South adhered to the code of honor and a handful of members were celebrities in dueling circles.[32] One of the most vocal opponents of the petitions, Hammond of South Carolina, understood honor to be "that principle of nature which teaches us to respect ourselves, in order that we may gain the respect of others." The southern code of honor directed gentlemen to demonstrate valor and to exact revenge against familial and community enemies, a requirement that could be fulfilled by dueling. In fact, the House was filled with celebrities in dueling circles who were not beyond reacting to statements made on the floor of Congress by throwing down the gauntlet.[33] In February 1838, for example, Representative Henry Wise, a major participant in the petition debate, acted as a second in a duel fought with rifles over remarks made in the House by the Maine Democrat Jonathan Cilley. Cilley was killed by William Graves, a first-term Whig from Kentucky, when, after surviving the initial exchange, Wise urged the two to fire again. Outrage over the Graves-Cilley affair was directed not so much at the principals as at the seconds, namely Wise, who was held responsible for failing to stop the needless violence. Adams responded by sponsoring a bill, the Prentice-Adams Act, which outlawed dueling in the District of Columbia.[34]

The deeply gendered southern code of honor clashed directly with northern principles of humane sensibility and the political identity constructed in

---

[31]Richards, *Congressman John Quincy Adams*, p. 15.
[32]Ibid., p. 132.
[33]Ibid.
[34]Marjorie G. Fribourg, *The U.S. Congress: Men Who Steered Its Course, 1787–1867* (Philadelphia, 1972), p. 214; Miller, *Arguing about Slavery*, pp. 282–83.

antislavery petitions. Indeed, by the beginning of the nineteenth century, while the code of honor and its enactment in dueling held sway in the South, both practices had almost completely disappeared in the North.[35] Instead, as the rhetoric of the petitions reflected, northern culture was attached to beliefs in legal equality and domestic virtue that were intended in theory, at least, to erase class privilege. In the North, "honor" had been replaced by "respectability" and "domestic and civic virtue," which for men included temperate behavior rather than indulgence in substances such as alcohol and tobacco. Not only did the manners of men differ, but so, too, did norms governing the behavior of women. "Antebellum Yankee women," explains Wyatt-Brown, "at least those in the upper and middle classes, had begun to question, with increasing insistence, their age-old subjection." When northern women claimed new privileges for themselves, southern men perceived their behavior as threatening deeply ingrained norms of gender conduct and reacted by articulating long-held assumptions about proper female conduct.[36]

In addition to violating elite southern notions of proper behavior, whether intentionally or not, the language of women's antislavery petitions registered with southern gentlemen as insults to their honor. They fell into the category of insult that demanded a duel, the petitions "gave the lie" to slaveholders— they unmasked the public appearance of slaveholders as differing from their true nature.[37] Particularly offensive to southern honor were petitions that accused gentlemen of sexual indiscretions with slaves, not because these accusations were untrue (they were true), but because they publicly exposed sexual misconduct with slaves. In the system of meaning sustained by the southern culture of honor, the women petitioners had violated standards of proper conduct by confronting gentleman with lying about their sexual behavior. This accusation disgraced not only the man, but also his wife and children.[38]

Had they been uttered by an individual, imputations like those contained in the petitions surely would have invited a duel. Dueling with thousands of distant petitioners was impossible, but there was available a similar form of social drama through which southerners could reassert their honor. That

[35]Kenneth S. Greenberg, "The Nose, the Lie, and the Duel in the Antebellum South," *American Historical Review* (1990):58.

[36]Wyatt-Brown, *Honor and Violence in the Old South*, pp. 85, 86.

[37]Greenberg, "Nose, Lie, and Duel," pp. 62–63.

[38]Wyatt-Brown, *Southern Honor*, p. 308.

form was oratory. Indeed, the duel and the oration shared profound similarities in goals, forms, and styles.[39] In southern political culture, oratory was viewed as an opportunity for a "public display" of character, thus, eloquence was considered a core value in the politics of honor.[40] "Oratory, or the art of speaking well," proclaimed *Lord Chesterfield's Advice to His Son on Men and Manners*, a popular early American guide to gentlemanly behavior, "is useful in every situation of life, and absolutely necessary in most. . . . A man cannot distinguish himself without it."[41] So tightly connected were oratorical performance and elite southern gender norms that the plantation class considered "eminence in war and eloquence in council the marks of illustrious manhood."[42]

No nose was pulled, no gauntlet thrown down, and no pistol drawn, yet the prolonged exchange in the House between sponsors of antislavery petitions and southern firebrands was for slaveholding members unquestionably a contest of honor. Though oratorical, it took on the emotions, the stakes, and the form of a duel. Slaveholding members bristled with insult, demanded satisfaction, and rose to defend the South. They asserted their masculinity, the quiet benevolence of their ladies, and the virtues of the South, while casting aspersions on the character of antislavery petitioners, northern representatives, and the northern people themselves.

In the oratorical duel sparked by presentation of women's antislavery petitions, southern representatives questioned the honor of northern women, and by implication northern men, to undermine the credibility of their accusers. The majority of southern responses attacked female signers as lacking the attributes of a proper lady. Northern women were characterized as flying wildly out of control and failing to recognize their place in society. Though he claimed to pay "cordial homage to the fair sex," Virginia's Henry Wise stated that he believed woman's sphere of action was drawn clearly and that she should not move beyond it: "Woman in the parlor, woman in her proper sphere, is the ornament and comfort of man; but out of the par-

[39]Kenneth S. Greenberg, *Masters and Statesmen: The Political Culture of American Slavery* (Baltimore, 1985), pp. 38–41.

[40]Greenberg, *Masters and Statesmen*, pp. 12–15.

[41]Craig Thompson Friend, "Belles, Benefactors, and the Blacksmith's Son: Cyrus Stuart and the Enigma of Southern Gentlemanliness," in *Southern Manhood: Perspectives on Masculinity in the Old South*, ed. Craig Thompson Friend and Lorri Glover (Athens, Ga., 2004), p. 106.

[42]Richard M. Weaver, *The Southern Tradition at Bay: A History of Postbellum Thought*, ed. George Core and M. E. Bradford (New Rochelle, N.Y., 1968), p. 72.

lor, out of her sphere, if there is a devil on earth, when she is a devil, woman is a devil incarnate!"[43] Another Virginian professed that "there is no man on this floor who has a higher admiration of the female character than I." Yet he was forced to confess that he did not like to see women "madly shooting out of their proper sphere, and undertaking to control national politics."[44] Likewise, North Carolina's Jesse Bynum preached, "It was not in the field, nor is it in the cabinet, where the counsel of lovely woman has been found most potent; to adorn her sex, she is destined for a different sphere."[45] The House referred all memorials relating to the Texas question to the Committee on Foreign Affairs, which was charged with composing a report about the content of the petitions and the expediency of granting their requests. On June 14 the report was presented by the committee's chairman, Benjamin Howard of Maryland. Annoyed by the preponderance of petitions from females, Howard expressed his "regret" that so many of the memorials were signed by women. It was inappropriate for women to petition their legislators, he said, because females were afforded ample opportunity for the exercise of their influence by approaching their fathers, husbands, and children in the domestic circle and by "shedding over it the mild radiance of the social virtues, instead of rushing into the fierce struggles of political life." By leaving their proper sphere, Howard charged, women were "discreditable, not only to their own particular section of the country, but also to the national character."[46]

Another shot fired against northerners was aimed at the physical appearance and sexuality of the women petitioners. Drawing from a poem, Bynum held that women who abandoned their proper sphere inevitably lost their femininity: "women become most mannish grown" when they "assume the part that men should act alone."[47] Bynum implied that the female signers were unappealing to men by dismissing them as "old grannies and a parcel of boarding-school misses." Likewise, James Garland of Virginia revealed

---

[43]*Register of Debates*, 24th Cong., 1st sess., 1835, p. 2032.
[44]Ibid., p. 2064.
[45]Ibid., 2d sess., 1837, p. 1337.
[46]John Quincy Adams, *Speech on the Right of the People, Men and Women, to Petition; on the Freedom of Speech and Debate in the House of Representatives of the United States; on the Resolutions of Seven State Legislatures and the Petitions of More than One Hundred Thousand Petitioners, Relating to the Annexation of Texas to this Union. Delivered in the House of Representatives of the United States, in fragments in the morning our, from the 16th of June to the 7th of July, 1838, inclusive* (Washington, D.C., 1838), pp. 76–77.
[47]*Register of Debates*, 24th Cong., 2d sess., 1837, p. 1337.

that he was certain that the petitioners were "old maids."[48] William Cost Johnson of Maryland implied that female petitioners were exhibiting inappropriate sexual behavior. He bid northern representatives to instruct their women petitioners "to attend to knitting their own hose and darning their stockings, rather than come [here] and unsex themselves, be laid on the table, and sent to committee to be reported on."[49] With these words Johnson not only accused northern women of excessive public displays that invited sexual response, but also he implied that northern men were unable to control their women. Garland depicted them as available for sexual conquest. In one instance, he responded to the comment of a northern congressman that female petitioners, who had been called murderers by some representatives, were "like those of Macbeth—they only 'murder sleep.'" It seemed from this remark, said Garland, that "one of the peculiar virtues of these females is, to disturb his slumbers." He suggested that the northern representative "take one of these interesting, charming ladies for his wife." Such a pairing, chuckled Garland, "would lessen the ranks of the abolitionists [by] one" and would prevent Granger "further disturbance of his midnight slumbers." Garland ended by calling this solution "a powerful soporific, and a very pleasant one in the bargain."[50] In the course of his joke, Garland both impugned the northern representative's manhood by suggesting that he lacked sexual experience and reduced the female petitioners to outlets for male sexual desire.

Other speakers jealously defended the virtues of southern women, which they perceived to have been dishonored by the petitioners. John Patton of Virginia compared what he interpreted as the hostile actions of northern women to the restrained behavior of southern ladies, stating that "they must be very different from their sex of any class that I have been acquainted with, if they would persevere in any course that went to hazard everything dear to their sex." He warned that if the women petitioners were to continue along their present course, "they would hazard the life and safety of the dear and tender offspring clinging to the bosoms of their own sisterhood." Patton professed to be certain that if northern women were informed as to the effect they were producing "upon the helpless, defenceless objects of their blind charity, they, being Christians, (as all women are, or should be)

[48]Ibid., 1st sess., 1835, p. 2064.
[49]*Congressional Globe*, 26th Cong., 1st sess., 1840, p. 450.
[50]*Register of Debates*, 24th Cong., 1st sess., 1835, p. 2064.

would leave the thing to God."[51] Bouldin proclaimed that it was unnecessary for northern women to petition Congress "to preserve the ladies of the South from corruption." He promised to draw no comparisons between ladies from different sections, but he beseeched female petitioners "to give themselves no further trouble about the ladies of the South." There was no danger, he said, that slavery had or would corrupt southern women, who did not "suffer by comparison with the fair in any part of the world, in any quality that could adorn or ornament the sex, or render it lovely."[52] Bouldin later refuted more bluntly claims that slavery tainted southern women: "Who, for pure, feminine modesty, and unsuspected chastity, as well as every other quality that can recommend her to the love and admiration of stranger or acquaintance, stands better in the eyes of the world than the southern female? Is it supposed that she will suffer by comparison with females in any nonslaveholding state?"[53]

In the very act of defending the honor of their women and attacking the enemies of the South, slaveholding members demonstrated that despite the condemnations in the petitions, they were men of honor. Southern representatives repeatedly asserted and enacted their honor by pledging to defend the South and in so doing demonstrating their valor. Garland, for one, assumed the role of the noble protector of helpless women and children in the face of the imminent danger posed by abolitionist petitions. Were the abolitionists to incite a slave rebellion that would result in "blood reeking for the bosoms of our wives and children," Garland vowed that southern husbands and fathers would "revenge to the utmost their blood upon the heads who shed it."[54]

While southern representatives attempted to reassert their honor and manhood, they also sought to denigrate that of northerners. Indeed, southern firebrands accused northern representatives who did not act to quell antislavery petitions as less than honorable and less than manly. Bynum, for example, urged members from New England—and especially Adams—to spurn the petitions of "old maids, grannies, and children." The reason was clear—the petitions were not manly and neither was any member who presented them. Bynum proclaimed, "There is not an idea connected with any

---

[51]Ibid., 1836, pp. 2170–71.
[52]Ibid., 1835, pp. 2002–4.
[53]Ibid., 1836, p. 2234.
[54]Ibid., 1835, pp. 2066–69.

part of the subject that deserves the name of manliness, and becoming the consideration of an intelligent statesman." He singled out the people of Massachusetts for rebuke, and, in a thinly veiled reference to the aging Adams, shamed them for allowing women to become political agents who were "urging their imbecile, timid men to action." Bynum predicted that when agitation over slavery resulted in civil war, female abolitionists and their allies would flee the scene: "Where, then, will be found their women and children, who crowd this House with silly petitions? Where their priests? In the tented field? No, sir, but skulking, shivering, shrinking from danger and responsibility, and even then denying the part that they had once taken in getting up this tragic drama. Will their women then be seen in the field, amid the clangor of arms and the shouts of victory, or heard in the cabinet with the cries of their children around them?" Bynum demanded that "the hardy sons of New England" answer these questions.[55]

Adding to accusations that male abolitionists were dishonorable because they threatened the Union and caused innocents to suffer, southerners attacked abolitionists as unmanly. Garland singled out the British abolitionist George Thompson, who had been "lecturing and propagating his incendiarism" in the North, as lacking masculinity. According to Garland, when an anti-abolitionist mob rushed Thompson during a visit to Boston, the Englishman could not defend himself and hid behind women. When indignant citizens surrounded Thompson and breathed threats in order to suppress his lectures, reported Garland, he was saved by his "charming female followers." According to Garland, these "blessed, pious old maids" carried Thompson away unseen—"in the midst of a cloud"—and he escaped untouched "entirely through female intervention." So it was, implied Garland, that proper gender roles were reversed—the cowardly, feminized male abolitionist was rescued from the hostile mob by his charming, masculinized female followers.[56] Thompson was just one example marshaled by southern members to illustrate the lack of manhood among abolitionists. Garland claimed that in general the abolitionists were "midnight murderers," not "open and manly murderers." They were cowards, not men, he explained, because they dared not show their faces in the South to directly propagate their schemes. Instead, lacking the manly trait of bravery, they stood at a distance, "safely

[55]Ibid., 2d sess., 1837, pp. 1329, 1337.
[56]Ibid., 1st sess., 1835, p. 2067.

moored behind the laws and institutions of independent States," in order to artfully excite slaves to the work of destruction.[57]

In sum, southern opponents of female antislavery petitions spurned the memorials' conservative characterizations of women's prayers on behalf of the slave as extensions of Christian duty, interpreting them instead as radical attempts to justify women's incursion into the exclusively male realm of congressional debate. Southern representatives, moreover, considered the accusations voiced in the petitions to be assaults on the honor of the South and its people. Deeply offended, southern representatives vociferously demanded satisfaction and oratorically exacted revenge by dissecting the character of northern women petitioners and their supposed male protectors. In the course of doing so, the southern representatives conflated acceptable gender behavior with constitutional rights. Adversaries of the women petitioners argued that because it was improper for women to petition Congress, they had no right to petition Congress. Women, they maintained, moreover, could not reason logically nor act independently—they lacked basic qualifications for republican citizenship—and therefore their petitions should not be seriously considered. Opponents denied that petitioning against slavery was an extension of female moral duty, instead labeling it as a clearly political action related to a clearly political subject. By bursting into congressional debate over the political issue of slavery, detractors maintained, northern females acted in such an unbecoming, unwomanly manner that their reputation, if not their sanity, was doubtful, and the House had no obligation to hear the requests of such deluded individuals. This objection amounted to denying women the right of petition because exercising that right fell outside norms of respectable womanly behavior. Slaveholders also developed a second level of arguments to build a republican rationale for denying women the right of petition, and, more generally, claims to citizenship. Women, they maintained lacked the requisite virtues of republican citizenship: they could not deliberate rationally, act independently, nor fulfill a citizen's obligation to serve in the military. Certain members went so far as to suggest that women possessed no claims whatsoever to citizenship. "Have women, too, the right of petition?" Wise demanded at one point in the debate. "Are they citizens!"[58]

---

[57] Ibid.
[58] Ibid., pp. 2032–33.

"Adding one injustice to another"

There were few northern representatives willing to defend the antislavery petitioners and even to respond to generalized attacks on the North. But there was one Yankee who shirked southern threats and who insisted that the abolition petitions be heard in the House. He repeatedly defended the character of petitioners, male and female, and threw the character of slaveholders into question. This man was, of course, John Quincy Adams, who had earned the appellation "Old Man Eloquent." During the course of the nine-year debate over the presentation of antislavery petitions, Adams delivered hundreds of speeches defending the right of petition on various grounds and especially the First Amendment. Besides addressing constitutional issues, he recognized that the debate rested on more than logical argument, that it was rooted in a cultural conflict between the sections. Despising dueling and the bravado of southern men of honor, the cantankerous Adams repeatedly used southern oratorical forms to parody southern firebrands and expose them as ridiculous.

A major weapon in Adam's rhetorical arsenal was the accusation of hypocrisy against members who fancied themselves gentlemen of honor, but who turned a blind eye to ungentlemanly behavior. When Adams presented a petition from "nine ladies" of Fredericksburg, Virginia, Representative Patton, who had lived in that city, assailed Adams for bringing before the House a petition from "mulatto" women of "infamous character." Adams responded by asking who it was that had made them infamous? Then he threw the House into an uproar by stating that it was most likely white men who had made these women "infamous." In support of this claim, Adams noted that "there existed great resemblances in the South between the progeny of the colored people and the white men who claimed possession of them." Southern members erupted with anger, for Adams had stabbed brutally at the heart of southern honor.[59] Not only had he defended the morality of "mulatto women," who were despised by Patton and southern elites in general, but he had accused southern men of sexual misconduct with black women—a charge often made in abolitionist petitions, particularly those from women, but heretofore veiled in silence on the floor of Congress. Adam's accusation also upset southern members because it was true. Slave owners

---

[59]Ibid., 2d sess., 1837, pp. 1675–76.

commonly raped and otherwise engaged in sexual activity with slaves, and as long as they discreetly observed the social rules, no retribution would follow. Foremost among those rules was that of silence in public about these liaisons.[60] Adams had lifted the veil of silence.

Yet another rhetorical strategy employed by Adams was to adopt the touchy, easily provoked demeanor of southern members in order to justify taking more of the House's time to discuss the abolition petitions. Adams responded to Howard's June 14, 1838, report cited above by mimicking the southern gentlemen's habit of jealously defending their women against the slightest insult. "Sir, was it from a son—was it from a father—was it from a husband, that I heard these words?" demanded Adams. "Does this gentleman consider that women, by petitioning this House in favor of suffering and distress, perform an office 'discreditable' to themselves, to the section of the country where they reside, and to the nation?" Before unleashing his rhetorical firepower, Adams offered Howard a chance to retract his assertion: "I have a right to make this call upon him. It is to the wives and to the daughters of my constituents that he applies this language." Like a valorous southern gentleman, Adams seized upon Howard's remarks as an insult to his women and to his section. Following the requisite form of language exchanged in an affair of honor, which, of course, often resulted in a duel, Adams confronted Howard with a description of how his honor had been injured and how he had been not been treated with due courtesy.[61] Adams insisted that if Howard refused to retract the insulting comments, he would be required to respond forcefully. And he did so not with a duel of weapons, but with a duel of words. In fact, by insisting that he must defend the honor of northern women, Adams justified holding forth on the floor of Congress for more than four days, during which time he defended the character of northern female petitioners.[62]

Adams proceeded to demonstrate that Howard's principle that women should have nothing to do with political affairs possessed no grounding in the Bible. He cited the case of Deborah, a judge and prophetess during the infancy of the Jewish nation, of Jael, who slew the enemy of her nation, and of Esther, who saved the Jews by petitioning. Turning to secular history,

---

[60]Wyatt-Brown, *Honor and Violence in the Old South*, p. 105.
[61]Greenberg, "Nose, Lie, and Duel," p. 62.
[62]Adams, *Speech on the Right of Petition*, pp. 76–77.

Adams challenged Howard to "find there that it is 'discreditable' for women to take any interest or any part in political affairs." Adams bid opponents of female petitioners to examine the character of Aspasia, an Athenian woman whom Socrates praised as "an excellent mistress of the art of rhetoric." Knowing that any encomium to southern womanhood required mention of Sparta's brave mothers, Adams asked whether they had "forgotten that Spartan mother, who said to her son when going out to battle, 'My son, come back to me *with* thy shield, or *upon* thy shield'?"[63] In so doing, once again he seized common forms of southern oratory to at once parody his opponents and use their own words against them.[64]

To stir patriotic sentiments, Adams also discussed heroines of the American Revolution. After recalling the work of the "ladies of Philadelphia," who outfitted Washington's troops when they were destitute of clothes, he quoted from another history of the Revolution, which said that "the LADIES of South Carolina conducted themselves with more than Spartan magnanimity." Adams had special praise for the women of Charleston, who petitioned for the release of Colonel Hayne. In the midst of adducing this example, Adams shouted, "Where is the chairman of the Committee on Foreign Relations?" But Howard was not in the House chamber. Adams railed, "I want him to discuss this point. Here were women who entered deeply into concerns relating to their country, and felt that they had other duties to perform, besides those to the domestic comforts of their husbands, brothers, and sons. They petitioned! I want him to listen to their petition, all glorious to their memories as it is!" He then proceeded to read the rather lengthy petition.[65] But Adams did not stop there. He called up the example of Deborah Gannett, who had dressed in men's clothes, joined the patriot army, and fought for three years until she was wounded. Members of the House were aware of Gannett's feats because within recent memory they had voted to give her husband a military pension based on the services of his wife and had praised her on the grounds that she had "fought and bled for human liberty." After commending Gannett's actions, which involved rushing physically into "the vortex of politics," Adams asked how Howard could conceivably think it wrong for women to petition on a matter of politics.[66]

---

[63]The frequency and function of classical allusions in southern oratory are discussed by Wyatt-Brown in *Honor and Violence*, p. 45.

[64]Adams, *Speech on the Right of Petition*, p. 80.

[65]Ibid., pp. 70–72.

[66]Ibid., pp. 72–73.

Adams aimed his last example from the Revolution directly at Howard, who had returned to the chamber. He recounted that the ladies of Baltimore won praise from all over the country by making summer clothing for the army of Lafayette. "Sir," said Adams, "was it from the lips of a son of one of the most distinguished of those ladies of Baltimore—was it from the lips of a descendant of one of the most illustrious officers in that war that we now hear the annunciation that the political and public services of women are to be treated with contempt? Sir, I do hope that honorable gentleman, when he shall reply to this part of my argument, will modify his opinions on this point."[67]

Howard was not about to wait for a chance to reply. He rose and begged permission to speak. Adams yielded the floor. Howard argued that he saw "not the slightest resemblance" between the conduct of the ladies of Baltimore during the Revolution and that of the women who were petitioning Congress against the admission of Texas: "When the relatives and friends of women are in the field, struggling amidst perils and sufferings for the independence of the country, undergoing all sorts of hardships and privations, without sufficient food or raiment, nothing could be more becoming to the female character than that, by the exercise of their needle, or influence, or industry, they should try to alleviate the toils of their gallant defenders." Howard protested vociferously against classifying the generous and patriotic ladies of the Revolution with the female petitioners who publicly opposed the annexation of Texas. He also upbraided Adams for likening the petitioners to Aspasia, who was "notorious for profligacy of her life," and Gannett, who had "usurped the habiliments" of her sex and put on men's clothes in order to associate with men. Surely, said Howard, the representative from Massachusetts could find more appropriate models for the "modest and virtuous girls of New England." With this argument, Howard questioned the very foundation of Adams's morals by implying that he possessed skewed perceptions about gender. Howard was saying, in so many words, "It figures that a Yankee would view a prostitute and a masculine woman as ideal." In his rejoinder, Adams accused Howard of harboring an opinion about women much like that entertained by the Turks—women have no souls. This opinion, said Adams, was not shared by the nation generally, and it reflected cruelly on the conduct and character of the women of the Republic.[68]

---

[67]Ibid., p. 75.
[68]Ibid., pp. 75–76.

In the course of defending the character of petitioning women, Adams prescribed standards of proper feminine behavior that differed significantly from the southern ideals of women. Instead, he recommended a three-pronged test by which one could determine whether women were acting properly when they voiced their opinion about controversial issues. When presented with such a circumstance, professed Adams, one must inquire "into the motive which actuated them, the means they employ, and the end they have in view." Adams then applied this test to the case at hand, the petitions against annexation of Texas. As for the motive, he said, it was of the "highest order" of purity: "They petition under a conviction that the consequence of the annexation would be the advancement of that which is sin in the sight of God, viz: slavery." The means were appropriate, Adams said, because it was Congress who must decide the question, and it was Congress to whom the women must petition. Echoing a justification offered by the female petitioners themselves, he said, "It is a petition—it is a prayer—a supplication—that which you address to the Almighty Being above you. And what can be more appropriate to their sex?" As for the end sought by female petitioners, it, too, was virtuous, pure, and of the most exalted character—"to prevent the perpetuation and spread of slavery through America."[69] In contrast to Howard's condemnation, Adams said, "the correct principle is, that women are not only justified, but exhibit the most exalted virtue when they do depart from the domestic circle, and enter on the concerns of their country, of humanity, and of their God." Adams concluded his argument by exalting the benevolence of northern women by stating that the female petitioners, by discharging their duty to God have "manifested a virtue which is even above the virtues of mankind, and approaches to a superior nature."[70]

But Adams did not stop with defending the character of female petitioners and the propriety of their actions in relation to their duty as women. He went one step further to expose Howard's attacks on the character of female petitioners as having the ultimate goal and effect of denying women the right of petition. Adams admitted that Howard had not directly contested the right of women to petition. "But he had," said Adams, "represented the exercise of it as disgraceful to those women who petitioned, and as discreditable to their own section of the Union, and to the nation at large. Now to say,

[69]Ibid., p. 81.
[70]Ibid., p. 68.

respecting women, that any action of theirs was disgraceful, was more than merely contesting their legal right so to act: it was contesting the right of the mind, of the soul, and the conscience." This was no "light question," insisted Adams; no mere quarrel over the honor of a few women. Instead it concerned "the very utmost depths of the Constitution of the country" and affected "the political rights of one half of the People of the nation."[71]

In a few short breaths Adams exposed the conflation of character and rights that since the writing of the Constitution had served to limit women's citizenship by depicting them as unfit to belong to the polis. And Adams pushed even further. He interpreted Howard as denying women the right of petition because they had no right to vote, and then he demanded: "Is it so clear that they have no such right as this last? And if not, who shall say that this argument of the gentleman's is not adding one injustice to another?"[72] Adams questioned the very assumption that the Constitution denied women the right to vote. He suggested that the reason women did not vote was custom rather than lack of a right to the franchise. And he implied that outright denial of women's right to vote was an "injustice," as was the denial of their right of petition. His was a radical assertion, for it would be another eight years before the women of New York petitioned their legislature for the vote, a decade before the Declaration of Sentiments of the Seneca Falls woman's rights convention would assert that women possessed the right of suffrage, and more than eighty years before women were granted the right of suffrage.

Conclusions

The debates in Congress over antislavery petitions were at their fiery core a battle over what should be the proper conception of the American character. In their petitions, northerners articulated a free-labor, middle-class morality, embracing it as a standard of judgment by which slaveholders could only be found immoral. Perceiving the petitions as an insult to their very way of life, slaveholding members performed the norms of southern masculinity. They fell back upon the language of dueling, a form of ritualized violence through which such gentlemen were accustomed to avenging their

---

[71]Ibid., pp. 77–78, 74.
[72]Ibid., p. 77.

honor. While using oratory to reassert their honor by acting as manly protectors of family and home, southern firebrands attempted to masculinize women petitioners while emasculating male abolitionists and northern representatives. Fully apprehending but thoroughly despising the behavior required by the southern code of honor, John Quincy Adams chose to parody slaveholders' bristly, melodramatic oratory. These exchanges, which increased animosity among members of Congress, were also put on display in the nation's newspapers.

Caught up in the debates over antislavery petitions, especially those from women, were ferocious contests for political power in the republic and claims to American citizenship. Indeed, the debates occasioned by appearance of women's antislavery petitions in Congress challenged the rationale for denying women their Constitutional rights. The standard of character had long been employed to limit groups of Americans from full practice of their rights as citizens. In the early republic it was the supposedly dependent nature and depraved character of the propertyless male that rendered him unqualified to vote. In 1787 it was the questionable patriotism of Quakers that jeopardized their right to petition Congress. In the writing of the Constitution, it was the allegedly brutish character of the African that excluded slaves from full personhood and freedom. And, in southern representatives' responses to female antislavery petitions, it was women's allegedly emotional, unintelligent, and sexually desperate behavior that justified denying them the right of petition. When Adams held forth on the floor of the House demanding that the constitutional right of petition no longer be held hostage to the approval of the character of the petitioner and that despite custom women may indeed possess the right to vote, he opened the door to a radical refashioning of the polis.

David Zarefsky

Debating Slavery by Proxy

The Texas Annexation Controversy

FOR ALMOST TWENTY-FIVE years, from the Missouri controversy until the mid-1840s, slavery was kept off the agenda for mainstream public debate. The two major political parties had both northern and southern wings, with no wish to antagonize either. In Congress, the Missouri debates made people aware of the volatile nature of the issue. Only two new states, one slave and one free, were brought into the Union. President Andrew Jackson stifled his desire to aid the Republic of Texas, delaying even diplomatic recognition until his last day in office. Neither he nor his successor, Martin Van Buren, responded favorably to overtures from the Texans seeking annexation to the United States. The House of Representatives went so far as to adopt a "gag rule," refusing to receive petitions advocating abolition, not because most of its members supported slavery but because they recognized how dangerous the public airing of the issue could be.

This state of affairs abruptly changed in the spring of 1844, when the administration of John Tyler, prompted by motives ranging from exaggerated fears of a British abolitionist conspiracy to the precarious political position of President Tyler, sent to the Senate a treaty by which Texas should join the Union.[1] Texas had been a Mexican province, settled largely by U.S. nationals attracted to the fertile soil of east Texas. Many were slaveholders who largely ignored Mexican law when it abolished slavery. Threats of stepped-up enforcement were among the factors spurring the successful Texas

---

[1] *Senate Executive Journal*, 28th Cong., 1st sess., Apr. 22, 1844, pp. 257–61.

revolt that resulted in the independent, slaveholding republic. But the new nation fell upon hard times. That, together with Mexico's threat to try to recapture its renegade province, led the Texans to seek annexation. The Tyler administration took seriously the rumors that, if that prospect failed, Texas would seek a deal with Britain, agreeing to abolish slavery in return for commercial and financial advantage.

Tyler's message requesting ratification subordinated the slavery question, perhaps deliberately. The president stressed national benefits to annexation and then explained how each section would gain. The North would gain markets for manufactured goods; the West, for animals and raw materials. For the South there would be peace of mind from the removal of a threat to its peace and tranquility on its southwestern border. In context, this meant that the South need not worry that fugitive slaves might seek a haven in a free Texas. But that oblique line was the only reference to slavery in the message. Tyler then maintained that these national and sectional benefits, though real, were insignificant when compared to the urgency of protecting the nation against a possible British threat.[2]

Unfortunately, Tyler's secretary of state was not so circumspect. John C. Calhoun had been named to the post after the accidental death of Abel P. Upshur. Both were committed annexationists and obsessively proslavery, but Calhoun was less under Tyler's control. He completed the negotiations with the Texans. He also answered a letter his predecessor had received from British foreign minister Richard Pakenham, denying rumors of possible British intervention in Texas but expressing the wish that Texas and all the world might abolish slavery and announcing that Her Majesty's government was "constantly exerting itself" to bring about this result. The reference to constant exertions probably was a rhetorical flourish suggesting sincerity of commitment, but Calhoun took it as a literal statement of Britain's intention. He lectured his counterpart about the benefits of slavery and announced that this British threat forced the United States to annex Texas as an act of self-defense of our right to form our own domestic institutions in our own way. Not only did Calhoun write the letter and send it to Pakenham, but he also included it among the documents sent to Congress along with the treaty.

---

[2]Ibid.

Some northerners seized upon the letter as confirmation that there was a southern plot to annex Texas in order to spread slavery, an allegation previously having been made by "fanatics" such as Benjamin Lundy and former president John Quincy Adams.[3]

So the Senate had a choice. It could either debate the treaty while downplaying the slavery issue, as Tyler had done, or it could magnify the significance of the slavery issue, as Calhoun had done. In fact, it did some of both. The debate, as recorded in the *Congressional Globe*, was brief and underdeveloped. Texas had not yet become the "hot issue" that would dominate the fall election campaign.

Rather than focus on slavery, some senators stressed the threat of possible British involvement to American economic freedom and national security. Although Thomas Hart Benton (D-Mo.), an opponent of immediate annexation, pointed out that the British government gave the allegations of a plot "no less than four full, broad, direct, unqualified denials,"[4] Arkansas Democrat A. H. Sevier insisted that these denials came "in the face of her public avowal that she is the advocate of [slavery's] abolition throughout the world."[5]

Another popular theme in the defense of annexation was that Texas was merely being "reannexed." According to this view, Texas was part of the Louisiana Purchase—certainly a contestable claim—and the United States unwisely and perhaps illegally had given it up in 1819 in return for claim to Florida. Now was an opportunity to rectify the error. Senator Robert J. Walker (D-Miss.) explained, "The question, then, of reannexation is a question of honor and good faith. We bound ourselves, in 1803, to admit the people of Texas now into the Union. They have never released us from that obligation." Walker went on to insist that "if we would not trample upon their rights, and upon the faith of treaties, and the obligation of contracts, they will and must be admitted into the Union."[6] The unstated portion of Walker's argument is that the status of Texas in 1803 somehow creates a presumption in favor of annexation in 1845. Texas need only call us on our pledge and we would be obligated to respond. Tennessee Whig Senator Spencer

---

[3] *Senate Documents* 341 (Serial No. 435), 28th Cong., 1st sess.
[4] *Congressional Globe*, 28th Cong., 2d sess., 1844, app., p. 484.
[5] Ibid., 1st sess., 1844, app., p. 559.
[6] Ibid., app., p. 550.

Jarnagin, however, argued that the "reannexation" claim was internally flawed: If Texas was ours to begin with, why did we need a new treaty to make it so, and how could Texas be competent to execute such a treaty?[7] Nevertheless, several of the defenders of annexation referred to it consistently as reannexation, adopting the term that was also in the Democratic party platform.

To add urgency to the decision, some supporters relied on what is known in rhetoric as the locus of the irreparable, the theme that if we forgo action now, the opportunity will never again present itself. We cannot afford the luxury of calm reflection and lengthy deliberation, because the situation will get away from us. Illinois Democrat Sidney Breese advanced this theme, noting that "this is the third time Texas has consented to [annexation]." If she is rejected once again, Breese rhetorically asked, "is it not more than probable such a revulsion of feeling will be produced by it, throughout the whole republic, as to change her love for us into hate, and her desire for a union with us into a position by which she could annoy and harass us?"[8] Similarly, Pennsylvania's James Buchanan, the future president, asserted, "Should we fail to embrace the present 'golden opportunity' for consummating the union between the two republics, another may never be afforded."[9] The locus of the irreparable creates pressure for a decision by heightening the risks of inaction. Nevertheless, other senators, such as Thomas Hart Benton (D-Mo.) and John M. Berrien (W-Ga.), denied or trivialized the claim. Berrien, for example, pointed out, "If the people of Texas sincerely desire this union they will not cease to cherish it because of this delay."[10] And Benton warned his colleagues that the "now-or-never" argument was "the potent argument when reason fails. Now or never is the address to the fears when the judgment refuses to yield."[11] These are attempts to diminish the rhetorical power of the argument by naming it for what it is.

Stressing the fear of English intrigue, insisting on "reannexation," and stressing that the moment not seized would be lost, were three of the common arguments for annexation that managed largely to avoid the question of slavery. They might have reflected their authors' genuine convictions, but they also were proxies for the issue that many did not want to acknowledge.

---

[7]Ibid., app., p. 682.
[8]Ibid., app., p. 543.
[9]Ibid., app., p. 726.
[10]Ibid., app., p. 704.
[11]Ibid., app., p. 575.

Similarly, some annexation opponents did not want to ground their objections in slavery either. Among their assertions were that annexation was unconstitutional, that it would trigger war with Mexico, that it reflected partisan motivation rather than sound public policy, and that it was inevitable so did not need to happen immediately. Tennessee's Senator Jarnagin, for instance, insisted that the Constitution gives no power to annex a foreign land by treaty; he denied that any act, such as the Louisiana Purchase or the acquisition of Florida, could serve as precedent for such an illegal use of power.[12] Benton believed that the proper approach was to negotiate with Mexico, since she had retracted her diplomatic recognition of Texas. Proceeding with annexation, he believed, would entail an unjust and unconstitutional war with Mexico.[13] Benton saw evidence of partisan motive in the fact that when the treaty was submitted to the Senate, the chair of the Foreign Relations Committee was asked to take no action on it for forty days, precisely the amount of time until the Democratic party would have held its presidential nominating convention (in which it could declare itself on the issue).[14] And he also asserted that "reunion" between Texas and the United States would have happened naturally, because of geographical and cultural proximity, were it not for the fact that "this insidious scheme of sudden and secret annexation, and its miserable pretexts, was fallen upon by our hapless Administration."[15] In short, both supporters and opponents of the Texas treaty could debate the question without bringing the slavery issue to the surface.

But it did not stay far submerged. Among both supporters and opponents there were references to slavery, sometimes by the same people who focused on other issues too. Some treaty supporters appealed for votes from moderate antislavery men by espousing what is known as the "diffusion thesis." The premise of this argument is that, since the foreign slave trade was illegal, the total size of the slave population was relatively fixed. If slaves went to Texas, they would have to come from somewhere. And they would come from areas where the soil was relatively depleted, compared to the virgin lands of the West. Thinning out slavery in the less fertile upper South might actually lead to its gradual abolition there, repeating the pattern that had characterized the Middle States some forty years before. In other words,

[12]Ibid., app., p. 682.
[13]Ibid., app., p. 476.
[14]Ibid., app., p. 482.
[15]Ibid., p. 653.

paradoxical as it sounds, spreading slavery to Texas could be defended as a means to weaken slavery elsewhere. Buchanan, for instance, asked rhetorically whether "the acquisition of Texas be the means of gradually drawing the slaves far to the South, to a climate more congenial to their nature; and may they not finally pass off into Mexico, and there mingle with a race where no prejudice exists against their color?"[16] And New Hampshire Democrat Levi Woodbury, believing that ratifying the treaty "cannot add to the whole number of slaves now in Texas and the United States together," believed that dispersing the number among a wider space would gradually "tend to make freedom less expensive."[17]

Other slavery-related arguments sought to appeal more directly to the South. Senator Sevier of Arkansas urged annexation to foil an assumed abolitionist plot by Great Britain, who sought to level the playing field after her own abolition of slavery drastically raised the price of cotton from the West Indies.[18] Though speaking in the House of Representatives, where he would not vote on the treaty, Alabama Democrat James E. Belser made clear that since the constitutional compromises sanctioned slavery, southerners were every bit as much entitled to the admission of new slave states as northerners were to the admission of new free states; Texas annexation was the means to this goal, and northerners were obligated to support it.[19]

More shrill, however, were the arguments of those who *opposed* the treaty because of its slavery implications, although even here this argument did not dominate the debate. Indiana Whig Senator Albert S. White presented a memorial from a meeting of Quakers in Indianapolis condemning annexation because "it would have the effect of upholding, continuing, and extending slavery in the United States."[20] Both Benton and William S. Archer (W-Va.) complained that the nature of the issue had been skewed by Calhoun and turned into a debate about slavery. Benton said, "The difficulty now is in the aspect which has been put upon it as a sectional, political, and slave question; as a movement of the South against the North, and of the slaveholding States for political supremacy,"[21] and Archer likewise lamented,

---

[16]Ibid., app., p.722.
[17]Ibid., app., p.767.
[18]Ibid., app., p. 559.
[19]Ibid., app., p. 525.
[20]Ibid., p. 647.
[21]Ibid., app., p. 485.

"Our Secretary of State . . . has changed the entire aspect of the question."[22] Few, however, went as far as did Ohio Whig Joshua Giddings, speaking in the House of Representatives: "The object and purpose for which it is now sought to annex Texas to the United States is clearly and unequivocally set forth in the official correspondence [of] the Secretary of State . . . In every letter of that correspondence the object is frankly avowed, without any apparent delicacy or attempt at concealment." Moreover, Giddings added, "The same object of maintaining the slave trade between the slave-breeding States of this Union and Texas, and the perpetuating slavery in Texas, is the avowed object of nearly every democratic paper south of Mason and Dixon's line, by nearly every address upon that subject, and by the proceedings of nearly all the public meetings held in the slave States for the purpose of promoting the cause of annexation." He noted the irony that the same supporters of annexation speak of "extending American liberty to Texas."[23]

For the most part, however, the arguments in the treaty debate are incompletely developed. There is little follow-up on the statements I have quoted, and little direct engagement with the arguments of the other side. The controversy was approached gingerly, and much of the dispute was carried out in terms of other matters that could serve as proxies for the issue of slavery.

Perhaps because of Calhoun's overt appeal, seven northern Democrats, along with the majority of Whigs, voted against the treaty, which was defeated by a vote of 16 to 35. That might have been the end of the matter, but Tyler, determined on annexation, now announced that a treaty was not necessary anyway. Taking advantage of a constitutional ambiguity, he now proclaimed that a joint resolution—requiring only a majority vote in each house, rather than two-thirds of the Senate—would do the job. But Congress preferred to await the results of the 1844 election.

Once it was known that James K. Polk had won the election—even though his key victory in New York came about because Henry Clay lost antislavery votes to the abolitionist James G. Birney—Tyler promptly proclaimed the election a mandate for annexation and called on Congress to pass the joint resolution. This occasioned a new round of debate, in the early weeks of 1845, in both houses. Compared to the earlier Senate debate, this one was more extensive, more thorough, more harsh—and more focused on slavery.

---

[22]Ibid., app., p. 695.
[23]Ibid., app., pp. 704–5.

Like the president, many supporters of the resolution proclaimed the election results as a mandate. According to this view, there was nothing more to debate; the election results rendered the verdict of the people and now it was the duty of Congress to act on that judgment. For example, Pennsylvania Democrat Charles J. Ingersoll said in the House that "he had, at every meeting in his district during the canvass, said that if elected he should deem himself instructed to vote for the immediate reannexation of Texas" and estimated that 2.0 million of the 2.7 million votes cast in the 1844 election came from annexation supporters.[24] Congressman James E. Belser (D-Ala.), indicating that no further debate was necessary, said that "this was a question which had been already decided by that omnipotent tribunal, the people, and sufficient had been said upon it, throughout this Union."[25] Similar statements were made by other senators and representatives.[26] This judgment, of course, was consistent with the argument of President Tyler.

Widespread as this claim was, however, it was by no means universal. Maryland Whig Congressman J. P. Kennedy, acknowledging that at first the meaning of the election had seemed clear, said that the view was now changing.[27] Maine Whig Luther Severance interpreted the election as generally endorsing annexation, but not necessarily right away.[28] Congressman George Rathbun (D-N.Y.) was skeptical: "It had been said that the people settled this question in the late election, but how was the truth?" he asked. Knowing the circumstances of the New York vote, he had good reason to be skeptical.[29] These doubts may have delayed a rush to judgment, but it is hard to doubt that the popular interpretation of the 1844 election results moved the presumption in the direction of action.

Nor was much attention given in this second round of debate to the dangers of war with Mexico. One sign of the shifting public opinion was that this prospect was less clearly a deterrent to annexation. Congressman Ingersoll denied that annexation would bring war; he promised that Mexico would be satisfied with the explanations we would offer and concluded, "It offers me great satisfaction to be authorized to state that hostilities are not probable with Mexico."[30] Others were less sanguine but insisted that the prospect of

---

[24]Ibid., 2d sess., 1845, pp. 85, 87.
[25]Ibid., p, 87.
[26]See, for examples, ibid., pp. 118, 136, 140, 297.
[27]Ibid., p. 124.
[28]Ibid., p. 142.
[29]Ibid., p. 176.
[30]Ibid., p. 86.

war should not stand in the way of annexation. For example, Ohio Democratic Congressman John B. Weller said that if annexing Texas brought war, "for one, I say, let that war come; ay, let it come: we will have right and justice on our side, and the God of our fathers will go with us and help us anew."[31]

Returning to the theme of Tyler's message the previous spring, one theme of this debate was that there were nationwide benefits to annexation. Stephen A. Douglass, for example, while still in the House (and not yet having dropped the second "s" from his last name), referred to the markets that would be opened to northern manufacturers as well as to the security that would come about from "obtaining better borders."[32] Ohio's Congressman Weller cited the "vast market for the pork, beef, and breadstuffs of the Northwest," a market for northern manufactured goods, control of the navigation of the Gulf of Mexico, and advantages in wartime. No one would be injured, save possibly for "the cotton and sugar regions of the South."[33] Some members of Congress explicitly denied these expansive claims, but not many.[34] The other element of Tyler's original position, fears about British action in Texas, was reasserted and again challenged. It does not appear that there was much progression in this argument between the two phases of the congressional debate.

What did receive significantly more attention was the relationship between slavery and annexation. Several members of Congress averred that the prospect of bringing in a slave state was sufficient reason to prevent annexation, but others argued just the opposite. Indiana Whig Congressman Caleb Smith, referring to the variety of proposals on the table, found none "which settled the important question of slavery"[35] and believed that the nation could not afford to defer this issue for another time. Congressman Charles Hudson (W-Mass.) and Congressman Giddings of Ohio both referred specifically to the statements of Upshur and Calhoun to establish that "the basis of this [annexation] scheme was the extension and strengthening of the system of slavery,"[36] and they objected to annexation for just this reason. These arguments were not much changed, except perhaps in their intensity.

On the other hand, a larger number of senators and congressmen were prepared to argue that the slavery question was not sufficient reason to

---

[31] Ibid., p. 119.
[32] Ibid., p. 96.
[33] Ibid., app., p. 83.
[34] See, for example, ibid., p. 176.
[35] Ibid., p. 108.
[36] Ibid., pp. 160, 169.

oppose annexation. If Whigs still thought otherwise, they were answered by Ohio Democrat John B. Weller, quoting "the great embodiment of the Whig party," Henry Clay, who had written in one of his "Alabama letters" during the late presidential campaign that "the subject of slavery ought not to affect the question one way or the other."[37] This by itself largely undercut the credibility of the Whig opposition. Illinois Democrat Orlando Ficklin trivialized this opposition by saying that only a "comparatively very small number" of statesmen believed that we had no right to acquire Texas, and that they resided "for the most part, in sections of country strongly infected with the fanatical spirit of political abolitionism."[38]

Congressman Belser of Alabama then put the matter straightforwardly: slavery was sanctioned by the Constitution "and could not be done away with without destroying that compact." This being so, he reasoned, "if the people of the North and Northwest had a right to new States in which the institution of slavery did not exist, the people of the South had an equal right to be surrounded by States with institutions similar to their own, to secure their safety."[39] To object because one was opposed to slavery was beside the point. Indiana's Robert Dale Owen similarly argued that Texas should be annexed despite whatever concerns one might have about slavery, because the real issue is whether the benefits of annexation outweigh the harms.[40] And New York Democrat Chesselden Ellis went further, maintaining that to object to annexation on the basis of slavery "strikes at the very foundation of the Union itself."[41]

For his part, Ohio's Congressman Weller trivialized the issue by reducing it from principle to numbers. Noting that there were about 25,000 slaves in Texas, he asked, "Are our domestic institutions so insecure that, if twenty-odd thousand negroes be thrown upon us, they will be demolished?"[42] Weller thereby rendered the problem insignificant and also suggested that his critics lacked confidence in the democratic institutions they purported to defend. Congressman William L. Yancey (D-Ala.) also attacked annexation opponents by accusing them of "an unmanly shrinking from the responsibilities

[37]Ibid., p. 118.
[38]Ibid., p. 184.
[39]Ibid., p. 88.
[40]Ibid., p. 111.
[41]Ibid., app., p. 141.
[42]Ibid., app., p. 83.

imposed by the constitution—a cowardly desire to weaken the slaveholding section by every means which perverted talent can devise."[43]

Some of these same senators and congressman argued the "diffusion thesis," largely unchanged from the previous spring except sometimes in the specificity of the predictions. Indiana's Robert Dale Owen, for example, was confident that permitting slavery in Texas would lead to its abolition in Kentucky, Virginia, Maryland, and Delaware.[44] Other Congressmen made similar predictions. The contrary voices were fewer, such as Illinois Whig Congressman J. J. Hardin. He refuted the theory by observing that, if it were true, slaves would have been withdrawn "from Maryland, Virginia, and Kentucky to the rich lands of the Mississippi," but that had not happened.[45] Hardin's empirical test did not shake the confidence of legislators who were convinced that annexing Texas would help and hurt the strength of the institution at the same time.

Perhaps the clearest evidence that slavery was not a deterrent to annexation is that some of its strongest supporters consistently described annexation as extending the blessings of liberty, as if there were no conflict between liberty and slavery. Especially revealing in this respect is the fact that Texas supporters could talk about annexation as extending the blessings of liberty and freedom, notwithstanding the fact that they supported the extension of slavery. Perhaps the paradigm case is a statement by House Democrat William W. Payne of Alabama: "Here is a proposition for extending the area of freedom, and spreading the blessings of our free and glorious institutions over a vast territory; and, instead of meeting it on its merits, involving the extension of the principle of civil and religious liberty, and involving the happiness of unborn millions, he saw gentlemen rising in their places and harping on the worn-out theme of slavery."[46] For Payne and like-minded colleagues, slavery was so small a matter that it did not even raise to the level of consciousness the incongruity of championing freedom and liberty while sanctioning an institution that embodied their opposite.

I have suggested that there was a shifting of momentum between the first congressional debate and the second: more of a presumption in favor of annexation, more willingness to address the topic of slavery directly, more

[43]Ibid., app., p. 88.
[44]Ibid., app., p. 100.
[45]Ibid., p. 141.
[46]Ibid., p. 174.

of a tendency to see it as bound up with the question of annexation, and less willingness to see it as a deterrent to annexation. These shifts mark subtle but significant changes in public opinion and a considerable weakening of the separation between the issues of slavery and territorial growth.

But I do not mean to suggest that the outcome of the second debate was predetermined. For one thing, there was a new issue: the constitutionality of the use of a joint resolution. Earlier, some legislators had objected to the constitutionality of annexation by treaty; now, some argued that the Constitution contained no sanction for treating with another power by means of joint resolution. Indiana Whig Congressman Samuel C. Sample reasoned that legislation could not be a satisfactory way of proceeding, since what one legislature could do, a subsequent one could undo. Ridiculing the argument that the House had a right to act because the Whig-controlled Senate had voted against the treaty, and so there was no other way to accomplish the goal, he said, "This was a new mode of settling constitutional questions, viz; by a hop, a skip, and a jump over the constitution."[47] But others disdained this objection. For instance, South Carolina's Democratic Congressman Robert Barnwell Rhett pointed out that the Constitution gives Congress the power to admit new states and does not specify the means.[48] This issue proved to be a wedge dividing the Democrats in Congress. The House voted to annex Texas by joint resolution; the Senate, also committed to annexation, preferred to defend its institutional prerogatives by renegotiating a treaty. Finally, in the conference committee, Senator Walker proposed passing both bills of annexation and allowing the president to choose between them. This compromise narrowly passed the Senate, 27 to 25. Although supporters of the compromise probably thought that the incoming President Polk would make the choice, it reached Tyler three days before his term expired and he decided to do it, picking the method of joint resolution.

In his recent book, Professor Silbey suggests that the annexation of Texas was a pivotal moment leading the nation on the path to civil war.[49] This reading of the congressional debates of 1844 and 1845 helps to make clear why. Subtly these debates reveal a shift in public understanding of what the slavery question was. Earlier it was understood to be the question: If the

---

[47]Ibid., app., p. 72.

[48]Ibid., p. 166.

[49]Joel H. Silbey, *Storm over Texas: The Annexation Controversy and the Road to Civil War* (New York, 2005).

southern states wish to have slavery, is it anyone else's right to interfere? The generally accepted answer was no, which is why mainstream politicians saw no need to allow the question to intrude into public debate. There was nothing they could do about it anyway.

But with the Texas annexation controversy, the nature of the question changed. Mixing the issues of slavery and expansion turned the question into one of the status of the virgin lands in the West, the property of the whole country. Here it was less clear that there was nothing that could be done. People who were willing to tolerate slavery where it existed, out of reverence for the Constitution, could oppose its extension into new lands. When the debate shifted from one about slavery itself to one about its extension, the political landscape shifted as well. The Whigs could not hold together their intersectional coalition; the Democrats tilted more to the South; and an amalgam of forces opposing the extension of slavery coalesced into the new Republican party. The stage would be set for the escalation of conflict into secession and civil war. And the pivotal events that started the nation on that path occurred in 1844 and were captured in the congressional debates about Texas.

2: The Politics of Slavery in the District of Columbia

A. Glenn Crothers

The 1846 Retrocession of Alexandria

Protecting Slavery and the Slave Trade
in the District of Columbia

IN SEPTEMBER 1846 Alexandrian citizens gathered "around the public square, *en masse*," to celebrate the results of a referendum taken to decide whether the town and surrounding county, a part of the District of Columbia since 1791, should return, or "retrocede," to Virginia. According to the recent act passed by Congress, a vote of the region's white male citizens was required before the retrocession of the portion of the district south of the Potomac River could proceed. The crowd greeted the results of the vote, 763 to 222 in favor of retrocession, with "the loudest cheers, and a salvo from the artillery." After the overwhelming vote in favor of a return to Virginia, all that remained was the president's signature. The successful referendum was the culmination of a more than decade-long campaign to remove Alexandria from the district, and supporters had reason to celebrate. "Young folks lighted torches," the crowd produced "flags, banners, and transparencies" to herald the event, "fire arms . . . were discharged, rockets, squips and crackers were let off, and general joy and enthusiasm prevailed." After a series of "eloquent speeches," "the crowd formed in procession" to cross "the old line that used to divide us from Virginia" and fire "upon the soil of our State . . . a National Salute of RETROCESSION."[1] The rhetoric is revealing. With

---

[1] *Alexandria Gazette*, Sept. 4, 1846. For additional descriptions of these celebrations, see Mark David Richards, "The Debates over the Retrocession of the District of Columbia, 1801–2004," *Washington History* 16 (Spring/Summer 2004):72; and Harold W. Hurst, *Alexandria on the Potomac: The Portrait of an Antebellum Community* (Lanham, Md., 1991), p. 4.

retrocession the residents of Alexandria and its hinterland turned south, in the process abandoning a fervent nationalism that had defined the town and region before 1820. Alexandrians' allegiance was now to the state of Virginia —"our state"—rather than to the nation and its federal district. In redrawing the border of the district white Alexandrians were choosing sides in a broader sectional divide.

Of course, supporters of the return to Virginian sovereignty emphasized more pragmatic and politically acceptable reasons for retrocession. Returning to Virginia, supporters argued, would end the disfranchisement from which Alexandria's voters suffered under federal jurisdiction; it would ensure that Alexandria was no longer neglected by a national legislature that lacked the time or interest to protect the region's welfare; and it would enable the town's economy, which had been moribund for decades, to revive and prosper. Behind these arguments, however, lay a more complicated reality linked to the partisan divides of the 1830s and 1840s and the increasingly vociferous national debate over slavery and abolition. The district's unique legal status—the ten-mile square over which most politicians agreed Congress had sovereignty—made it subject to the political agendas of congressmen of different political stripes. Radical or Loco-Foco Democrats tried to implement their hard currency and antibank agenda within the district; states' rights and proslavery Democrats and Whigs tried to reduce congressional spending within the district in order to minimize federal power; and most portentous for slaveholding Alexandrians, abolitionists in the mid-1830s sought to end slavery and the slave trade within the district, initiating a massive petition campaign designed to overwhelm Congress. These various attacks on the interests of the town enabled local leaders to forge a broad and unlikely coalition that included probank and prodevelopment Whigs, local Quaker merchants, slaveholding merchants and planters, and local slave traders. But town leaders also needed allies in Congress. They turned to states' rights and proslavery southerners, men like R. M. T. Hunter of Virginia and John C. Calhoun of South Carolina, who viewed retrocession as part of a broader campaign to protect the institutions and interests of the South.

In short, though some locals supported retrocession for reasons other than the protection of slavery, the symbolic significance of the district and the hardening of the border between slavery and freedom during the sectional crisis of the 1840s and 1850s transformed a campaign to protect local interests (including slavery) into part of the larger national struggle over the future of slavery in the United States. What is striking is how rarely historians of the broader sectional conflict, the slave trade, and even the conflict over slavery in the middle ground between slavery and freedom, have recognized the significance of Alexandria's retrocession. With a few notable exceptions, the redrawing of the district's boundaries has gone unmentioned.[2] And most of the small number of local historians who have examined the subject deny explicitly that slavery and the slave trade were prime factors in the campaign for retrocession.[3] The reasons are readily apparent. In order to foreclose the possibility of antislavery politicians using Alexandria to forward their political agenda, supporters of retrocession both in and out of Congress deliberately downplayed the sectional implications of redrawing the district's borders and studiously avoided any direct mention of slavery. As a result, historians have overlooked the significance of retrocession, despite the fact that as early as the late 1830s both proslavery southerners and antislavery northerners recognized its sectional implications. Still, the timing and rhetoric of the campaign, and the regional and political context in which it took place, reveal the

[2]Though studies of the domestic slave trade recognize the District of Columbia's central role in it, Alexandria's retrocession receives at best passing mention; see, for example, Robert H. Gudmestad, *A Troublesome Commerce: The Transformation of the Interstate Slave Trade* (Baton Rouge, 2003), pp. 35–37, 77–78, 180–89; Michael Tadman, *Speculators and Slaves: Masters, Traders, and Slaves in the Old South* (Madison, Wis., 1989), pp. 11–82; and Frederic Bancroft, *Slave Trading in the Old South* (1931; Columbia, S.C., 1996), pp. 45–66, 91–92. Broader studies of the politics of the antebellum era also ignore Alexandria's retrocession; see, for example, Sean Wilentz, *The Rise of American Democracy: Jefferson to Lincoln* (New York, 2005); and William W. Freehling, *The Road to Disunion*, vol. 1, *Secessionists at Bay, 1776–1854* (New York, 1990). For studies that do note the importance of Alexandria's retrocession on the slave trade in the district and the region and see it as part of the larger antebellum sectional debate, see Constance McLaughlin Green, *Washington: Village and Capital, 1800–1878* (Princeton, 1962), pp. 86, 173–74; and Mary Beth Corrigan, "Imaginary Cruelties? A History of the Slave Trade in Washington, D.C.," *Washington History* 13 (Fall/Winter 2001–2):9, 21–22, 24–25.

[3]Richards, "Debates over Retrocession"; John Hammond Moore, "The Retrocession Act of 1846: Alexandria and Arlington Return to the Fold," *Virginia Cavalcade* 25 (Winter 1976):126–35; Moore, "Alexandria and Arlington 'Come Home': Retrocession, 1846," *Northern Virginia Heritage* 3 (Oct. 1981):3–9, 20; Robert L. Scribner, "In and Out of Virginia: Alexandria Was Orphaned by an Act of Her Son," *Virginia Cavalcade* 15 (Autumn 1965):4–8; and Amos B. Casselman, "The Virginia Portion of the District of Columbia," *Records of the Columbia Historical Society* 12 (1909):115–41. For the one local historian who connects slavery and retrocession, see Dean C. Allard, "When Arlington Was Part of the District of Columbia," *Arlington Historical Magazine* 6 (Oct. 1978):36–47. The small number of biographies of R. M. T. Hunter, the Virginia congressman who pushed the retrocession act through the House, also fail to link the return to Virginia to slavery; see Richard Randall Moore, "In Search of a Safe Government: A Biography of R. M. T. Hunter of Virginia," Ph.D. diss., University of South Carolina, 1993, pp. 148–49; and R. R. Anderson, "Robert Mercer Taliaferro Hunter," *John P. Branch Historical Papers of Randolph-Macon College* 2 (1906):27–28.

close links between the slave-based economy of the town and region and the desire to return to Virginia.

The turn to the south represented a dramatic turnabout in Alexandrians' vision of the future. Nearly sixty years earlier, in 1790, led by regional and national leaders who believed that the Potomac watershed would link the western country to the east, the town and its hinterland—extending from Alexandria west along the Potomac River to the upper Shenandoah Valley —embraced a fervent nationalism. For many locals, these aspirations were confirmed by the rapid development of the regional economy after northern Virginia farmers shifted from tobacco to wheat in the 1780s. The region was soon home to a variety of transportation improvements, financial institutions, and spin-off manufacturing enterprises and saw rapid urban development. At the center of this development was the port of Alexandria, which local boosters believed would become the entrepôt of a commercial and manufacturing empire and would soon eclipse rival ports such as Baltimore and Philadelphia. As unrealistic as these goals seem in retrospect, they provided the basis for a strong sense of national identity. Instead of looking south, northern Virginians before 1820 saw the Potomac as a link between the sections, a common transportation and commercial artery that would help bind west and east (not north and south) into a common unit.[4]

Northern Virginians' post-Revolutionary boosterism was not unique, of course, but its extravagant nature and nationalistic tone is striking. By the mid-1780s, many Alexandrians believed, like printer William Scott, that the town "bid fair to be soon classed amongst the first trading towns in the United States." One resident was so taken with his town's possibilities that in 1785 he wrote a letter, published in the local newspaper, to "a Gentleman in Philadelphia" that urged the Philadelphian to relocate to Alexandria because such a move could only better his situation. Local boosterism reached a peak in 1789 and 1790 when the region competed for the site of the new

---

[4]Kenneth Bowling, *The Creation of Washington, D.C.: The Idea and Location of the American Capital* (Fairfax, Va., 1991); A. Glenn Crothers, "'The Projecting Spirit': Social, Economic, and Cultural Change in Post-Revolution Northern Virginia," Ph.D. diss., University of Florida, 1997; Joel Achenbach, *The Grand Idea: George Washington's Potomac and the Race to the West* (New York, 2004). My thinking about the link between economic function and the development and transformation of regional identity draws from Kim M. Gruenwald, *River of Enterprise: The Commercial Origins of Regional Identity in the Ohio Valley, 1790–1850* (Bloomington, Ind., 2002); see also Gruenwald, "Space and Place on the Early American Frontier: The Ohio Valley as a Region, 1790–1850," *Ohio Valley History* 4 (Fall 2004):31–48.

federal city. Alexandria's civic and commercial leaders believed that the port would furnish an ideal site for the permanent seat of Congress, and they filled the local press with glowing descriptions. Most significant, in May 1789 printer Samuel Hanson published a portion of Samuel Morse's *The American Geography* that described the Potomac River and its environs in glowing terms. The Potomac River, Morse noted, would soon be opened to navigation to the "western country," enabling the produce of the region to flow eastward. The result, he predicted, would be a prosperous and united nation, with Alexandria "one of the most thriving commercial places on the continent." Thus, Morse linked Alexandria's prosperity to the future expansion and growth of the United States—and Alexandrians embraced this nationalist image.[5]

In late 1789, local residents launched a national campaign to make the case for Alexandria. Joined by five Georgetown merchants, five of Alexandria's leading residents issued a broadside arguing forcefully for a Potomac site for the new capital. To make their case, the authors made two central arguments: the particular advantages of the surrounding countryside and the national benefits to be gained from a Potomac site. The authors effusively praised the "fertility of soil and salubrity of air" in northern Virginia, described at length the abundance of natural resources in the region, and noted the site's defensibility. So hyperbolic were these claims that one northerner was led to comment wryly that Virginians "seemed to think the banks of the Potomac a Paradise, and that river a Euphrates." But the centerpiece of the broadside focused on the national benefits of the Potomac site. The "river Potomack," they noted, lay "nearer the center of the Union, than any other considerable river," and was "more advantageously situated for preserving an intercourse with the inhabitants of the Western territory." Given the youth and fragility of the nation, this was a significant consideration, and in order to stress the point the authors included an extended passage describing the "extensive inland" navigation to which the Potomac connected. In short, the Potomac offered incomparable national benefits, making it the most propitious site for the new national capital.[6]

[5] *Virginia Journal and Alexandria Advertiser,* Apr. 15, 1784, Apr. 21, 1785, May 11, 1786, May 21, 1789; Jedidiah Morse, *The American Geography; or a View of the Present Situation of the United States of America* (1789; reprint ed., New York, 1970), pp. 363–64, 381.

[6] "Gentlemen, the Permanent Seat of Congress . . . ," Broadside, Dec. 7, 1789 (Alexandria, Va., 1789); Fisher Ames, quoted in the *Virginia Centinel* (Winchester), Sept. 30, 1789; see also Donald Sweig, "A Capital on the Potomac: A 1789 Broadside and Alexandria's Attempts to Capture the Cherished Prize," *Virginia Magazine of History and Biography* 87 (Jan. 1979):74–104.

After the passage of the Residence Act in July 1790, Alexandrians celebrated that the president included their town within the District of Columbia's "ten mile square." Indeed, an "American," writing in the local newspaper, presented to the public a "Rhapsody, [on] the effect of a delightful prospect of the Patomack." Disdaining "grovelling state prejudices," the writer explained how locating the capital in a "central position" promised to benefit both the region and nation. The "free exercise of legislative power," he noted, would attract Americans to the Potomac "like the blood in a well formed body" comes "regularly to the heart, to receive and communicate equal vigour through the whole frame." "Here kinsmen will meet, and exchange the various comforts of their different climes. . . . Here the necessaries of life may come from the West or from the East, downstream or by the tides; and aid from either quarter, if danger should appear in the other." As part of the new national capital on the Potomac, Alexandria would help bind a far-flung and disparate nation both politically and economically, leading to the growth and prosperity of both. For Alexandrians and northern Virginians in the 1790s, then, the destinies of the nation and their region were inextricably linked.[7]

Similar sentiments appeared throughout the 1790s and into the first decade of the nineteenth century. As long as the regional economy thrived—as it did up to the War of 1812—the region's residents embraced economic nationalism. The community's responses to early retrocession proposals provide one measure of the depth of its nationalism before the 1830s. When disgruntled northern congressmen suggested in 1803 and 1804 that the territory Virginia and Maryland transferred to Congress in 1800 be retroceded back to the respective states, Alexandria's leaders responded aggressively. Recognizing that the ultimate goal of these proposals was to remove the capital from the Potomac altogether, Alexandria's leading citizens tartly informed Congress "of their disapprobation of" the motion. Pennsylvania politicians led further efforts to remove the capital in 1807 and 1808, arguing that the district should be transferred back to Maryland and Virginia because it was unhealthy, unfinished, and expensive. Albert Gallatin added that situating the capital on the Potomac was the only bad decision George Washington ever made. In response, Alexandria's civic leaders once more sprang into action, preparing a petition for Congress that opposed retrocession. Still con-

---

[7] *Virginia Gazette and Alexandria Advertiser,* Aug. 19, 1790.

vinced in 1808 that the town and region could and would be the political and economic focal point of the nation, local luminaries strongly resisted any attempt to remove the national government.[8]

In the years after the War of 1812, however, dreams of commercial glory slowly evaporated as European markets for Chesapeake products closed and the Potomac was eclipsed by the Mohawk River and the Erie Canal as the primary conduit between America's eastern ports and the Midwest. The stagnation of the regional economy altered the outlook of many of the town's and region's inhabitants. Though attempts to bolster regional economic development continued throughout the antebellum period, and Alexandria remained the focus of these efforts, the grandiose visions of the immediate post-Revolutionary years could not be sustained. As a result, the national orientation of many Alexandrians began to erode. Beginning in the 1820s, but accelerating in the next two decades, the region started looking south for commercial links and models of economic development. Left behind by northern economic development, Alexandria and northern Virginia retrenched and turned to more traditional economic practices—particularly, slavery and the slave trade. In the years after 1820, northern Virginia turned south, and the port of Alexandria stood at the center of this economic and cultural transformation.[9]

The rising popularity of retrocession provides one measure of the changes taking place. In the past, proposals to cede most of the district back to Virginia and Maryland had been initiated within Congress by opponents of the Potomac site. In contrast, in the early 1820s a growing number of Alexandria residents believed that the town should return to Virginia's jurisdiction. In the previous decade the town had suffered through the War of 1812 and a decreased overseas demand for American grains. Meanwhile, the ongoing

---

[8]*Letter from the Mayor of the Town of Alexandria . . .*, Dec. 6, 1804 (Washington, D.C., 1804); Margaret Bailey Tinkcom, "Caviar along the Potomac: Sir Augustus John Foster's 'Notes on the United States,' 1804–1812," *William and Mary Quarterly*, 3rd ser., 8 (1951):93; Bowling, *Creation of Washington*, pp. 241–43; Constance McLaughlin Green, *Washington: Village and Capital, 1800–1878* (Princeton, N.J., 1962), pp. 29–30.

[9]The story of northern Virginia's economic stagnation and its implications for slavery has been told by a number of historians, but see especially Avery O. Craven, *Soil Exhaustion as a Factor in the Agricultural History of Virginia and Maryland, 1606–1860* (Urbana, Ill., 1926); Brenda E. Stevenson, *Life in Black and White: Family and Community in the Slave South* (New York, 1996), pp. 25–29, 175–86; and Lewis Cecil Gray, *History of Agriculture in the Southern United States to 1860*, 2 vols. (New York, 1941), 2:909–15.

Panic of 1819 promised continued hard times. The port's economic difficulties
were reflected in its stagnant population growth. While the population nearly
doubled between 1800 and 1810, exceeding 7,200 in the latter year, a decade
later the town had only 8,200 residents. In addition, supporters of retrocession noted that congressional largesse had been extended to Washington
City at the expense of Alexandria—as was required by federal law—and
pointed to that community's rapid growth, from 3,200 residents in 1800 to
over 13,000 in 1820, to make their point. Led by Steven Thomson Mason,
town residents launched their first retrocession campaign in 1824, petitioning
Congress for a removal to Virginia. Mason, however, had limited support.
In the 1820s few Alexandrians believed that retrocession was the solution to
the town's deepening economic woes. Mason's opponents argued that if
Alexandria returned to Virginia (and Georgetown to Maryland), the region
would lose the national government and with it the promise of future prosperity. Faced with this division of opinion, Congress ignored the petition and
Alexandria remained part of the district. Eight years later, as the town's economy continued to stagnate and its population fell, a similar campaign found
broader support. Still, an 1832 referendum revealed that most Alexandrians
—419 versus 310 for returning to Virginia—still saw their future within
the district.[10]

By 1840, in contrast, support for retrocession had risen sharply. Indeed, a
second referendum held in October 1840 revealed that a large majority of
Alexandrians—606 in favor versus 211 opposed—now supported a return to
Virginia.[11] What had happened between 1832 and 1840 to bring about this
reversal of public sentiment? The 1840 referendum was preceded by a long
newspaper debate over retrocession, which constituted the most extensive
public discussion of the issue that would take place in Alexandria. Proponents of a return to Virginia emphasized the disfranchisement of Alexandria's voters and the town's stagnant economy, which they linked directly to
the residents' lack of political rights and congressional disregard for the welfare of the southern portion of the district. And, indeed, they had much to
complain about. Between 1830 and 1840 Alexandria's population had grown

[10]*Alexandria Gazette,* Jan. 7, 8, Oct. 14, 1819, Jan. 25, 1832, Aug. 31, 1840; Henry Howe,
Historical Collections of Virginia . . . (Charleston, 1845), pp. 534, 543; Green, *Washington,* 86–88;
Richards, "Debate over Retrocession," pp. 60–61. See *The Question of Retrocession, Stated and
Discussed* . . . (Georgetown, D.C., 1826), for the concurrent debate in Georgetown over
retrocession.
[11]*Alexandria Gazette,* Oct. 14, 1840.

but only nominally, and various internal improvement initiatives designed to improve the local economy had mired the town in debt and produced few tangible results. Meanwhile, cities such as Baltimore and Washington that Alexandrians had once viewed as rivals had grown far more rapidly and eclipsed the Virginia port.

The lack of political representation—a problem still not solved in D.C.—was a constant irritant for Alexandria residents. The February 1801 act that established congressional control over the district included no provisions to enable residents to vote in national elections or for representatives in Congress. Though a number of residents protested this provision, the mercantile community believed that federal rule and spending would ensure the town's economic success and were willing to live without political representation. The initial enthusiasm for congressional control, however, soon waned. By the terms of the act that created the district, no federal buildings could be built in the portion of the district ceded by Virginia, depriving Alexandria of the most direct source of federal aid. But the problem lay deeper still. Congress, finding the ongoing expense of overseeing the district burdensome and having no compunction to answer to nonvoting district residents, was often slow to respond to the needs of local residents. As a result, Alexandria remained burdened with the legal statutes that had been inherited from Virginia in 1801, and which Congress lacked the time or inclination to update. Equally distressing, Alexandrians discovered that as a result of their unequal legal status they could not, according to the federal court, successfully sue state residents outside the district—as Alexandria resident Richard Bland Lee learned from his own experience in 1824. Over time, locals became convinced that living subject to congressional rule and taxation without representation was both unjust and jeopardized their legal rights and economic welfare. As the Alexandria town council's 1845 petition requesting retrocession pronounced, "all government . . . but self-government is bad and . . . a despotism."[12]

---

[12]Green, *Washington*, pp. 24–26, 86–88; Joseph Martin, *A New and Comprehensive Gazetteer of Virginia and the District of Columbia* . . . (Charlottesville, 1835), p. 478; William Francis Smith and T. Michael Miller, *A Seaport Saga: Portrait of Old Alexandria, Virginia* (Norfolk, 1989), p. 56; Robert M. T. Hunter, *Speech of the Hon. R. M. T. Hunter, of Virginia, on the Subject of the Retrocession of Alexandria to Virginia . . . May 8, 1846* (Alexandria, D.C., 1846); "Memorial of the Committee of the Town of Alexandria for Retrocession," [1845], in William Tindall, *Origin and Government of the District of Columbia* (Washington, D.C, 1909), pp. 108, 110. See also Allard, "When Arlington Was Part of the District of Columbia," pp. 36, 42; Richards, "Debates over Retrocession," pp. 60–62; and Moore, "Retrocession Act of 1846," pp. 126–35.

The stagnation of Alexandria's overseas trade after 1820 had a profound effect on local attitudes. Between 1790 and the late 1810s the port of Alexandria thrived. When northern Virginia's farmers switched from tobacco to grains in the post-Revolutionary era, the export economy of the port thrived. In 1800, for example, over 160,000 barrels of flour were inspected at the port, rising (with some dramatic yearly fluctuations) to 209,000 barrels in 1817. However, this peak would never again be reached. In 1830, for example, flour inspections fell to just over 160,000 barrels, and by 1840 they plummeted to just under 80,000. The loss of European markets after the Napoleonic Wars played a crucial role in this decline, as did Virginian farmers' inability to compete with the grain producers of the West, who by the 1820s could ship their produce directly to eastern markets such as New York City. As the Alexandria market worsened, flour and wheat prices fell and remained low (despite a brief rise in the late 1830s) until the mid-1850s. Complaints about the low prices offered at Alexandria became a regular theme in the correspondence of the region's farmers, and many sought alternative outlets for their produce. Nathan Lupton decided in the 1840s that he could obtain a better price for his Shenandoah Valley flour in the Baltimore market. Alexandria boosters countered with glowing descriptions of the Alexandria market, but such propaganda could not negate the economic impact of the decision of farmers such as Lupton to abandon Alexandria. Nor could it halt the erosion of economic nationalism in the town and region.[13]

Still, the optimism of the region was not so easily extinguished, particularly after Congress and the states of Virginia, Maryland, and Pennsylvania chartered the Chesapeake and Ohio Canal between 1824 and 1826. The C&O's promoters envisioned a national project that would link the District of Columbia to the Ohio River at a cost—according to the U.S. Corps of

---

[13]For flour inspections, see Crothers, "Projecting Spirit," pp. 68–81; Arthur Peterson, "The Alexandria Market Prior to the Civil War," *William and Mary Quarterly*, 2nd ser., 12 (1932), pp. 104–14; Gray, *History of Agriculture*, 2:816–20, 914–15, 1039; and *Alexandria Gazette*, Apr. 2, July 2, Oct. 2, 1840, Jan. 5, 1841. For Alexandria boosterism, see *Alexandria Gazette*, Sept. 29, 1840, Apr. 3, Sept. 9, 1841, and Mar. 31, 1842. For examples of local farmers complaining about stagnant prices, see Samuel Kelly to David Lupton, Apr. 22, 1820, Lupton Family Papers, 1745–1895, VHS; and Seth Smith to Jacob Smith, Sept. 28, 1842, Apr. 21, 1843, in Clarence H. Smith Papers, 1775–1955, Indiana Historical Society, Indianapolis. For Nathan Lupton's dealings with Baltimore merchants, see Charles A. Gambrill to Nathan Lupton, Jan. 28, 1843, Lupton Family Papers, VHS; and Orndorff & Co. to Nathan Lupton, Nov. 26, 1842, Lupton (Bond) Family Papers, 1792–1962, Swarthmore College Friends Historical Library, Swarthmore, Pa.

Engineers—of $22 million. Despite the expense, the canal, by promising to revitalize the local economy, for a time revived the flagging economic nationalism of the region. The town of Alexandria subscribed for $250,000 worth of shares on the condition that a lateral canal be constructed to the town. In 1830, Congress chartered the Alexandria Canal Company to build this extension, the centerpiece of which was a 1,500-foot-long aqueduct between Georgetown and the south shore of the Potomac. Construction began in July 1831, with backers estimating the canal's cost at just over $200,000.[14]

In the 1830s Congress agreed to contribute $400,000 for the construction of the canal, but its costs soon exceeded the original estimates and town leaders turned again to Congress for help. They believed their case was legitimate. As Edgar Snowden—mayor of Alexandria, editor of its newspaper, and president of the canal company—noted, "Here we have no public money expended—no public buildings—no 'extra appliances and means to boot,' on which our neighbors on the other side of the Potomac, rely." "Thus situated," he concluded, "we look to the liberality of Congress, to compensate us, in some measure, for the deprivation which we suffer." No further congressional aid, however, was forthcoming, and the costs of canal construction fell to the town and its taxpayers. To help sustain local support, town leaders breathlessly described the completion of each phase of the canal and reminded the town's inhabitants that the sacrifices and expense would eventually be worth it. "We trust," wrote one correspondent, that this "stupendous work . . . may be as useful and profitable in its results, as it is bold in its design, and successful in its execution." Another observer, writing in 1842, as the aqueduct was close to completion, announced that "the great work in question, is regarded, and will be for ages . . . as a stupendous monument of the indomitable energy and persevering industry of the good people of Alexandria." "When the waters are let in the Canal," he concluded, "public exhibitions of pleasure will be far greater than at any time" since construction began.[15]

[14]Walter S. Sanderlin, *The Great National Project: A History of the Chesapeake and Ohio Canal* (1946; reprint ed., New York, 1976), pp. 179–82, 316; Ronald E. Shaw, *Canals for a Nation: The Canal Era in the United States, 1790–1860* (Lexington, Ky., 1990), pp. 98–126; John Lauritz Larson, *Internal Improvements: National Public Works and the Promise of Popular Government in the Early United States* (Chapel Hill, 2001), pp. 89–90, 230–31.
[15]*Alexandria Gazette,* July 28, 1840 (Congress's contribution), Jan. 23, 1840 (first quotation), Sept. 9, 1840, Oct. 4, 1842.

The town completed the canal in 1843, but by that time the project's costs exceeded \$1.2 million—an amount that was borne primarily by the town of Alexandria and investors in the company. Still, the extravagant rhetoric of the canal's boosters seemed not entirely misplaced in the early 1840s. After the completion of the aqueduct Alexandria became the major, if unofficial, terminus of the C&O, and it carried large quantities of coal to Alexandria from western Maryland and some produce from the Shenandoah Valley. However, the canal never lived up to its supporters' extravagant expectations. By the 1850s, according to economic historian David Meyer, it had "transmogrified into a coal canal" with "little developmental impact on wheat farming" or the regional economy.[16]

The reason for its limited success is easy to discern. The Baltimore and Ohio Railroad, chartered in Maryland the same year as the C&O, soon superseded the C&O as the main conduit for the produce of the Potomac River watershed. As early as the 1830s Shenandoah Valley farmers enthusiastically invested in and used one of the B&O's branch lines, the Winchester and Potomac Railroad. As a result, the C&O was completed only to Cumberland, Maryland, and never enjoyed the volume of traffic its boosters anticipated. The Alexandria canal, meanwhile, was plagued by freshets and prohibitive maintenance costs and left the town seriously indebted. Indeed, when Congress added a provision to the 1846 retrocession act stipulating that the federal government would not be responsible for Alexandria's canal debt, some town residents opposed the return to Virginia. They feared that paying off the town's debt would require a sharp rise in local taxes. Their opposition collapsed only after Virginia came to the town's aid, guaranteeing some of the Alexandria Canal Company's bonds (amounting to three-quarters of the town's debt) and purchasing a significant block of the company's stock.[17] In 1846 Alexandrians looked south for aid rather than to the national government.

---

[16]Larson, *Internal Improvements*, pp. 89–91, 149–93, 221–22, 230–32; Sanderlin, *Great National Project*, p. 182; Smith and Miller, *Seaport Saga*, pp. 54, 72; Hurst, *Alexandria on the Potomac*, pp. 4–5; Peterson, "Alexandria Market," pp. 109, 111; David R. Meyer, *The Roots of American Industrialization* (Baltimore, 2003), pp. 151–52.

[17]Larson, *Internal Improvements*, pp. 89–91, 149–93, 221–22, 230–32; Sanderlin, *Great National Project*, p. 182; Hurst, *Alexandria on the Potomac*, pp. 2–3. For the success of the Winchester and Potomac Railroad Company, see *Alexandria Gazette*, Aug. 16, 1842; the article reported that in 1840 the railroad transported over 160,000 barrels of flour to the B&O and from there to Baltimore, and in the first seven months of 1842 it carried over 100,000 barrels. Many local farmers invested in the railroad. For example, Joel and Jonah Lupton, Frederick County

If town leaders believed the federal government had failed to support the canal project adequately, they were even more disenchanted with congressional attempts to dismantle the district's banks. Indeed, their disgruntlement over congressional "experiments" with D.C. banks reignited the retrocession campaign in 1840. The political battle over district banks began in 1834 when the failure of the Bank of Maryland forced three local institutions to suspend specie payments on their bank notes and led to the failure of the Bank of Alexandria, which had operated profitably since 1792. The suspension and bank collapse prompted the House Committee on the District to investigate local bank practices, and their report, issued shortly before the banks' charters were due to expire, brought to light the self-interested and financially risky lending practices and excessive paper money issues of some local institutions. Led by antibank Democrats, Congress threatened to shut down the district banks, but ultimately rechartered seven of them. Democrats ensured, however, that Congress kept the banks on a short leash, renewing their charters for only four years. In 1838, with the charters once more up for renewal, Congress granted them only two years.[18]

Months later, with the country in the midst of a severe economic depression, district banks once again suspended specie payments, like banks throughout the United States. Banks outside the district, however, were not under the direct authority of Congress, which in 1840 was dominated by antibank Democrats who wished to restrict paper issues and return the country to hard currency. Local banks' decision to suspend specie payments gave hard-money supporters an opportunity to put their principles into action. The Whig merchants of Alexandria, strong supporters of their local banks, reacted to debate in Congress, which dragged on for months in the spring of 1840, with anger. In April, Whig supporters met to decry politicians who considered "the ten miles square . . . as a field upon which experiments in legislation might be safely tried by political quacks . . . regardless of the wishes . . . of

farmers, each purchased ten shares in the Winchester and Potomac Railroad Company in 1831. Thereafter, it became their primary means for transporting produce to market; see Jonah Lupton Receipt, Aug. 3, 1831, and Joel Lupton Receipt, July 22, 1831, Lupton Family Papers, VHS. The debate in Congress over Alexandria's debt can be followed in the *Congressional Globe*, 29th Cong., 1st sess., 1846, pp. 778–79, 781, 1046; the debate in town can be followed in *Alexandria Gazette*, June 12, 17, 1846; and Moore, "Debates over Retrocession," pp. 69, 71.

[18]Green, *Washington*, pp. 124–25; Richards, "Debates over Retrocession," p. 66; Hurst, *Alexandria on the Potomac*, p. 2.

the people." The legislation that Congress ultimately produced in July re-chartered district banks for four years "to enable them to wind up their affairs—and for no other object." On July 7 town leaders held a public meeting that denounced the legislation and appointed a committee of thir-teen "to adopt such measures as they may deem necessary to carry into effect the unanimously expressed desire of this meeting, that the Town and County of Alexandria be RETROCEDED to the State of Virginia as soon as practi-cable." Retrocession was necessary, the meeting resolved, because "a major-ity" of Congress view "the District of Columbia . . . as a field for legislative experiments." They "deem it right," the resolution continued, "to exercise their ingenuity in untried schemes upon the rights and property of the people of the District, regardless of their welfare." The only way "to relieve us from . . . political bondage," town leaders concluded, was a return to Virginia.[19]

In the wake of the public meeting, the columns of the *Gazette* were filled with the debate over retrocession. The war of words addressed a wide range of issues—the constitutionality of retrocession, the economic benefits of re-turning to Virginia, and the need for Alexandrians to regain their political rights in order to protect their interests—but the debate also made abun-dantly clear that the crux of the matter was not simply the survival of the district's banks. Indeed, the language of the town meeting points to the broader issues involved. In the previous decade the District of Columbia had become for politicians of many stripes "a field for legislative experi-ments . . . upon the rights and property of the people" who resided there. One writer addressed these broader issues in an allegorical "History of Delphi," which likened D.C. to Delphi of the Greek confederacy. Delphi, the writer explained, was the seat of "the Oracle" of the Greek confederacy—that is, the Capitol—and was overseen by the "Commission"—that is, Congress. Unfortunately, because Delphians lacked political rights and responsibilities, their "district" soon became "a mere colony of dispirited idlers and eman-cipated slaves." The commission, meanwhile, did nothing to address the needs of Delphians, but instead performed "the most unusual experiments upon" them. Specifically, the commission, controlled by Phillip (that is, Martin Van Buren) and his allies (antibank Democrats), ordered all of Delphi's olive

[19]*Alexandria Gazette*, Apr. 18, July 8, 9, 1840. The *Gazette* published the congressional de-bates over the District Bank Bill in Congress at great length; see Apr. 4, 11, 17, June 17, 18, July 3, 4, 8, 1840. On the antibank and hard money ideology of Loco-Foco Democrats, see Bray Hammond, *Banks and Politics in America: From the Revolution to the Civil War* (Princeton, N.J., 1957), esp. pp. 490–99; and William M. Gouge, *A Short History of Paper Money and Banking in the United States*, pts. 1 and 2 (Philadelphia, 1933).

trees (that is, banks) chopped down, "though the inhabitants not only depended upon them in a great measure for food," but had "for a long time past," used "the *leaves* of these olive trees" as "*currency.*" Moreover, the removal of the olive trees was not, the author insisted, "a casual and accidental abuse of power"; rather, it was (and here the author lapsed into the present) "but one of a series of outrages which we may certainly expect if . . . our relations to the government remain what they are at present." "The regulation of [Dephi's] affairs," the author concluded (restoring his allegorical prose), "nearly formed a pretext for a civil war, or at least a dissolution of the Grecian confederacy."[20]

Another correspondent, "One of the People," dropped such allusive references altogether. "Can . . . the People of Alexandria," the writer asked, "safely dispense with a right which is so highly and properly valued by all around us?" "In the opinion of a large portion of the people of the United States," he continued, "we are . . . mere subjects of the Government, to be disposed of . . . agreeably to the views which others entertain of public expediency." Alexandrians' right to hold "at least one important species of property" survived, he noted, only because politicians dared not touch a "correlative right" enjoyed by "the people of Virginia and Maryland." Coming directly to the point, "One of the People" asked, "Who doubts but that if this consideration did not interpose, the institution of slavery would be instantly abolished, without reference to the views or interests of the people of the District?" "What chance is there left for" our property rights "amidst the experiments of party and in the war of opinions"? The district, he added, had become "subservient to [the] designs" of "moral or political fanaticism" in Congress. As a result, politicians had "no time to spa[re on] any . . . species of social melioration" embraced by district residents, but "can listen to pe[ti]tions without number for the abolition of slavery among us." Here was the crux of the issue. If banks were subject to congressional "experiments," so, too, were other types of property, including slaves. As another writer who labeled himself "Working Man" noted, "the citizens generally, and the property holders in particular, are in favor of Retrocession to Virginia, so . . . they can be free from the jurisdiction of an experimenting Congress."[21]

At base, then, Alexandrians embraced retrocession in order to protect their rights to property, including the right to own slaves, from an "experimenting

---

[20]"History of Delphi," *Alexandria Gazette*, Sept. 2, 3, 22, 1840.

[21]"One of the People," *Alexandria Gazette*, Oct. 9, 10, 12, 1840; "Working Man," *Alexandria Gazette*, July 22, 1840.

Congress." But Loco-Foco Democrats were not the only or even the most dangerous threat. Town residents were only too aware of the broader debates in Congress in the 1830s and 1840s over the issues of slavery and freedom— debates in which the district played a central role. In the mid-1830s northern abolitionists, under the newly formed umbrella of the American Anti-Slavery Society, began a petition campaign to end slavery and the slave trade in the District of Columbia, the one portion of the country over which Congress had complete authority, and thus slavery's most vulnerable point. Abolition- ists also understood the symbolic value of ending slavery within the national capital, particularly because of the district's infamous slave trade. Fueled by a series of publications highlighting the horrors of the "man trade" in the "Metropolis of Liberty," abolitionists pronounced the trade a national "shame," "an outrage upon public sentiment" in which they were directly implicated by the spending of federal tax dollars within the district. "Surely," concluded one antislavery pamphlet, "there is no authority, divine or human, to establish and maintain slavery and the slave trade at the nation's capital. So far as they exist there, they are in defiance of God's commands and in violation of our own fundamental national law."[22]

In an attempt to silence the slavery debate in Congress, both the House and Senate instituted gag rules in 1836 that automatically tabled all anti- slavery petitions. Most proslavery southerners viewed the gag rule as an essential measure to protect the institution throughout the South and the territories from federal intrusion. For proslavery (and classically trained) politi- cians such as John C. Calhoun, the district was the southern "Thermopy- lae"; here, "on the frontier," the abolitionist enemy had to be confronted. The Senate gag lasted until 1850 and effectively ended debate on the subject within its walls. In contrast, the House gag immediately aroused controversy, as a group of northern congressmen, led by John Quincy Adams, used every opportunity to remove the gag, which they viewed as a violation of free

[22]E. A. Andrews, *Slavery and the Domestic Slave-Trade in the United States* . . . (1836; reprint ed., Detroit, 1969), pp. 95–143 (esp. pp. 122–25); Jesse Torrey, *A Portraiture of Domestic Slavery in the United States* . . . (1817; reprint ed., St. Clair Shores, Mich., 1970), pp. 41–52; *Slavery and the Slave Trade at the Nation's Capital* (New York, n.d. [1846]), p. 2; see also Corrigan, "Imaginary Cruelties." On the abolitionist petition campaign, see James Stewart, *Holy Warriors: The Abo- litionists and American Slavery* (New York, 1976), pp. 81–93; Richard S. Newman, *Transformation of American Abolitionism: Fighting Slavery in the Early Republic* (Chapel Hill, 2002), pp. 131–51; and for the central role of women in the campaign, Susan Zaeske, *Signatures of Citizenship: Petition- ing, Antislavery, and Women's Political Identity* (Chapel Hill, 2003).

speech. In nearly every session of Congress over the next eight years, the debate raged for days and weeks. As R. M. T. Hunter, the proslavery Virginia congressman who shepherded the retrocession act through the House, noted to his wife in December 1841, "it was extremely fortunate" that he had got to Congress early. "On Monday," he wrote, "the South lost the anti-abolition rule by three votes," and Hunter's vote was needed to the next day to reinstate it. "All is well," he happily reported, "we have saved the rule." Despite the efforts of southern politicians such as Hunter, the House voted in December 1844 to rescind the measure.[23]

For slaveholders in the district the petition campaign and the ensuing House debate was an ominous development, posing a direct threat to their property and what they believed were their constitutional rights. In Alexandria, Edgar Snowden publicly voiced the anger and worry of the town's elite in the pages of the *Gazette*. Most revealing was his increasing disgust with Adams, or "Old Man Eloquent." After Adams raised the issue again in late-1840, Snowden pronounced that "it is unfortunate for Mr. Adams that he ever came to the House of Representatives." Adams, the editor conceded, "is honest and sincere. But he is also wrong headed and obstinate." The following June, when Adams once more attempted to rescind the rule, Snowden adopted less conciliatory language. "Respect for" Adams's "age, services, and talents will not prevent us," Snowden stated, "from speaking of his malignant and incendiary conduct." Four days later Snowden erupted, "the nation is *cursed* with John Quincy Adams and his abolition petitions!" By early 1842, the editor denounced Adams as "a malicious political incendiary" who "adds the passion of a fanatic to the obstinacy of a mule . . . when he tries to force on the reluctant and unwilling House Abolition petitions."[24]

Perhaps nothing infuriated Alexandria's leaders more than Adams's June 1842 attempt to use a House bill to enable Alexandria residents to elect the mayor directly as an opportunity to attack the suppression of black rights

---

[23]John C. Calhoun, quoted in Avery Craven, "The 1840s and the Democratic Process," *Journal of Southern History* 16 (1950):167; Robert M. T. Hunter to Mary Eveline Hunter, Dec. 1841, in Martha T. Hunter, *A Memoir of Robert M. T. Hunter, with an Address on His Life by Col. L. Quinton Washington* (Washington, D.C., 1903), p. 95. On the congressional battle over the gag rule, see William Lee Miller, *Arguing about Slavery: The Great Battle in the United States Congress* (New York, 1996); Freehling, *Road to Disunion*, pp. 308–52; and Daniel Wirls, "'The Only Mode of Avoiding Everlasting Debate': The Overlooked Senate Gag Rule for Antislavery Petitions," *Journal of the Early Republic* 27 (2007):115–38.

[24]*Alexandria Gazette*, Dec. 14, 1840, June, 11, 15, 1841, Jan. 6, 26, 1842.

within the district. In response to a Jacksonian Democrat attempt to change the wording of the bill to include all adult "white male citizens" among the voters, Adams introduced an amendment to strike out the word "white." In the ensuing debate, Adams asked why "a tincture on the skin could deprive a man of" voting rights? If Congress "were to give that power, by this law, to the white people of Alexandria . . . with what consistency could they refuse it to the colored man, who was a citizen, who paid taxes, who was ready and perhaps many of them actually shed their blood for the defence of our country"? Outraged southern congressmen were soon on their feet attacking Adams. Such questions, they pronounced, had been "settled when the Constitution itself was framed"; there could be no reason for such an amendment other "than to increase irritation in the South." Members "who found their happiness promoted by exciting the South," exclaimed Cost Johnson of Maryland, were to be pitied, and they certainly had no business "making the District of Columbia the arena for their everlasting experiments on every new fangled notion."[25] Caught between the agendas of Jacksonian Democrats and abolitionists, Alexandria town leaders could only fume as the House tabled the bill.

But Snowden left no mistake about which meddling politicians he feared and despised most. "The Northern people," he emphatically declared, "have no *right* to interfere in our domestic matters."[26] As in the rest of the district, Alexandria's free black population grew rapidly after 1820—at the same time its white population was stagnant. Soil exhaustion, the abandonment of labor-intensive tobacco planting for grain production, and significant white out-migration lowered demand for enslaved labor in the early nineteenth century and convinced significant numbers of slaveholders to manumit their slaves. As a result, the free black population of Alexandria nearly doubled between 1810 and 1840 to more than 1,600, or almost 20 percent of the total population. White Alexandrians worried about what one newspaper correspondent denounced as a "filthy and abandoned" population, "steeped in infamy, bloated by disease, and too lazy to live by honest industry." The town council apparently agreed, promulgating a series of municipal regulations that required free blacks to possess valid free papers and a license that

---

[25]Ibid., June 4, 1842.
[26]Ibid., Dec. 13, 1842.

was "revocable at pleasure" to reside within the town limits. The council also proscribed meetings and assemblies, restricted the sale of liquor, and the playing of all games of chance among the free black and enslaved persons. The town even prohibited autonomous African American religious meetings. When "James Evans and other colored persons" requested permission in May 1842 to hold services without "the presence and direction of a white person," the town council tabled their petition without discussion.[27]

If some slaveholders chose to manumit their slaves, many more chose to sell them to the Deep South, raising demand for the services of professional slave traders. Indeed, as early as 1802 local antislavery activists noted that Alexandria had become "a place of deposit" for slaves transported from northern Virginia and Maryland to the Deep South. The transport of slaves by sea also began early; in 1809 the Alexandria Marine Insurance Company insured slave vessels bound for New Orleans. As the major port on the Potomac, it made sense for slave dealers to establish their businesses in Alexandria. Equally important, an 1812 federal law that allowed Alexandria residents to bring slaves into the district while prohibiting those on the Maryland side from traveling to Alexandria to buy slaves for resale had the unintended consequence of compelling slave traders to establish their businesses in Alexandria. In the process, the town became a principal center of the slave trade. By the late 1820s at least four substantial slave trading firms headquartered in the town. The most notorious of these and, according to contemporary Moncure Conway, among the largest in the country was the partnership of Isaac Franklin and John Armfield. By 1834, Franklin and Armfield owned a large slave pen in the town and shipped fifteen hundred to two thousand slaves yearly to the Deep South, both by land and in their fleet of four vessels. Two years later, they sold the business to George Kephart,

---

[27]On the economic changes in the upper Chesapeake South and its impact on slavery in the region, see Stevenson, *Life in Black and White*, and Barbara Jeanne Fields, *Slavery and Freedom on the Middle Ground: Maryland during the Nineteenth Century* (New Haven, Conn., 1985). On the rise of the free black population in Alexandria, see Martin, *Gazetteer*, pp. 179–80; and Hurst, *Alexandria on the Potomac*, 126. The newspaper also reported white and black population changes regularly; see, for example, *Alexandria Gazette*, Nov. 17, 1841. Denunciations of free blacks: *Alexandria Gazette*, Dec. 3, 6, 1841. On the municipal edicts regulating black life, see *Laws of the Corporation of the Town of Alexandria, D.C.* (Alexandria, D.C., 1844), pp. 54–60; *Alexandria Gazette*, May 31, 1842.

who throughout the 1840s advertised the purchase of slaves for southern markets. By the 1830s, then, the slave trade had become a "vital component" of Alexandria's economy, linking it and the region's slaveholders to the Deep South.[28]

Despite the growing slave trade, the town and the region remained home to a significant enslaved population. Though the number of slaves in Alexandria fell sharply in the decade after 1830, over a thousand enslaved people —some 13 percent of the total population—still resided in the town in 1840. This was, however, a deeply restive population. While northern abolitionists bombarded Congress with petitions to end slavery in the district, and a few northern politicians agitated the issue on every occasion that offered, slaveholders worried about an apparent flood of runaway slaves, many of whom, they believed, were encouraged by abolitionists. In March 1840 district residents learned that Leonard Grimes, a Washington City free black hack driver of "good character," had helped "several slaves" escape from Loudoun County to Canada the previous November. Two years later, the *Gazette* reported that a local farmer, after procuring "the consent of his field and family hands," decided to move west to Missouri. The day before he was to depart, however, he discovered that "suddenly all his negroes were missing," taking with them the property that "had been abundantly provided by the careful and considerate owner." After twelve of his slaves ran off the same year, John Thomson Mason, a member of the House from Maryland, received a letter from northern abolitionist Gerrit Smith informing him that his former property "were safe and in good health, and contented," and "on their way to the Canada." In this environment, Fontaine H. Pettis, a Virginia lawyer living in New York City who specialized in "catching fugitive slaves," believed he would find a ready market in the district and advertised his services in the *Gazette*. Worry about fugitives also made some slaveholders easy marks

---

[28]"Minutes of the Proceedings of the Tenth American Convention for Promoting the Abolition of Slavery and Improving the Condition of the African Race, Assembled at Philadelphia . . . 1805," *The American Convention for Promoting the Abolition of Slavery and Improving the Condition of the African Race: Minutes, Constitution, Addresses, Memorials, Reports, Committees and Anti-Slavery Tracts*, 3 vols. (New York, 1969), 1:371–76; Insurance Policy No. 2157, Marine Insurance Company of Alexandria, Virginia: Insurance Policies, May 18, 1807–November 8, Virginia Historical Society, Richmond, Virginia; Moncure Daniel Conway, *Testimonies Concerning Slavery* (1864; reprint ed., New York, 1969), p. 21; *Alexandria Gazette,* Jan. 7, 1840, Aug. 17, 1842 (Kephart); Gudmestad, *Troublesome Commerce*, pp. 1–2, 18–19, 26–27, 32 (quotation), 38 (federal law), 154–56; Tadman, *Speculators and Slaves*, pp. 11–82; Bancroft, *Slave Trading in the Old South*, pp. 50, 59–64, 275–76.

for a few "speculating" northerners who used runaway slave advertisements to identify erstwhile owners. Putative slave catchers, the *Gazette* reported, informed slaveholders that their human property had been recaptured, but could not be returned until expenses were covered. Once paid, of course, the slaveholder never heard from the northerner again.[29]

Such scams were possible because the number of runaways continued to rise. The Georgetown paper reported in November 1842 that at least one hundred runaways have "within the last month . . . clandestinely left their owners," and "reports from all parts of the District and surrounding country" confirmed "numerous cases of negroes absconding." Unable or unwilling to believe that enslaved people wanted freedom, slaveholders asserted that a "well-concerted scheme for the escape of slaves from this neighborhood has been, for some time in operation." "This is," a correspondent to the *Gazette* noted in late 1842, "the first fruits of the new scheme entered into by the negroes of the North and their brethren the Abolitionists." "Societies are formed, the members of which pay a weekly subscription, for the purpose of raising funds to assist the liberation of slaves, by paying so much a head for every one successfully got off." Other slaves, another correspondent reported, escaped on foot to Chambersburg, Maryland, where they caught the railroad to Pennsylvania and freedom. The "nefarious designs of mischievous fanatics," another writer apprehensively noted, have filled the "Maryland and District papers" with "advertisements for the recovery of lost slaves." "The excitement," the report concluded, "is great indeed." In fact, slaveholders had real reason to be excited—and deeply anxious. As historian Stanley Harrold and others have argued, abolitionists helped support an active, interracial abolitionist community within the district, one that drew broad support from the region's large and growing free black population.[30]

In short, by the early 1840s Alexandria's slaveholders and town leaders believed that district slavery and the slave trade, both vital components of the town and the region's economy, were under siege, and local elites agreed that retrocession to Virginia was necessary to protect themselves from an

---

[29]Hurst, *Alexandria on the Potomac*, p. 126; *Alexandria Gazette*, Mar. 2, 17, 1840, Apr. 12, 1841, May 3, Nov. 1, 1842.

[30]*Alexandria Gazette*, Nov. 1, 1842. On the presence of a "subversive" community in the district, see Stanley Harrold, *Subversives: The Antislavery Community in Washington, D.C., 1828–1865* (Baton Rouge, 2003); Josephine F. Pacheco, *The Pearl: A Failed Slave Escape on the Potomac* (Chapel Hill, 2005); and Hilary Russell, "Underground Railroad Activists in Washington, D.C.," *Washington History* 13 (Fall/Winter 2001–2):28–49.

"experimenting Congress." When the measure finally came before Congress in the mid-1840s, however, few contemporaries linked it to slavery—though both northern and southern newspapers had done so in the late 1830s. Most pointedly, the *Southern Agriculturalist* of Charleston, South Carolina, urged "all the slave-holding States" to support "a retrocession of the District of Columbia to the States of Virginia and Maryland." With Congress "no longer the local legislature" of the district, the paper continued, "the abolitionists would be driven from the ground . . . forever." Likewise, a New York paper noted two years later that "the slavery question will undoubtedly be set at rest . . . by the retrocession of the District of Columbia to its original donors, the States of Maryland and Virginia." However, the editor was far less sanguine about the impact of retrocession. "The question then will not be slavery or abolition in the District," he added ominously, but "Union or Disunion!" The Cincinnati *Philanthropist* also feared the consequences of retrocession and recommended that slaveholders abandon schemes to return the district to Maryland and Virginia. Altering the ten miles square, the paper argued, would set a constitutional precedent and enable antislavery forces to move the "seat of government to a free soil." Abolitionists, the paper concluded, would hail such a result "as a triumph over the spirit of slavery" and "a national sentence of condemnation on the whole system of slavery."[31]

Knowing the political and ideological pitfalls that could befall any measure dealing with the district, local supporters of retrocession in 1845 and 1846—in contrast to the more open debate that took place in 1840—studiously avoided any mention of slavery in their public statements. By the mid-1840s they had seen how district affairs could be manipulated for political gain by a variety of ideologues, though most noisily and dangerously by abolitionists, and they had no desire to see their measure founder in sectional and partisan debates. Instead, the 1845 petition that officially enunciated the town council's reasons for retrocession focused above all on the disfranchisement of Alexandria voters. "We are," the petition declared, "a disfranchised people" who live in a "state of vassalage," "deprived of all those political rights and privileges so dear to an American citizen." Equally problematic, the town and county was burdened by an antiquated and confused legal code that Congress lacked the time to "modify and reform." Unlike D.C. residents across the river, moreover, Alexandrians received no federal spending to compensate for their loss of political and legal rights. The petitioners also pointed out that

---

[31] *Southern Agriculturalist and Register of Rural Affairs* (Charleston) 11 (Sept. 1838):9; *New World* (New York), Aug. 1, 1840; *Philanthropist* (Cincinnati), Apr. 24, 1838.

Congress would save money, as much as $50,000 a year, if Alexandria returned to Virginia. The balance of the petition addressed constitutional objections to retrocession, arguing that implicit in Congress's "right to acquire territory" was "the right to abandon" it. Finally, the petition pointed to recent federal decisions—namely, the annexation of Texas in 1845 and the Ashburton Treaty of 1842, which established the Maine-New Brunswick border—to prove that the federal government could and did relinquish territory when Congress believed it was in the national interest.[32]

If public statements of town officials avoided any direct reference to slavery or the slave trade, their backdoor politicking revealed more clearly the issues at stake. In their search for congressional allies, town leaders identified two of the most solidly prosouthern and proslavery politicians in Congress, John C. Calhoun of South Carolina in the Senate and R. M. T. Hunter, Calhoun's Virginia lieutenant, in the House. For a solidly Whig elite, which had in the early 1840s derided Hunter for weakness and indecision and labeled Calhoun the "nullifier," turning to these two sometime Democratic politicians seems a curious choice. However, by the mid-1840s the *Gazette* began to embrace the Calhounite notion that only a united South, free from partisan attachments and committed to states' rights, could effectively defend the region's interests from northern attack. "The true safety of the South," wrote Snowden in late 1842, "lies *in itself*, and it can have but little to fear from foreign interference, if it preserves itself intact at home." In 1843–44, when Calhoun sought support in Virginia for the Democratic presidential nomination, he and Hunter increasingly looked to the *Gazette* as an ally. Snowden's "Editorials," Virginian Edward Dixon informed the South Carolinian in 1843, express "the kindest feelings towards you" and a "great respect and admiration for your character and talents." Long infuriated by political interference in district matters, town leaders appreciated a politician who rejected out of hand any "petition which proposed to give the Federal Government a cognizance over the institution of slavery."[33]

---

[32]"Memorial of the Committee of the Town of Alexandria for Retrocession," *Origin and Government of the District of Columbia*, pp. 108–13.

[33]*Alexandria Gazette*, Dec. 13, 1842, July 11, 1840; Edward Dixon to John C. Calhoun, June 8, July 25, 1843; Calhoun, "Remarks upon the Reception of an Abolition Petition," Mar. 12, 1846, all in Robert L. Meriwether et al., eds., *The Papers of John C. Calhoun*, 28 vols. to date (Columbia, 1959–), 17:xxi, 238, 315, 22:683. On Calhoun's attempts to create a purified states' rights party, see Freehling, *Road to Disunion*, pp. 271–72, 289–310. On Hunter's political career in the 1840s and his devotion to a similar states' rights position, see Moore, "In Search of a Safe Government," pp. 51–152; and Anderson, "Hunter," pp. 8–32.

Indeed, it was Hunter, by 1846 a member of the House Committee on the District, who became the spokesman for Alexandria's proretrocession elites. He introduced the legislation and in May 1846 made an extended speech in the House on its behalf. Hunter's address was a masterpiece of indirection that at the same time reflected clearly the profound shift in the sectional identity of Alexandria's leadership. Aside from an allusive reference to "fugitives from justice" whom local authorities had difficulty retaking because of the absence of comity between D.C. and the states, Hunter made no overt reference to slavery or the slave trade. Instead, he focused on the issue of states' rights, arguing that a smaller district would decrease congressional power and thereby lessen the "temptation" of Congress to "exercise . . . powers within the States, which many of us believe to be forbidden by the Constitution," although it was currently exercised legally "within the District." Among these powers, Hunter listed congressional control over district banks, education, and internal improvements, but he pointedly avoided any mention of slavery. Following the lead of Alexandria's petitioners, Hunter also focused on the disfranchisement of Alexandria's citizens and the antiquated and confused legal code with which they were saddled. The result, Hunter argued, was that the town's economy and population "has been nearly stationary" since 1815. Largely abandoned by Congress, and lacking access to the state of Virginia's fund for internal improvements, Alexandria's sea traffic had declined precipitously and its economy had stagnated. Meanwhile, many residents had left the port because, Hunter asserted, "they cannot enjoy within it, the rights of men or the privileges of freemen."

Hunter also dismissed constitutional objections to retrocession, likening the district to the federal government's "forts, arsenals, and dockyards," which the government could "jettison" at will when they were "found to be useless." But the most striking portion of his speech was his vision of what Alexandria might have been "had she remained an integral portion of Virginia," and what she could become once free from congressional oversight. Invoking with a sectional twist the grandiose visions of early national town boosters, when Alexandria seemed poised to serve as the commercial link binding the nation together, Hunter asserted that had Alexandria not become part of the district the town would by now be "a flourishing depôt of the commerce of the western portion" of Virginia. Instead of its present decline, the port would have become "the keystone in a great arch of commercial interests which would bind eastern and western Virginia together," "the golden link which . . . would have united the interests and healed the divisions of the two sections" of the state. Retrocession, in contrast, promised to revive the city and help residents realize the economic rewards commensurate with their "natural advantages." Remove Alexandrians from their present "state of semi-bondage," Hunter concluded, and you will "awaken in them the energies of freemen" and enable them to transform Alexandria into "a large and flourishing place."[34]

The bill sparked extended debate within the House, though only one congressman, Erastus D. Culver of New York, explicitly linked retrocession to slavery in the district. Culver first moved that the bill be amended to allow all male citizens of Alexandria—not just white males—to participate in the proposed retrocession referendum. Equally provocative, he asserted that if after retrocession Virginia had the power to legislate upon all matters in Alexandria, including slavery, then "certainly Congress itself possessed that power" while Alexandria remained under her "exclusive jurisdiction." Culver, for one, saw the implications of the legislation for the future of slavery within Alexandria. He also asked Hunter to rewrite the "preamble" of the bill to reflect "the whole truth concerning the causes which had tended to bring it forward." In particular, he believed that the legislation, by reducing the size of the district, was designed to hinder the flight of "fugitive slaves" to D.C., where slaveholders had more difficulty recapturing them. Finally, he expressed his disquiet with the idea that retrocession would place "1,000 or 1,500 slaves under the jurisdiction of Virginia." The House, however, quickly turned aside Culver's amendment, and antislavery voices were heard no more during the debate.[35]

Instead, states' rights southerners voiced the greatest objections to retrocession, worried about the constitutional implications of Hunter's bill. William Payne of Alabama argued that Congress had only an "'exclusive' power of legislation" over the district, "not unlimited power." Congress, Payne asserted, was not "omnipotent within the district of Columbia," and thus while it had "the right to receive a district" because this was specified in the Constitution, "it had no right to transfer." For Payne, then, retrocession

---

[34]"Retrocession of Alexandria. Speech of Mr. R.M.T. Hunter of Virginia, in the House of Representatives, May 8, 1846," *Congressional Globe*, 29th Cong., 1st sess., 1846, app., pp. 894–98. See also "Retrocession of Alexandria to Virginia," House Report No. 325, 29th Cong., 1st sess., Feb. 25, 1846, in *Origin and Government of the District of Columbia*, pp. 102–8.
[35]*Congressional Globe*, 29th Cong., 1st sess., 1846, p. 778.

was dangerous because it enlarged the power of the federal government beyond what the Constitution specified. Along with western Virginia representatives such as Joseph Johnson, he also wondered if the real purpose of the bill was to increase the voting power of eastern Virginia in the ongoing sectional contest over political representation in the state legislature. As a result of such concerns twenty-one southern congressmen voted against the bill. Clearly, as historian William Freehling reminds us, in 1846 the ongoing agitation over slavery at the national level had not yet created a unified South. What historian William Cooper labels the "politics of slavery"—attacking political opponents for being weak on slavery—most certainly existed in the South by the mid-1840s, but debates over local issues or how best to defend slavery could diffuse such attacks. For Payne, and for the small number of fellow southerners who joined him in opposing the bill, the small victory of returning Alexandria to Virginia did not warrant abandoning either localist concerns or larger principles—states' rights and a strict construction of the Constitution—upon which the defense of southern interests depended.[36]

Still, fifty-one southern representatives (or 71 percent) voted for retrocession. In the Senate, where Calhoun served as the primary defender of the bill, the vote was even more lopsided, with only three southern senators opposing and nineteen supporting the bill. A solid South may not yet have existed, but for most southern congressmen the retrocession of Alexandria was perceived as a sectional issue. Alexandria's free and enslaved African American community also recognized the implications of retrocession. The act as passed stipulated that a referendum be held in Alexandria before the separation from the district could occur. African Americans, denied by the terms of the act from voting, watched the count with growing dismay. Writing to abolitionist Gerrit Smith, "two colored men of Alexandria," recalled that "on the day of the election" "the poor colored people of this city . . . were standing in rows on either side of the Court House, and, as the votes were announced every quarter of an hour, the suppressed wailings and lamentations of the people of color were constantly ascending to God for help and succor, in this the hour of their need." Under congressional authority,

---

[36]Ibid., pp. 778–81; Freehling, *Road to Disunion*, pp. 289–307, 599–600n19. On the "politics of slavery," see William J. Cooper, *The South and the Politics of Slavery, 1828–1856* (Baton Rouge, 1978). On the east-west sectional contest within antebellum Virginia, see William Shade, *Democratizing the Old Dominion: Virginia and the Second Party System, 1824–1861* (Charlottesville, 1996), pp. 54, 262–83; and Charles H. Ambler, *Sectionalism in Virginia from 1776–1861* (Chicago, 1910).

local African Americans had managed to secure limited privileges, including meeting "for the purpose of religious worship" and Sunday schools for their children. They feared that "when the Virginian laws are extended over us . . . our schools will be broken up, and our privileges . . . will all be taken away." "The laws of Virginia," the writers concluded, "can hardly be borne by those colored people," and "in the spring," after Virginia extended its jurisdiction over the town, "forty or fifty colored families would be glad to leave for some free State, where they can educate their children and worship their God without molestation." Their predictions proved accurate; after decades of growth, between 1850 and 1860 the free black population of Alexandria fell from 15 to 11 percent of the total population.[37]

Indeed, in the years following the passage abolitionist voices and proslavery forces recognized the consequences of the act. In the wake of its passage, the New York publication *Morris's National Press* lamented, "there is something painful in this act of retrocession." Further north, the antislavery *Boston Recorder*, noting the impact of retrocession on Alexandria's black population, ruefully stated in 1847 that such "considerations should have prevented the passage of the law." Likewise, John Quincy Adams, who voted against the act but made no objection to it during the House debates, announced in November 1846 that "the Act retroceding the County of Alexandria to the State of Virginia" is "unconstitutional and void." In contrast, southern politicians quickly realized how retrocession transformed the debate over slavery in the district, placing the slave trade beyond the reach of abolitionist agitation. During the debates over the Compromise of 1850, Henry Clay argued that southerners could have no objection to ending the slave trade in Washington "now that a large portion of the District has been retroceded to Virginia" and no "motive or reason" remained "for concentrating slaves" in the district for sale to the Deep South. Indeed, in response to Alexandria's retrocession and the 1850 congressional ban of the slave trade, a number of Washington slave traders moved their operations across the river. For Alexandria's leaders, retrocession ensured that their slave property and the slave trade, an important component of the local economy, remained free from federal interference. As an added bonus, Virginia law required

---

[37]Richards, "Debates over Retrocession," p. 70; *Boston Recorder*, Jan. 7, 1847; Hurst, *Alexandria on the Potomac*, p. 126. For Calhoun's Senate speech, which also avoided the question of slavery and instead focused on the constitutionality of the act, see "Remarks on the Retrocession to Virginia of Part of the District of Columbia," July 2, 1846, in *Papers of Calhoun*, 23:266–68.

that manumitted blacks leave the state within a year, a measure that probably contributed to proportional decline of the town's troublesome free
black population.[38]

Little wonder, then, that Alexandria merchants Francis Smith and Robert
Brockett heaped such effusive praise on Calhoun after his Senate speech.
Both he and his ally Robert Hunter had played key roles in ensuring the
passage of retrocession. But that Alexandria's overwhelmingly Whig leadership had turned to proslavery, states' rights, and Democratic politicians reveals the underlying issue at stake in the retrocession battle. By the 1840s,
Alexandria suffered from a stagnant economy, a half decade of abolitionist
attacks on the property rights of slaveholders, and an unsympathetic Congress that provided little economic aid to the town and appeared to invest time
on district affairs only when it suited the political and ideological agendas of
the members. These various sources of discontent enabled retrocession advocates to build a broad base of support. But at its core the return to Virginia was designed to protect Alexandrians from the "tremendous power
resident in Congress, which extends to all our property, and is liable to be
extended at any moment" by an "experimenting Congress." Protection of
slavery and the slave trade lay at the heart of the campaign, which was led,
both locally and in Congress, by men deeply invested in the slave economy
and culture of the district and the South. In 1866, Ohio Senator Benjamin
Wade argued that retrocession was "gotten up" by "the secessionist politicians
of old Virginia," men who viewed the act "as preparatory to the secession
of the States that took place afterward." He was not far wrong. In choosing to
return to Virginia, Alexandrians abandoned their post-Revolutionary economic nationalism and embraced instead a sectional—or, more accurately,
a southern—economic and cultural orientation.[39]

---

[38] *Morris's National Press* (New York), July 18, 1846; *Boston Recorder,* Jan. 7, 1847; John Quincy
Adams, quoted in *Liberator,* Dec. 4, 1846; Henry Clay, "Compromise Resolution," *Congressio-
nal Globe,* 31st Cong., 1st sess., 1850, app., pp. 121, 122 (see also Corrigan, "Imaginary Cruel-
ties," pp. 21–25); Michael A. Ridgeway, "A Peculiar Business: Slave Trading in Alexandria,
Virginia, 1825–1861," master's thesis, Georgetown University, 1976, pp. 92, 120, 131; Philip J.
Schwarz, *Slave Laws in Virginia* (Athens, Ga. 1996), pp. 53–57.

[39] Francis L. Smith and Robert Brockett to Calhoun, July 2, 1846, in *Papers of Calhoun,*
23:268; "One of the People," *Alexandria Gazette,* Oct. 12; "Working Man," *Alexandria Gazette,*
July 22, 1840; Wade, in *Congressional Globe,* 39th Cong., 1st sess., 1866, pp. 3576–82, 3701–9
(quotations pp. 3578, 3705); see also Bowling, *Creation of Washington,* p. 243.

Mary Beth Corrigan

"Whether they be ours or no, they may be heirs of the kingdom"

The Pursuit of Family Ties among Enslaved People in the District of Columbia

IN HIS 1844 *Narrative,* Frederick Douglass commented on the distinctive-ness of urban slavery: "I had resided in Baltimore but a short time before I observed a marked difference, in the treatment of slaves, from that which I witnessed in the country. A city slave is almost a freeman, compared with a slave on a plantation. He is much better fed and clothed, and enjoys privi-leges altogether unknown to the slave on the plantation."[1] To a large degree, historians have agreed with Douglass's characterization. Richard Wade, whose 1964 study *Slavery in the Cities* still shapes the historical debate, con-curred that urban slavery provided a level of autonomy nonexistent on plan-tations. Enslaved people in the urban areas had greater access to freedom, whether through manumission or escape, and participated in communities that included free blacks. Wade pointed out that the hiring-out system en-abled enslaved people to save their wages and purchase their own freedom. As they frequently traveled between work sites in the cities and neighboring countryside, enslaved men in particular used this time away from their owners or employers to meet friends in markets and other public spaces. In addition,

I am grateful to Beatriz Betancourt Hardy, who carefully read and commented upon a draft of this essay.

The quotation in the title is from Paul Edmonson, quoted in Harriett Beecher Stowe, *A Key to Uncle Tom's Cabin* (1853; reprint ed., Bedford, Mass., 1998), p. 156.

[1] Frederick Douglass, *Narrative of the Life of Frederick Douglass: An American Slave* (New York, 1968), p. 50.

the ability to secure living-out privileges, enabling an enslaved person to live outside their owner's household, was nearly unique to urban areas.[2]

While the flexible work arrangements, mobility, proximity to free blacks, and access to freedom support Douglass's effusive characterization of urban slavery, the fractured family life described by most historians of urban slavery belies his characterization of urban slaves as "almost a freeman." Wade wrote: "To be sure, urban proximity permitted wider opportunity for the choice of mate, and 'living out' secured a portion of privacy to some which was almost wholly absent in rural areas. Yet, the greater instability of slavery in the towns meant that attachments were seldom permanent."[3] Wade cites the gender division of labor and the size of the slaveholdings as the principal reasons for the continual disruptions to family life. Throughout the South, the demand for enslaved workers to serve as domestics far exceeded other occupations. Therefore, women well outnumbered men in the enslaved populations of the urban South. This disproportionately high sex ratio curtailed the opportunity for long-lasting, monogamous relationships, according to Wade and others. Urban slaveholders rarely owned more than three slaves, so urban slaves rarely lived with family members.[1]

This chapter explores how enslaved men and women in the District of Columbia confronted the harsh realities of urban slavery to establish and maintain enduring kin relationships. Indeed, Wade and others have correctly pointed out that enslaved men and women rarely lived with their families in the same household. Focusing on the separation of husbands and wives, these historians have ignored the impact of the slave system upon the parent-child relationship. Slave owners routinely and systematically separated parents from their children as well; they frequently separated even the youngest children from their mothers. Though generally unable to nurture their nu-

[2]Richard Wade, *Slavery in the Cities: The South, 1820–1860* (New York, 1964).
[3]Ibid., p. 117.
[1]This essay is based largely upon research initially presented in my dissertation, "'A Social Union of Heart and Effort': The African American Family in the District of Columbia on the Eve of Emancipation," Ph.D. diss., University of Maryland, College Park, 1996. For other characterizations of the pernicious impact of urban slavery upon the family life of slaves, see Barbara Fields, *Slavery and Freedom on the Middle Ground: Maryland during the Nineteenth Century* (New Haven, Conn., 1985), pp. 24–28, 30–31; Brenda Stevenson, *Life in Black and White: Family and Community in the Slave South* (New York, 1996), pp. 206–257; Midori Takagi, *"Rearing Wolves to Our Own Destruction": Slavery in Richmond, Virginia, 1782–1865* (Charlottesville, 1999), pp. 66–67, 97–102; Vivienne L. Kruger, "Born to Run: The Slave Family in Early New York, 1626–1827," Ph.D. diss., Columbia University, 1985.

clear family relationships within a single household, enslaved people negotiated for privileges, established communal ties, carved spaces within their neighborhoods, and created time to maintain ties with their kin. These niches provided opportunities for enslaved people to meet their family members without the intrusions of their owners. Urban enslaved people used their relative independence to create a community that nurtured their family relationships and touched the lives of the enslaved throughout the region.

Until approximately ten years ago, few studied the lives of enslaved people of the District of Columbia. Instead, academic and popular historians alike concentrated on the free black population, seemingly with good reason, as it outnumbered the enslaved population by more than three to one in 1860. Recent work has concentrated instead on the relatively small population of enslaved residents of the district. Their ties to black and white abolitionists from the North—pressing for abolition within the district, in particular —have constituted the focus of study. Most of the essays in this volume contribute to a growing literature that describes the cooperative network between abolitionists and the enslaved community of the district. This essay has benefited from their insights but concentrates instead upon the ways that the enslaved people lived with the realities of their status.[5]

To a greater extent than most southern cities, the district provided its enslaved population the chance to forge meaningful ties with free black people. At the time of the district's establishment in 1800, enslaved people constituted nearly one out of four residents, while free black people accounted for nearly one out of twenty. Once the land was cleared and the construction of the capital began, the slave system began to break down, as employers rarely needed steady, year-round labor characteristic of tobacco plantations. Increasingly, employers turned to free black laborers, hired for terms as short as one day. The free black population grew so quickly that by 1830 it outnumbered the enslaved population. From that point onward, the enslaved population decreased in absolute numbers and as a portion of the district's

---

[5] The National Underground Railroad Network to Freedom, a program of the National Park Service charged with the identification of sites related to the Underground Railroad, has played a large role in sparking interest in the abolitionist network in the district. There have been a large number of publications as well, the most comprehensive of which is Stanley Harrold's *Subversives: Anti-Slavery Community in Washington, D.C., 1828–1865* (Baton Rouge, 2003). Two noteworthy books on the *Pearl* have also received widespread attention: Josephine F. Pacheco, *The Pearl: A Failed Slave Escape on the Potomac* (Chapel Hill, 2005), and Mary Kay Ricks, *Escape on the Pearl: The Heroic Bid for Freedom on the Underground Railroad* (New York, 2006).

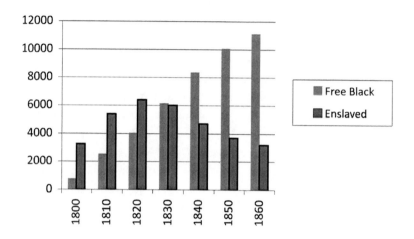

FIG. 1. The free black and enslaved populations in the District of Columbia, 1800–1860. *Sources:* U.S. Census Bureau, *Fifth Census or Enumeration of the Inhabitants of the United States, 1830* (Washington, D.C., 1832), pp. 10–11, 160–63; idem, *Sixth Census or Enumeration of the Inhabitants of the United States in 1840* (Washington, D.C., 1841), pp. 470–71; idem, *The Seventh Census of the United States: 1850* (Washington, D.C., 1853), pp. 232–35; idem, *The Population of the United States in 1860,* prepared by Joseph G. Kennedy (Washington, D.C., 1864), p. 588.

population as a whole. In 1850 free black people outnumbered the enslaved by a margin of nearly three to one (fig. 1). This urban population distribution was, in fact, a distinctive characteristic of the Chesapeake. The only other southern city with a larger free black than enslaved population was Baltimore, where the proportion was nearly nine to one in 1850.[6]

The free black people of the district built a strong community that embraced enslaved people. Churches stood at the center of this community. In the beginning of the century, free and enslaved African Americans attended church with white congregants. Invariably, they suffered indignities such as segregated seating and the refusal of white ministers to perform key sacraments such as baptism. Only the Catholic Church retained a significant portion of its free and enslaved congregants. Priests did not exclude them from the sacraments, yet Catholics relegated African Americans to separate bal-

---

[6]For the comparative data, see J. D. B. DeBow, *Statistical View of the United States: Compendium of the Seventh Census* (Washington, D.C., 1864), pp. 397–98; and Wade, *Slavery in the Cities,* pp. 325–30.

conies during services. Black Protestants, however, soon began to invest in the establishment of their own churches. By 1820 three churches exclusively served free and enslaved blacks: "The Little Ark," later known as Mount Zion United Methodist Church, formed by members of the Montgomery Street Methodist Church; "Little Ebenezer" formed by members of Ebenezer Church in Washington; and Israel A.M.E., which first met in a ropewalk and then a schoolhouse, until the purchase of a church on Capitol Hill. By 1860 this community had formed fourteen churches of various denominations, including Presbyterian and Baptist. These churches supported the aspirations of the community in key ways. Each congregation sanctioned the formation of families in the administration of baptisms and marriages, provided funerals and sometimes burial grounds to its members, and maintained Sunday schools, if not day schools. In addition, several, if not all, of these churches participated in the abolitionist network that facilitated the escape of enslaved people from the district and points south.[7]

The growth of the free black community in the district alarmed its white residents, who tried to stem the population increase and limit its ties to enslaved people. The backlash was in full throttle by 1827, when the corporation of Washington required its free black residents to register with the mayor to gain a permit allowing them to live and work in the city. That same year, the city required a permit for all public assemblies of free black people and imposed a ten o'clock curfew. Two events in 1831 further inflamed anxieties regarding the free black population: Nat Turner's Rebellion, which white people throughout the Chesapeake erroneously attributed to free black people and the publication of *The Liberator* by William Lloyd Garrison, who advocated abolition in the district as part of the campaign to end slavery in the nation.

Local events triggered an explosion of tensions that led to another clampdown. In August 1835 the Washington police reported the attempted murder of Anna Maria Thornton, the widow of William Thornton, architect

---

[7]Mary Beth Corrigan, "The Ties That Bind: The Pursuit of Community and Freedom among Slaves and Free Blacks in the District of Columbia, 1800–1860," in *Southern City, National Ambition*, ed. Howard Gillette (Washington, D.C., 1995), pp. 75–78; Mary Beth Corrigan, "Making the Most of an Opportunity: Slaves and the Catholic Church in Early Washington," *Washington History* 12 (2000):90–101. Pauline Gaskins Mitchell, "The History of Mt. Zion United Methodist Church and Mt. Zion Cemetery," in *Records of the Columbia Historical Society* 51 (1984):103–4; *Special Report of the Commissioner of Education*, 41st Cong., 2d sess., 1870, H. Ex. Doc. 315, pp. 217–19.

of the Capitol, and the arrest of Reuben Crandall, a physician accused of distributing antislavery literature. Rumors that a free black restaurant owner, Beverly Snow, insulted white women prompted the angry crowds awaiting the verdict of the Crandall trial outside the courthouse to destroy the property of free blacks and schools run by John Cook and Mary Wormley, both leaders of the free black community. The Washington City Council imposed restrictions aimed at arresting the growth of the free black population. It prohibited the licensing of free black people as independent proprietors (a law subsequently deemed a denial of the right to property by the circuit court), increased the number of sponsors necessary to require a certificate of freedom from two to five, and widened the scope of the curfew. The capture of the *Pearl* and the abolition of the interstate slave trade prompted the Washington City Council to enlarge the size of the police force and increase the fee for a certificate of freedom.[8]

White employers could not easily sate their demand for a compliant unskilled labor force without employing free black men and women in large numbers. In the cities and countryside alike, white employers sought laboring men for short-term jobs, often only for a day. Generally, the season defined the term of the job. In the summers, these unskilled laborers tended to find work in the countryside; the cities proved more remunerative in the winters. For many jobs, employers expected the laborers to work alongside enslaved laborers. White workers, even newly arrived immigrants, refused to compete against free black and enslaved laborers and even led work stoppages in protest.[9] As a result, the seasonal, intermittent, and unskilled work in demand throughout the region was often the only work available to free black laboring men. At the same time, white householders turned to free black women to serve as domestics. By the 1850s most took in washing, working on a daily basis for several households. Others worked steadily with white householders and usually lived with their own families rather than their em-

[8]Corrigan, "The Ties That Bind," pp. 79–80, 85. Southern cities and states generally enacted black codes to curb the growth of the free black population. For the standard on this subject, see Ira Berlin, *Slaves without Masters: The Free Negro in the Antebellum South* (New York, 1974), pp. 182–216. Leonard Curry included an account of Snow's Riot in *The Free Black in Urban America, 1800–1850: The Shadow of a Dream* (Chicago, 1981), pp. 98–100.

[9]See especially Peter Way, *Common Labor: Workers and the Digging of the North American Canals, 1780–1860* (New York, 1993), pp. 42–43, 87–88, 125–130, and Ira Berlin and Herbert Gutman, "Natives and Immigrants, Free Men and Slaves: Urban Workingmen in the Antebellum American South," *American Historical Review* 88 (1983):1175–1200.

ployers. Few native white women wanted such work; indeed, this flexible and fluid system enabled most to secure outside help for at least their washing and special tasks. Because of this labor market, far more free black women than men—by a margin of nearly three to two in 1850—resided continuously in the cities.[10]

Enslaved people assumed the same type of work roles, although their owners defined the terms of their work. Whereas free black people could effectively limit their availability to their employers, enslaved people could merely influence their owners to secure release time, travel passes, and other privileges. Most slave owners in the District of Columbia had significant ties to the countryside. Several maintained an urban seat and a farm, while others had brothers, sisters, or other family members who managed nearby farms. These economic and social ties enabled slave owners to distribute their slaves between urban and rural areas. If such transfers were unfeasible, the slave hiring system enabled owners to shift their slaves to where their work was demanded. Using these means, slave owners employed women in the cities far more frequently than men, who most often cultivated their farms. They so effectively exacted this division of labor that, within the urban enslaved population, women outnumbered men by nearly two to one in 1850.[11]

The District of Columbia provides a unique vantage point to examine the relationship between the relative autonomy of urban enslaved people and their ability to form and maintain families. Free black men and women established a viable community that embraced enslaved people as equal members, mitigated the conditions of their enslavement, and pressed for their freedom. In no small part because of this community, the enslaved people of the district secured privileges that provided them the type of autonomy described by Wade. At the same time, they encountered the worst conditions possible to maintain nuclear family households. The urban enslaved rarely lived with their entire nuclear family. Their owners disregarded their family ties, routinely separating husbands and wives as well as parents and children.

Enslaved people could hardly defend themselves against their owners' designs. At best, they merely influenced their household arrangements. They had no right to a family: though sanctioned by their community, their

---

[10]Corrigan, "A Social Union of Heart and Effort," pp. 334–35.

[11]Ibid., pp. 336–37. David Goldfield has argued that southern cities depended upon and were thereby shaped by the agricultural production and commerce of its region. *Cotton Fields and Skyscrapers: Southern City and Region, 1607–1980* (Baton Rouge, 1982), pp. 28–50.

marriages had no legal standing, and their children were their owners' property. Owners, in turn, routinely transferred, sold, or hired out their slaves
within the region to fill the various work roles needed. In addition, owners
sold a significant number to dealers, who in turn took them to slave markets
in the Lower South, particularly in New Orleans. As a result, enslaved people
in the district could expect frequent disruptions in their household arrangements. Even worse, these disruptions could take them outside the region so
that the threat of sale loomed large over the entire community.[12]

The census helps establish the contours of household arrangements in
the cities of Washington and Georgetown as well as surrounding countryside. This area included parts of Montgomery and Prince Georges County
in Maryland, as well as Alexandria and Fairfax Counties in Virginia. It also
included Washington County, one of three distinct political entities—including the cities of Washington and Georgetown—that comprised the District
of Columbia. Washington County surrounded these cities, and its economy
resembled that of Maryland and Virginia. The census for the District of
Columbia recorded the distribution of enslaved and free people, men and
women, as well as the young and old for each jurisdiction. Since the outlying
counties of Maryland and Virginia were far more extensive than Washington County, it is impossible to isolate the countryside immediately surrounding Washington and Georgetown. Yet, the census of the district recorded
separately the small agricultural Washington County and the cities of Washington and Georgetown and thereby provides a window into the demographic
patterns of the countryside, particularly the distribution of enslaved men,
women, and children between the city and countryside. The data reveals
when enslaved people could expect disruptions to their family ties, as the
work roles of children, teens, and adults were distinctive. Such transitions
often were marked by their transfer to and from the cities.

As in other southern cities, owners typically maintained smaller numbers
of slaves in the cities than in the countryside. In 1850 slightly more than half
of the slaveholders owned only one slave; more than nine out of ten slaveholders owned fewer than four slaves. Enslaved people probably lived with
at least one enslaved person, as only one out of four lived in solitary holdings. In all likelihood, they lived with fewer than three others, as nearly half

---

[12]Mary Beth Corrigan, "Imaginary Cruelties? A History of the Slave Trade in Washington, D.C.," *Washington History* 13 (2001–2002):4–27.

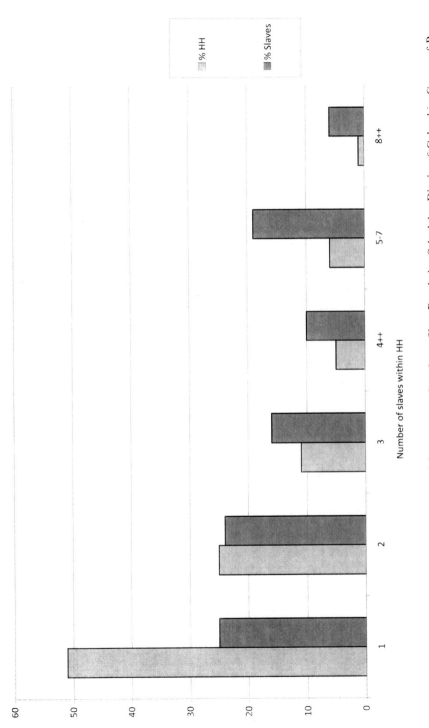

Fig. 2. Size of slave households in Washington and Georgetown, 1850. *Source:* Slave Population Schedules, District of Columbia, Census of Population, National Archives Manuscript Publications M432, Seventh Census of the United States, 1850, Record Group 29: Records of the Bureau of the Census, National Archives, Washington, D.C.

of the enslaved people lived in holdings of two to four (fig. 2). By contrast, slaveholders in Washington County, the area surrounding Washington City and Georgetown, established larger slave households. There, most included more than eight enslaved people. Nearly all of the enslaved of Washington County—close to nine out of ten—lived in residences of that size.[13] Not surprisingly, the urban enslaved had fewer opportunities to live with their kin than those living in the countryside.

Within the small urban residences, household composition appears random. Even in the larger residences, the enslaved quite often did not live with a family member. There was no kin relationship that owners as a group favored over the other. While individual owners might have enabled parents and children or husbands and wives to live together, owners generally did not protect these relationships. If fortunate enough to live with family members, the urban enslaved probably resided with lineal descendants; grandparents, parents, and children were more likely to live together than with spouses, siblings, or aunts and uncles. As owners depended upon the natural increase of their holdings, mothers often lived with one or two children. Owners usually retained only one or two women in their prime adult years so that there was a greater possibility for children to grow up in the presence of their grandmothers rather than aunts, as owners had probably sold or transferred them elsewhere. Caroline Mackall retained forty-five-year-old Maria Compton and her nine-year-old grandson Marlborough Wilson in Georgetown, while Maria's children and Marlborough's aunts and uncles resided and worked on the Mackall farm in Prince Georges County.[14]

Household composition depended largely upon the work roles assigned to enslaved people, not their kin relationships. The census reveals distinct patterns of distribution that undoubtedly affected kin relationships. During their prime work years, men and women were generally entrenched in their respective work roles. As a result, the sexual imbalance among enslaved adults

---

[13]From data collected from the Slave Population Schedules, District of Columbia, Census of Population, National Archives Manuscript Publications M432; Seventh Census of the United States, 1850, Record Group 29, Records of the Bureau of the Census, National Archives, Washington, D.C. For the table, see Corrigan, "A Social Union of Heart and Effort," p. 224.

[14]Petition 110, Records of the Board of Emancipation in the District of Columbia, 1862–63, National Archives Microfilm Publication M520, Record Group 217, Records of the U.S. General Accounting Office, National Archives, Washington, D.C.; Corrigan, "A Social Union of Heart and Effort," pp. 269–73.

in Washington and Georgetown was even higher than two women for every man, the ratio for these cities as a whole. Indeed, women between the ages of twenty and forty-nine outnumbered men by approximately nine to four. Correspondingly, in Washington County, adult men outnumbered women by eleven to ten.[15] This distribution of the enslaved workforce effectively prevented most enslaved men and women from living with each other.

Even though most enslaved men and women did not live with their spouses under these conditions, they nonetheless achieved a healthy rate of reproduction. Sexual activity among women began in their early teenaged years and continued through their childbearing years. By age twenty-two, most enslaved women had borne at least one child. In addition, in Washington and Georgetown in 1850 there were nearly three enslaved children under the age of five for every ten women of childbearing age (fifteen to forty-nine) (fig. 3). This ratio, known as the child-woman ratio, constitutes a measure of fertility when birth rates are not available. The enslaved of Washington and Georgetown achieved a healthy rate of reproduction—that is, men and women replaced themselves—yet the ratio was far lower than the enslaved population of the United States as a whole. Most owners promoted childbearing among their slaves to expand their holdings and the child-woman ratio suggests their success in doing so: there were more than seven enslaved children for every ten women of childbearing age throughout the enslaved population in 1850, far higher than the ratio for Washington and Georgetown.[16]

Unlike most slaveholders, many Washington and Georgetown slaveholders discouraged childbearing to increase their holdings. Instead, they sought to avoid pregnancies among their slaves and regarded children as a drain upon their mothers. Pregnancy weakened them, and childcare distracted them from their work. Susanna and Harriet Tobias claimed that the weight of thirty-eight-year-old Treacy enhanced her value, as at three hundred

---

[15]Calculated from figures in U.S. Census Bureau, *The Seventh Census of the United States: 1850* (Washington, D.C., 1853), pp. 233–34. For population tables showing the distribution of enslaved people by age and sex, see Corrigan, "A Social Union of Heart and Effort," pp. 336–37.

[16]Generally, the child-woman ratio denotes the number of children under five for every 1,000 women of childbearing age. Because of the classifications in the published censuses, my calculations include women up to the age of forty-nine. For a definition of the child-woman ratio, see Arthur Haupt and Thomas T. Kane, *The Population Reference Bureau's Population Handbook: International Edition* (Washington, D.C., 1989), p. 25. Marie Jenkins Schwartz explores the impact of slave owners' interest in reproduction upon the parent-child relationship in *Born in Bondage: Growing Up Enslaved in the Antebellum South* (Cambridge, Mass., 2000).

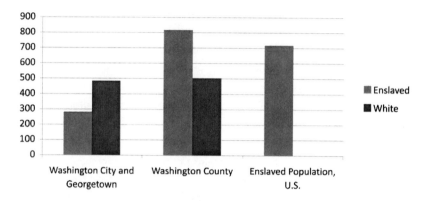

FIG. 3. The child–woman ratio among enslaved and white populations in the District of Columbia, 1850. *Sources:* U.S. Census Bureau, *The Seventh Census of the United States: 1850* (Washington, D.C., 1853), pp. 233–34; U.S. Department of Commerce, Bureau of the Census, "Population by Age, Sex, Race and Nativity, 1790–1970," in *Historical Statistics of the United States: Colonial Times to 1970, Part 1,* Series A-119-134 (Washington, D.C.), p. 18.

pounds she "was not liable to maternity." Other owners were smart enough to count on the fertility of their enslaved women. As a result, several frequently sold or manumitted women at the beginning of their childbearing years to avoid the burdens of owning enslaved children.[17]

Even among those who regarded children as an important value to their investment, urban slaveholders regarded children as a distraction to the workings of an urban household. Instead of maintaining them in Washington and Georgetown, many slaveholders transferred or sold children to farms in the countryside. The youngest children were certainly not protected; in fact, they were the most likely to reside in the countryside. In 1850 an especially large number of enslaved children under the age of five lived in rural Washington County, as there were more than eight children under that age for every ten women of childbearing age, above the seven to ten ratio for the enslaved population of the United States and well above the five to ten ratio among the white population of Washington City and Georgetown (see fig. 3). In this context, the ratio of nearly three to ten among the enslaved of those

---

[17]On Treacy, see petition 192; for other examples, see petitions 65, 285, and 385, Board of Emancipation Records, NARA, R. 2–3; on the manumission and trade of young childbearing women, see Mary Beth Corrigan, "'It's a Family Affair': Buying Freedom in the District of Columbia, 1850–1860," in *Working Toward Freedom: Slave Society and Domestic Economy in the American South,* ed. Larry Hudson (Rochester, N.Y., 1994), pp. 175–79.

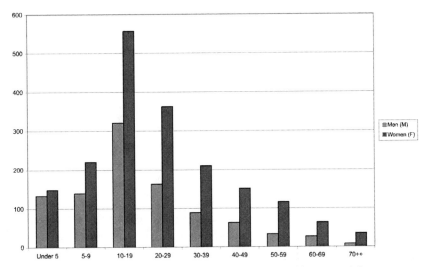

Fig. 4. The Distribution of Men and Women by Age in Washington and Georgetown, 1850. *Source:* U.S. Census Bureau, *The Seventh Census of the United States: 1850* (Washington, D.C., 1853), pp. 233–34.

cities was disproportionately low. Infrequent contacts with their mates probably accounted, in part, for the differential. Yet, these figures also suggest a high level of intrusion among the owners of the district, as they shifted children between the city and country.

Childhood was short for enslaved girls and boys who were expected to work at young ages. Girls and boys as young as seven and eight-years-old arrived in the cities from the countryside. Girls, however, outnumbered boys of that age by as much as three to two. In many cases, owners did not place them within their own urban residence but instead sought employers to hire out these girls for a small wage. As many as one out of ten enslaved girls (under age nine) residing in Washington and Georgetown worked for an employer instead of their owner. For their part, owners received wages between three and six dollars per month and relieved themselves of the burden of training them (fig. 4).[18]

Among enslaved teenaged women between the ages of ten and nineteen, these patterns were even more pronounced. Nearly one out of every three enslaved persons living in Washington and Georgetown were teenagers, and a disproportionate number of them—approximately seven out of every four

---

[18]Corrigan, "A Social Union of Heart and Effort," pp. 238–40.

—were women. One out of every four of these teenaged women (ages ten to seventeen) were hired out by these owners to another employer.[19] As their training ended and childbearing years commenced, owners frequently opted to transfer them back to the countryside, sell them, or retain them in the cities. They were more than twice as likely as men to stay, as adult enslaved women outnumbered men by more than nine to four (fig. 4).

Certainly, enslaved people could anticipate periods of instability. The teenaged years were fraught with peril. As they approached their prime, owners could sell young men and women at a high profit. Between the ages of eighteen and twenty-one, men and women had reached their peak value. They had not only acquired the skills necessary to fulfill their work role, but they also had reached physical maturity. Enslaved men could work at full strength, and women at the beginning of their childbearing years could enhance the holdings of a slaveholder. Owners intent upon selling these slaves often did so locally, yet they maximized their profits by selling them to the Deep South. Otherwise, owners transferred or hired out their enslaved men and women to enhance their own profits as much as possible.

Given that the division of labor separated men, women, and children, the enslaved people of the district needed to develop networks that enabled them to travel distances of several miles or more to see their family members. They could do little to disrupt the frequent transfers, slave hirings, and sale of their kin. At best, they sought to minimize the impact of these events. Sometimes, they successfully bargained to be transferred, hired out, or even sold to an owner or employer of their liking. More important, they tried to secure privileges that would enable them to manage visits to see their loved ones. Of course, they sought living-out privileges. Yet, they also needed to maximize their release time as much as possible. This time enabled them to travel and then enjoy their families and friends.

The work roles of men and women necessarily shaped their communities and thereby their family roles. The urban community, strengthened by the contributions of a large free black community, created opportunities for the enslaved of the district that did not exist in most cities. Enslaved women created strong neighborhood networks, with churches at their center that supported childcare and protected them from the worst effects of separation. Enslaved men reaped the benefits of these networks, as they frequently trav-

---

[19]Ibid., p. 239.

eled into the cities as part of their work and during their release time. Since they were able to visit family members in both the city and countryside, they facilitated communication between the countryside and the city so that everyone could maintain contact.

Despite their best efforts, however, enslaved people could never completely diminish the despair felt as they confronted their owners' power. Regardless of how deftly they negotiated with their owners, enslaved people only influenced their family arrangements, as they had neither marital nor parental rights. In an interview with Harriett Beecher Stowe, Amelia Edmonson expressed the anguish intrinsic to her status in a statement reprinted word-for-word in *A Key to Uncle Tom's Cabin*. Approximately sixty years old at the time of the interview, Amelia had a long and happy marriage to her husband, Paul, that led to the birth of at least fourteen children, thirteen living at the time of the interview. Despite her love for Paul, during their engagement she felt ambivalence rooted in her lack of parental rights: "Well, after a while, when I got engaged to Paul, I loved Paul very much; but I thought it wasn't right to bring children into the world to be slaves, and I told our folks that I never was going to marry, though I did love Paul."[20]

Ultimately, Amelia married Paul at the sanction of the African American community. Enslaved people participated in the same churches as free blacks, which apparently applied the same standards to them as free blacks. As Amelia explained, "Well, they told me I must marry, or I should be turned out of the church, so it was."[21] Obviously, African American churches took marriage seriously. No other institution promoted the goals of African Americans to extend their family ties as effectively as marriage. The Reverend John F. Cook, the free black pastor of Fifteenth Street Presbyterian Church, distributed a tract at the weddings of family and friends that outlined the responsibilities of married couples to the community as a whole: "Smaller communities are the nurseries of larger ones. At a certain time of life a transplantation is made, and the larger field of society takes its character from those qualities which were brought into it from the little inclosures of family life." The pamphlet emphasized the importance of children, as couples were

---

[20]Stowe, *A Key to Uncle Tom's Cabin*, p. 156; Stowe records Amelia Edmonson's age as seventy years, yet the census taker in 1850 recorded her age as fifty-eight, which is consistent with the youth of her children; 1860 Free Population Schedules, 5th Berry's District, Montgomery County, Maryland, p. 369, http://www.myancestry.com.

[21]Stowe, *Key to Uncle Tom's Cabin*, p. 156.

"the founders of a little community of rational and immortal creatures, who may hereafter found other small communities, and from whom, in the process of time, a *multitude* may spring . . . The members of your family are *immortals*. Such also will be their successors."[22]

These communally sanctioned marriages did not change the legal standing of marriage among the enslaved and did little to induce slave owners to protect the parental relationships of their slaves. Amelia Edmonson fully grasped this reality and expressed hopelessness to Mrs. Stowe. "Well, Paul and me, we was married, and we was happy enough, if it hadn't been for that; but when our first child was born I says to him, 'There 't is now, Paul, our troubles is begun, this child isn't ours.' And, every child I had, it grew worse and worse. 'O Paul,' says I 'what a thing it is to have children that isn't ours!'" She continued, "But, nobody knows what I suffered. I never see a white man come onto this place that I didn't think 'There, now, he's coming to look at my children;' and when I saw any white man coming by, I've called in my children and hid 'em, for fear he'd see 'em and want to buy them." Paul comforted his wife, at least somewhat. Drawing upon his religious faith and the values instilled by his community, he affirmed the humanity of his children: "Milly, my dear, if they be God's children, it an't so much matter whether they be ours or no; they may be heirs of the kingdom, Milly, for all that."[23]

Like other enslaved families, the Edmonsons encouraged their daughters to secure their freedom before their childbearing years. Milly explained to her daughters: "Now, girls, don't you never come to the sorrows that I have. Don't you never marry till you get your liberty. Don't you marry, to be mothers to *children that an't your own*." With the help of their fiancés, four Edmonson daughters raised the money to secure their freedom before marriage. One daughter had raised the money and shortly thereafter became ill. Reasoning that she had only months to live, her doctor advised her to keep the money to take care of herself. She answered, "If I had only two hours to live, I would pay down that money to die free."[24] As these and other enslaved women in the beginning of their childbearing years attempted to secure their freedom,

---

[22]James Bean, *The Christian Minister's Affectionate Advice to a Married Couple* (New York, 1815), box 20, folder 11, Cook Family Papers, Moorland-Spingarn Research Center, Howard University, p. 5.

[23]Stowe, *Key to Uncle Tom's Cabin*, p. 156.

[24]Ibid., p. 157.

their owners' desire to stem the increase of their holdings undoubtedly assisted them.[25]

Instead of scrimping to purchase their freedom, Mary and Emily Edmonson sought to achieve their freedom through escape. Hired-out servants living in Georgetown, thirteen-year-old Emily and fifteen-year-old Mary were removed from their parents only a short time in 1848 when they and more than seventy other enslaved people boarded the *Pearl*. Within one day of leaving the port of Washington City for its ultimate destination of Philadelphia, the ship was captured. As recrimination, Emily and Mary's owner sold them to a trader who transported them to New Orleans, where they met an older brother, Hamilton, also sold after trying to escape. The Edmonsons drew upon all the resources of their family and community, including its contacts with northern abolitionists, to secure the freedom of their girls. Their age certainly contributed to the intensity of the campaign. All sympathetic onlookers feared the possibility of sexual abuse following their sale in Louisiana. Though the resulting outpouring of donations from the North was truly extraordinary, the girls' motivation to escape was not. They feared the possibility of bearing enslaved children and the disruption to their family life as they approached adulthood. In the aftermath of the *Pearl*, the Edmonsons relied upon the same networks to purchase the freedom of Mary and Emily as nearly all enslaved people when raising the money for freedom.[26]

In lieu of freedom, enslaved people negotiated for privileges that permitted regular contact with family members. Enslaved people prized living-out arrangements more than any other privilege. When granted permission to live on their own, enslaved people typically lived within nuclear family households wherein couples not only shared meals and slept together but also raised their children together. Usually, they needed the cooperation of free black kin to win this concession from their owners. Enslaved men and women always appealed to the economic self-interest of their owners, who needed assurances that their slaves would receive the basic support of shelter, food, and even basic medical care. After Paul Edmonson secured his freedom by the will of his owner in 1835, Amelia gained permission to live with Paul. She even worked on her sewing tasks in his house. In addition, her owner stipulated that their children could live with him until they reached working age.

---

[25]Corrigan, "A Social Union of Heart and Effort," pp. 307–8, 314.

[26]Ricks, *Escape on the Pearl*, p. 12; Pacheco, *The Pearl: A Failed Slave Escape on the Potomac*, pp. 112–39; and John H. Paynter, *The Fugitives of the Pearl* (Washington, D.C., 1930).

This arrangement enabled Paul and Amelia to raise a large family together with minimal intrusion for the youngest children. From her owner's perspective, the couple's privacy encouraged childbearing and thereby an increase to her holdings, and Paul's farm and housing reduced the costs of provisions. In a similar fashion, John Harry of Georgetown permitted Henrietta Crusy, a servant, to live in a "hired house," where she bore ten children under her owner's "care and protection." In some cases, owners allowed their enslaved children to live with recently freed parents. Following her manumission in 1858, Cynthia resided with her enslaved son William. Likewise, Daniel Boston, a driver living on Capitol Hill, cared for his son Isaac.[27] For Henrietta, the arrangement gave her privacy with her husband and a place to raise her own children until they were ready to assume their work role.[28]

Living out arrangements enabled enslaved families to reap the benefits of the cooperative spirit within their neighborhoods. African American women within neighboring households helped each other raise their children. In many cases, these women shared ancestral ties, but often their networks included women who took on the obligations of kinship without any blood relation. These fictive kin thereby played an important role in the networks of women.[29] With the extension of these families, enslaved adults knew that their children would receive appropriate care as they met the demands of their owners. The kin networks also safeguarded enslaved children from the worst effects of separation from one or more parents due to the slave trade or hiring system. With their three children, Lucien and Mary Jones lived in Georgetown. Next door, Martha Gray lived with her enslaved husband, Michael Gray, whose visitation privileges enabled him to live with his family. Both couples benefited from the close friendship of the free black families headed by Julia Queen and Frank Newton.[30]

Wherever possible, the African American community buttressed such networks. Congregants of Holy Trinity Catholic Church in Georgetown used the sacrament of baptism to strengthen parental-child ties. All denominations

[27]Petitions 263, 393, Board of Emancipation Records, R. 3.
[28]Ibid.
[29]Herbert Gutman introduced the concept of fictive kin in *The Black Family in Slavery and Freedom, 1750–1925* (New York, 1976), pp. 216–27. James Borchert looked at extended kinship networks and the role of fictive kin in *Alley Life in Washington: Family, Community, Religion and Folk Life in the City, 1850–1970* (Urbana, Ill., 1980), pp. 77–79.
[30]1860 Free Population Schedules, R. 101: Georgetown, Ward 4, p. 170; Baptismal Register, 1835–1858 and 1858–1871, Holy Trinity Church Archives, Georgetown University.

held that during this ceremony the church accepted its new members and parents pledged to instruct their children in their religious obligations to prepare them for their roles within the community.[31] At Holy Trinity Catholic Church, the baptismal ceremonies of free blacks and slaves occurred within months after the birth of their sons and daughters. During baptisms, parents at once named their child and sought the support of kin and friends who would later help raise the child. Within the baptismal rites of the Catholic Church, parents named godparents, also known as sponsors, who agreed to care for their godchildren if orphaned, find a "good and virtuous nurse" in the event of the mother's death, and share in the religious instruction for these children.[32]

The free black and enslaved congregants of Holy Trinity Catholic Church embraced the practice of designating godparents as a means of bolstering the networks established within their neighborhood. Black parents made this practice their own. Nearly always parents chose a free black or enslaved godmother, instead of two godparents, for their children.[33] They did not conform to church teachings, as white parents always designated both a godmother and a godfather for their children at baptism. The frequent absences of men due to their work accounted in part for the preference for godmothers. In addition, the selection of women as sponsors stemmed from their role as nurturers of their children, a function that godparents performed alongside parents.[34]

Often, enslaved and free black parents chose one of their sisters or another family member as godmother, thereby augmenting the obligations already implicit in their kin relationship. Several sponsors had a surname in common with one of the child's parents. Henrietta Belt agreed in 1851 to become the godmother of Louis, the son of Richard Ford and Ellen Belt.

---

[31]Peter Collet, *Doctrinal and Scriptural Catechism* (New York, 1853), pp. 269, 271–72; *The Doctrines and Discipline of the African Methodist Episcopal Church*, 13th ed., rev. (Philadelphia, 1873), p. 20.

[32]Baptismal Registers, 1835–1858 and 1858–1871, Holy Trinity Church Archives, Georgetown University; Collet, *Doctrinal and Scriptural Catechism*, pp. 155–56.

[33]Margaret McAleer, "The Other Congregation: Patterns of Black Catholic Worship at Holy Trinity Catholic Church," seminar paper, Georgetown University, p. 30. See Baptismal Registers, 1835–1858 and 1858–1871, Holy Trinity Church Archives, Georgetown University.

[34]Margaret McAleer found that whites sponsored a mere 10 percent of the baptisms of free black and slave children performed between 1795 and 1845. McAleer, "The Other Congregation," p. 30; Baptismal Registers, 1835–1858, Holy Trinity Church Archives, Georgetown University.

Three years later, Martha Smith sponsored the baptism of Mary Henrietta
Smith, the daughter of an unmarried couple, Mary Jane Smith and John
Johnson. In February 1857, Catharine Becraft, who was herself childless,
sponsored the baptism of her nephew William Becraft Boudin, the son of
Sarah Ellen Becraft and Alexander Boudin. Two years later, Elizabeth Contee
presented Mary Florence, the daughter of Mary Contee and Benjamin
Grandison, for baptism.[35]

Usually, the sponsors were mothers themselves so that a baby and his or
her mother benefited from a godmother's practice in rearing young children. A godmother's maternal experience undoubtedly assisted new mothers
unfamiliar with tending young children. Henrietta Ross, a mother of three
children, sponsored three infant baptisms in 1860 alone.[36] A godmother was
often older than the mother of the newly baptized infant. In 1859 sixteen-
year-old unmarried mother Frances Newton selected Martha Gray, who was
approximately twenty years older, as her daughter's godmother. Even Gray
chose someone older than she. Thirty-seven years old when her son Charles
Robert was baptized, Martha and her husband Michael Gray selected a
woman three years older than herself as the baby's godmother.[37]

More often than not, the designation of godmothers by enslaved and free
black parents formalized loose bonds of kinship fostered within their neighborhoods. In May 1851, Monteville and Martha Herbert Daggs named
James and Catherine Young as godparents to Barbary Anne Herbert Daggs.
By 1860 the family of Monteville Daggs, including Barbary, lived in a household headed by James Young.[38] Parents often named neighbors as godparents. Henrietta Ross sponsored the baptism of Mary Emma Neale, the
daughter of Thomas and Sarah Neale, who lived within blocks of Ross.[39]

[35]Baptismal Registers, 1835–1858 and 1858–1871, Holy Trinity Church Archives, Georgetown University. Catharine Becraft, Sarah E. Boudin, and William Becraft Boudin appeared
in the same household in the 1860 census. Both Catharine and Sarah Becraft were listed in a
household headed by their father in the 1850 Free Population Schedules, R. 57: Georgetown,
Northwest, p. 230; 1860 Free Population Schedules, R. 101: Georgetown, Ward 2, p. 90.
[36]Baptismal Registers, 1858–1871, Holy Trinity Church Archives, Georgetown University;
1860 Free Population Schedules, R. 101: Georgetown, Ward 4, p. 186.
[37]Baptismal Registers, 1858–1870, Holy Trinity Church Archives, Georgetown University;
1860 Free Population Schedules, R 101: Georgetown, Ward 4, p. 170.
[38]By October 1860, Barbary Ann Daggs had died. Baptismal Registers, 1835–1858, and
Burial Registers, 1818–67. Holy Trinity Catholic Church Archives, Georgetown University;
1860 Population Schedules, Georgetown, Ward 2, p. 63.
[39]Entry for Dec. 31, 1859, Baptismal Registers, 1858–1860, Holy Trinity Church Archives;
1860 Free Population Schedules, R. 101: Georgetown, Ward 4, p. 186.

Though engaging in a practice unique to the Catholic Church, the congregants of Holy Trinity used the designation of godparents to advance goals common to all African Americans. They formalized relationships with extended kin—aunts, uncles, and friends—who lived in their neighborhood. As godparents pledged to educate and care for their godchildren throughout their lives, they also agreed to support these families as they encountered separations and other disruptions. On a daily basis, they helped each other with childcare responsibilities, assistance critical to women who worked long days inside the homes of wealthy white Georgetowners. Although the overwhelming majority did not seek the spiritual sanction of godparentage, enslaved people and free blacks formed ties with their neighbors that strengthened existing bonds of ancestral kinship and embraced fictive kin relationships as well.

Even if unable to reside near their kin, enslaved people enormously benefited from these neighborhoods. Given the prevalence of free black households, enslaved people of Washington and Georgetown could usually visit the homes of free black family members during their release time. Elizabeth and John Brent, the daughter and son-in-law of Amelia and Paul Edmonson, maintained their own residence in Washington City and regularly entertained their family. On weekdays and weekends, Elizabeth's sisters and brothers, hired out to work in Georgetown, visited and ate supper with them. Frequently on Saturdays their parents, Amelia and Paul Edmonson, traveled from the countryside to Center Market and then dined and lodged with the Brents. On Sundays, they often attended services at Asbury A.M.E.[40]

Enslaved men also brought crops to sell in the markets of Washington and Georgetown on at least a weekly basis. Often, these trips dovetailed their day of rest, Sunday, so that they had plenty of opportunity to visit their kin and friends. These men valued these contacts. Josiah Henson, once owned by a Montgomery County farmer, often recalled fondly his days in the markets of Washington and Georgetown. In his memoir, published in 1849, nineteen years after his escape to Canada, Henson hoped that "many respectable people, yet living there, may possibly have some recollection of 'Siah' or 'Si' . . . as their market-man." If not, he wanted them to know that he "remember[ed] them with an honest satisfaction." Harriett Beecher Stowe based Uncle Tom on Henson's story. When Henson returned to Washington

---

[40]Paynter, *Fugitives of the Pearl*, pp. 1–16, 37–46.

in 1877 to meet President Rutherford B. Hayes, he took pleasure in visiting his old haunts and meeting some of his old friends.[41]

Enslaved people did not necessarily need the sanction of their owners to visit their kin. As much as they tried, owners simply could not strictly control their slaves at every moment. There also were numerous places to hide in Washington and Georgetown. Often left unattended, nearly every enslaved person had the opportunity to slip away from their work to visit friends and family. Under the circumstances, enslaved workers took to "losing time"— that is, they slowed their work down or simply walked away from their jobs. While running errands, a domestic servant could stop to chat with neighbors. While waiting for his owners to finish their visits with friends, a coachman could have a drink with his kinsmen.[42]

Because of the nature of their work, men had more opportunities to "lose time" than women. Craftsmen could conduct their trade anywhere and often worked outside their owners' view. For other men, the regular treks between the countryside and the urban markets certainly increased their contacts with family and friends by simply delaying their return. Unsupervised, they had plenty of opportunity to connect with friends and family. They used these meetings to catch up with family news over dinner and at church. And they also engaged in carnal pleasures. They drank liquor and played games of chance. Card games were especially popular, and gambling invariably made things interesting. During their visits to the cities, single men sought out dances. Although the municipalities occasionally awarded a permit, these dances were illicit gatherings noted for their drinking, loud music, and festive costumes worn by women.[43]

The yard was an important gathering place for African Americans, enabling them to visit, take care of their children, play games, and flirt without immediate threat of owners or employers. Eastman Johnson depicted a yard in Washington City in his 1859 painting *Negro Life at the South* (fig. 5). An intermittent resident of Washington from 1844 to 1858, Johnson painted the dwelling and yard next door to his house on 246 F Street. The resulting

---

[41]Josiah Henson, *The Life of Josiah Henson, Formerly a Slave, Now an Inhabitant of Canada, as Narrated by Himself* (Boston, 1849; reprint ed., Chapel Hill, 2001), p. 20, http://docsouth.unc.edu/neh/henson49.html; "The Story of Josiah Henson," *Journal of Negro History* 3 (1918):21.

[42]On this form of resistance, see Takagi, *"Rearing Wolves to Our Own Destruction,"* pp. 46–52.

[43]*The Evening Star* (Washington, D.C.), Jan. 10, 1855.

FIG. 5. *Old Kentucky Home,* or *Negro Life in the Old South,* by Eastman Johnson, 1859, oil on canvas, Robert L. Stuart Collection. Courtesy of the New-York Historical Society. A resident of Washington City, Johnson painted this yard scene from his window on F Street, not in Kentucky, as its popular title suggests.

image, Johnson's most famous painting, captures the ambiguities of urban slavery. The viewer cannot tell whether enslaved or free blacks lived in the dwelling. Likewise, the status of the individuals in the painting cannot be discerned by sight. The light skin color of the woman talking to the muscular black man has suggested to some the possibility of an interracial relationship, although her dress instead indicates that she was probably an African American servant of mixed racial ancestry.

The fate of the painting is at least in part the product of these ambiguities. Unwilling to inflame the sectional debate in Washington, Johnson first debuted the painting in New York. One reviewer recognized the picture as representative of "several groups of Negroes enjoying the air, according to negro fashion, in the rear of one of those dilapidated houses common to Washington City." Otherwise, almost no one recognized the painting's source as urban, no less Washington. Northern abolitionists regarded the painting as evidence of the squalid conditions of slavery, whereas southern defenders of slavery found it substantiated the leisurely lifestyle provided by owners to their slaves. Within ten years the painting was exhibited as *Old Kentucky Home* and interpreted as a characteristic representation of domestic life on a Kentucky plantation. By and large, this interpretation has stuck. Only recently has art historian John Davis established the Washington provenance of the painting.[44]

Johnson based this illustration on his experiences in Washington, where the social life of African Americans depended on frequent visits to their homes. Given the residential distribution of enslaved people, free black people were more likely to control access to their own homes and thereby provide a semiprivate setting enabling men, women, and children to gather as depicted by Eastman. Regardless of who actually occupied this building, this scene was characteristic of the visits to the homes of free blacks, where enslaved and free gathered to mind young children, court, and relax. The scene shows a group that appears disconnected, although undoubtedly all are listening to the banjo player playing just outside the house. Child care is the dominant activity. One woman and child are perched outside the window taking in the scene in the yard. Another woman is dancing to the tunes with her young boy. At least one woman is working, preparing string beans for dinner. As she works, she is listening to a man whose more than casual interest suggests that the yard could be a setting for courtship. At least one child seems startled by the appearance of the white woman. Her entry into the yard serves as a reminder that the work demands placed upon African Americans could intrude on their social life at any time. Yet she appears more startled than anyone else in the yard, perhaps reacting to the banjo-playing, dancing, and housing conditions with the revulsion so characteristic of white residents of Washington and Georgetown.

She was entering a world that provided African Americans psychological release and enabled them to pursue relationships apart from their owners and employers. For enslaved people, the African American community took on special significance. Whether visiting the home of family and friends, worshipping in church, or gossiping with the neighbors, enslaved people were regarded as equal contributors and participants. This community en-

---

[44]John Davis, "Eastman Johnson's *Negro Life at the South* and Urban Slavery in Washington, D.C.," *Art Bulletin* 53 (1998):67–91; quotation from "Domestic Art Gossip," *Crayon* 6 (1859):125.

abled them not only to maintain family relationships but also to extend them. It hardly subverted their owners' agenda, as only a few of the enslaved achieved the ideal of a common household shared by a single nuclear family. Yet this community enabled the enslaved to have families that cared for and loved them as best they could. Best of all, perhaps, their families and communities existed independently of their owners, who universally underestimated the deep attachments held by the enslaved to their families and community. Any chance encounter with this community would stir apprehension on the part of any white interloper, such as the woman pictured in Eastman's painting.

Attachments fostered within the cities extended into the countryside. Men often bore the responsibility of conveying messages between relatives living in distant places. Adam Plummer, an enslaved man who worked the Riversdale Plantation near Hyattsville, Maryland, frequently traveled into Georgetown, where he could visit his mother-in-law as well as a son and a daughter. Twice a year, he secured the passes to travel approximately thirty miles by train to Mount Hebron near Ellicott City to see his wife, Emily. Since he was literate, they further maintained contact by writing letters. The whole family depended upon him to sustain the connections. His oldest daughter, Sarah Maranda, proved the most challenging. She always looked forward to his visits and his gifts, usually produce from his garden such as celery, eggs, and "a good slip of that grape vine." She even tried to visit him at Riversdale, but as "some of the family were sick I could not get off." Desperate, Sarah Maranda looked for her father in the city market on Sunday, one day after her grandmother spotted him, but missed him. Meanwhile, Adam faithfully reported news from her and others to his wife in distant Mount Hebron.[45]

Like other enslaved men, Adam Plummer took flak for the consequences of broken communication. During the late summer of 1860, Sarah Maranda's owner sold her to a slave trader who held her in an Alexandria pen for two months and then conveyed her to New Orleans. Sarah Maranda received no consoling messages or visits from her family during her stay in Alexandria. More important, none of them could try to find her a local owner or raise the money for her purchase. She unfortunately interpreted the silence as indifference. She wrote to her mother that she did not blame her mother, but thought "it very hard that father did not come to see me as he was

[45]Sarah Maranda Plummer to Adam Plummer, Dec. 2, 1859, in Carter Woodson, ed., *The Mind of the Negro as Reflected in Letters Written during the Crisis* (New York, 1926), p. 526.

nearer than you were." She left Alexandria thinking that she "may never expect to see" her parents again and instead only hoped that "in the good Providence of God I hope that we will meet to part no more."[46] It is not difficult to imagine Adam's distress that he could not meet her expectations during her crisis. The family had not learned of the sale until its completion but pledged to reunite with her. They brought Sarah Maranda home after the end of the Civil War in October 1866.[47]

The cities provided families like the Plummers a means of keeping in touch. The visits to the urban markets and nearby kin hardly compensated for a broken household. Yet enslaved people valued the ability to meet and greet their families and friends at the market, in the yards, at churches, and inside the homes with relatively little interference from their owners. These seemingly casual contacts could have great significance to enslaved people isolated in the countryside. Emily Plummer longed for Paul's letters, not just for news about him but also for news about her sons, daughters, and mother. The community recognized this role and embraced the enslaved from the countryside: men who visited the markets, the teenagers hired out to work as domestics, and those women who ultimately settled into service within an urban household. Altogether, they helped sustain the independent households, neighborhoods, and churches formed by free black and enslaved people.

The niches provided by the cities allowed the enslaved people of the region to maintain their family ties. Frederick Douglass was not necessarily ignoring the fractured family ties of the urban enslaved people when he claimed that one was "almost a free man" in the cities. They used their privileges primarily to enhance their family relationships, even though some family members lived as much as fifteen or twenty miles away. The urban enslaved used their relative autonomy primarily to pursue their own relationships. Contrary to Richard Wade's characterization, the urban enslaved developed strong commitments and long-lasting bonds to their family members, even though their household arrangements severely diminished their ability to provide food, shelter, and medical care to each other. When compared to others, whose owners likewise separated families, the enslaved of Washington and Georgetown sustained their families.

---

[46]Sarah Maranda Plummer to Emily Plummer, May 24, 1861, Woodson, *The Mind of the Negro*, pp. 527–28.

[47]In addition to the letters collected by Carter Woodson, see Nellie Arnold Plummer, *Out of the Depths or the Triumph of the Cross* (New York, 1997), esp. pp. 88–101.

Mary K. Ricks

The 1848 *Pearl* Escape from Washington, D.C.

A Convergence of Opportunity, Motivation,
and Political Action in the Nation's Capital

A N AUDACIOUS ESCAPE attempt on the Underground Railroad, involving nearly eighty fugitives on a fifty-four-ton schooner named the
Pearl, occurred in the unlikeliest of places—the nation's capital, with its almost nonexistent agricultural base. But it was the only city in slave territory
where such an ambitious event could have been organized, and it had greater
purpose than moving slaves north to freedom. Although the schooner was
captured and the fugitives returned to Washington, the failed escape became
a significant part of the ongoing debate over slavery.

The Escape

On the evening of April 15, 1848, the fugitives made their way through the
streets of Washington to board a hired schooner from Philadelphia named
the *Pearl*.[1] Among them were teenaged sisters Mary and Emily Edmonson and
their four older brothers, whose family's story is well documented. Harriet
Beecher Stowe, who later sponsored the sisters' schooling at Oberlin College,
wrote a chapter devoted to the Edmonsons and the escape attempt in her

---

[1]This chapter is adapted from Mary Kay Ricks, *Escape on the Pearl: The Heroic Bid for Freedom on the Underground Railroad* (New York, 2007), which details the planning, execution, and
aftermath of the attempted escape on the schooner *Pearl* in 1848.

1853 nonfiction book, the *Key to Uncle Tom's Cabin.* John Paynter, an Edmonson family descendant and graduate of Lincoln University (AB 1883, Hon. D.Litt. 1941), provided an extensively detailed account of the family's role in the escape. Paynter interviewed his great-uncle and *Pearl* fugitive, Samuel Edmonson, for a 1916 article, "The Fugitives of the *Pearl*," published in the first issue of Carter G. Woodson's *Journal of Negro History.* In 1930 Paynter wrote an expanded and partly fictionalized book of the same title.[2] Although both of his works are missing a number of important facts, most noticeably the pivotal role played by northern antislavery activist William Chaplin, an impressive amount of Paynter's story has been corroborated.

The six Edmonson siblings were enslaved because their mother was a slave. The law was clear at that time in all slave jurisdictions: a child's legal status flowed directly from the mother. It made no difference that their father was a free man who owned a forty-acre farm in Montgomery County, Maryland, a significant accomplishment when the small number of free black landowners possessed closer to a quarter acre in that area.[3]

The Edmonson offspring were hired out to work for prominent Washingtonians: Mary and Emily were placed in elegant homes and treated well, Richard was the coach driver for James Polk's secretary of the Treasury, and Samuel poured the wine and set the table for Joseph Bradley, Washington's most respected lawyer.

Other fugitives were owned by a disparate array of owners that included a grocer, a shoe manufacturer, the U.S. marshal for the District of Columbia, at least two physicians, a Baptist minister, a former U.S. congressman, and Dolley Madison, the much loved former first lady.[4]

The schooner, co-captained by Daniel Drayton and Edward Sayres, had arrived two days earlier at the busy main Seventh Street wharf in Washington and unloaded a cargo of wood purchased with money provided by Professor Charles Cleveland, the head of the Philadelphia Antislavery Society.[5] The wood not only camouflaged the schooner's purpose in Washington

---

[2] John H. Paynter, "The Fugitives of the *Pearl*," *Journal of Negro History* 1 (1916):243–64; Paynter, *Fugitives of the Pearl* (Washington, D.C., 1930). Because the 1916 article was largely incorporated into the 1930 book, all further references are to the book.

[3] Montgomery County Land Records, BS 7, 1935, 414–415, and STS 3, 1947, 198–200.

[4] *Drayton v. U.S.*, Trial Records of the U.S. District Court for the District of Columbia, 1838–61, RG 221, National Archives, Washington, D.C.

[5] Charles Cleveland to Wendell Phillips, Francis Jackson, and Lysander Spooner, Feb. 18, 1854, Spooner Papers, New-York Historical Society.

but also would be sold and the proceeds used to purchase supplies for the journey.

It was not the first time Cleveland had given Captain Drayton money to aid a slave escape from Washington. The summer before, Drayton was hired to transport an enslaved woman and several members of her family to Philadelphia. Drayton stated in his autobiography, written six years later with Richard Hildreth, the Boston abolitionist who assisted at his trial, that he had been approached by an unnamed black man in Washington who told him that the woman's free husband would pay him for the job. Drayton indicated that it was a chance encounter and all had gone well.[6]

In a letter Cleveland later wrote to prominent abolitionist Wendell Phillips, constitutional scholar Lysander Spooner, and attorney Richard Hildreth, he revealed his involvement in the earlier event. He reported that a financial dispute arose between Drayton and the escaping woman's husband that caused them to stall at the Frenchtown Landing at the top of the Chesapeake Bay in Maryland. The husband hurried to Cleveland's home in Philadelphia to get the money he needed to bring his family to freedom. After the family had been safely delivered, the husband returned to Cleveland's home with Drayton to resolve additional outstanding financial issues.[7]

In that same letter, Professor Cleveland reported that Drayton then came back alone to propose that the abolitionists purchase a ship which he could use in normal trade while at the same time assisting more families to escape, as the occasion would arise. A skeptical Cleveland dismissed his proposal but, with Drayton's urging, agreed to pass the idea on to others in the network.[8]

Six months later, in February of 1848, Cleveland was contacted by a "gentleman in Washington" who wrote that there were "two or three slave cases there of great distress—females who had for months been concealed by humane families to prevent them being sold; that it was exceedingly desirous that they should soon be got off."[9] He asked Cleveland to contact Drayton, or someone like him, indicating that he had either known of Drayton's proposal that abolitionists fund a vessel for him or knew him from the earlier escape from Washington.

---

[6]Daniel Drayton, *Personal Memoir of Daniel Drayton, for Four Years and Four Months a Prisoner (for Charity's Sake) in Washington Jail, Including a Narrative of the Voyage and Capture of the Schooner Pearl* (1854; reprint ed., New York, 1969), pp. 22–23.
[7]Cleveland to Phillips, Feb. 18, 1854.
[8]Ibid.
[9]Ibid.

Drayton made his way to Washington to "see what could be done" and agreed to take on the job.[10] He returned to Philadelphia and engaged Edward Sayres, the hired captain of the *Pearl*. The schooner's owner, Caleb Aaronson of New Jersey, would later issue a statement through his lawyer that he had known nothing of the illicit plan.[11]

For a fee of one hundred dollars, Sayres took on the dangerous job of carrying runaway slaves some one hundred miles down the Potomac River and then up the Chesapeake Bay to the same Frenchtown Landing in Maryland where Drayton had stopped in the previous escape.[12] There, "according to the arrangement with the friends of the passengers," they were to be met and carried to Philadelphia.[13]

The person from Washington who contacted Cleveland to solicit a ship was undoubtedly William L. Chaplin, the Harvard-trained lawyer, agent of the New York Anti-Slavery Society, and editor/correspondent for the *Albany Patriot*, the organ of the eight-year-old abolitionist Liberty party. In December 1844, Chaplin had arrived in Washington to join a residential interracial Underground Railroad cell that had been initiated by his colleague Charles Torrey in 1841. Both Torrey and Chaplin were strongly supported by the New York Anti-Slavery Society and closely linked to the Liberty party through the *Albany Patriot*.[14]

By 11 P.M. on the evening of the escape, after all the fugitives were loaded into the hold and the *Pearl* was ready to leave, the wind had completely died. After drifting less than a mile, the tide turned and they were forced to drop anchor to prevent the schooner from being pulled back up the river. The *Pearl* sat with slack sails until the sun began to rise and a small breeze finally picked up. The wind steadily increased and by afternoon the schooner was racing downriver.[15] If they continued at this speed, they would certainly be able to make the turn north into the Chesapeake Bay before anyone could reach them.

---

[10]Drayton, *Memoirs*, p. 24.

[11]*Baltimore Sun*, Apr. 24, 1848.

[12]Francis E. Newton, "Long Lost Frenchtown, Maryland: A Secret Station on the Underground Railroad," *Cecil Historical Journal* 4 (2004–5):2–5. Newton clearly establishes that the schooner's destination was Frenchtown, Maryland, and not Frenchtown, New Jersey, as had been previously believed.

[13]Drayton, *Memoirs*, p. 25

[14]Stanley Harrold, *Subversives: Antislavery Community in Washington, D.C., 1828–1865* (Baton Rouge, 2003), pp. 66, 70, 98–99.

[15]Drayton, *Memoirs*, p. 30.

Back in Washington that same Sunday morning, word spread quickly that a mass exodus or, depending on one's view, a grand theft had taken place. Residents were stunned at its scope. So unexpected was "this hegira of the servants," the *Georgetown Advocate* reported, "that one lady, on coming down to breakfast on Sunday morning, was surprised to find the fireplace cold and no breakfast prepared."[16] The *National Daily Intelligencer,* Washington's first newspaper, reported that "very great excitement has prevailed in the city and Georgetown, arising out of the fact that many citizens of the two places had been deprived of their servants, and its being ascertained that they had been taken on board a suspicious vessel which had brought wood to this city."[17]

A posse made up of a mix of Washington and Georgetown authorities, thrill seekers, and an owner with two slaves on the schooner quickly formed and learned that a small baycraft named the *Pearl* had unloaded a cargo of wood and then mysteriously disappeared without a word. According to John Paynter's account, the posse was tipped off by Judson Diggs, a free black man who reportedly attended Methodist prayer classes in the home of church leader John Brent, married to an older free Edmonson sister. Mt. Zion church records list several members of the Diggs family in Brent's Methodist class but not Judson Diggs.[18] While he may not have officially joined the class, he was widely known among the black community and likely spent time at the Brent home.

Francis Dodge, Jr., a member of a wealthy Georgetown shipping family and an owner of three women who had escaped from a slave trader, offered up his family's steamboat for the chase. Very early on Monday morning, the posse spotted the *Pearl* in a harbor at the mouth of the Potomac River where it had taken shelter from a fierce storm that blocked the small schooner from turning up into the Chesapeake Bay. Had the *Pearl* been able to make that turn as planned, it was unlikely that the posse would have pursued it; the steamboat was only insured to operate on the Potomac River.[19] The escape had come maddeningly close to succeeding, though word had gone out to authorities in Baltimore to look for the schooner.

---

[16] *Georgetown Advocate,* Apr. 19, 1848.

[17] *Washington National Daily Intelligencer,* Apr. 19, 1848.

[18] Paynter, *Fugitives,* pp. 69–74; Mt. Zion United Methodist Church Records, Washington, D.C.

[19] Drayton, *Memoir,* p. 31; *Drayton v. U.S.,* National Archives, Washington, D.C.

The *Pearl* was towed back to Washington and reached the jurisdictional waters of Washington, D.C., on Tuesday morning. A hostile crowd began gathering as the fugitives and the ship captains—the men tied together two by two, much like the slave coffles that were often led out of the city to walk to southern slave markets—were marched up to the D.C. jail located north of City Hall. The crowd escalated into a mob that swarmed the jail before moving on to the offices of the *National Era*, a moderate abolitionist newspaper purposefully located in Washington. Under the direction of Gamaliel Bailey, a Liberty party man who had once been the editor of the *Philanthropist*, an antislavery newspaper in Cincinnati, Ohio, the *Era* had been operating for eighteen months on Seventh Street, in an office across from the eastern facade of the Patent Office, today's Smithsonian Museum of American Art and the National Portrait Gallery.[20] Bailey became the focus of the crowd's wrath as they demanded that he remove his printing press from Washington. Gamaliel Bailey steadfastly refused to shut down his newspaper.[21]

It took three days, and support from President Polk, for the Washington authorities to bring the mob under control. While the president made clear in his diary that he had nothing but sympathy for the owners who had nearly lost extremely valuable property on an Underground Railroad escape, he also knew that riots in the streets of Washington would do his administration no good.[22] City officials agreed and deputized help for the small number of law enforcement officers in the city. The mob was met with one of the largest nonmilitary forces that had ever gathered in Washington, and the *Era* continued publishing without missing a scheduled issue of the weekly newspaper.[23]

The fugitives and the two ship captains fared less well. Notices in the local newspapers instructed owners to make their way to the jail to identify their property. Owners, slave traders, remnants from the mob of the night before, and the curious converged at the jail. So did antislavery Representative Joshua Giddings of Ohio; Edwin Hamlin, a former congressman and editor of the abolitionist *Daily True Democrat* newspaper published in Cleveland, Ohio; David Hall, a sympathetic local attorney from Vermont; and the bombastic and not very bright district attorney Phillip Barton Key, the son of Francis

[20]See Stanley Harrold, *Gamaliel Bailey and Antislavery Union* (Kent, Ohio, 1986).
[21]*New York Herald*, Apr. 21, 1848.
[22]James Polk, *The Diary of a President, 1845–1849* (New York, 1952), p. 320.
[23]*National Era* (Washington), Apr. 27 and May 4, 1848; *New York Herald*, Apr. 21, 1848.

Scott Key.[24] The unique positioning of the capital in a slave city had enabled both Giddings and Hamlin to play a direct role in the events that were swirling around the escape attempt. Giddings, anxious to assure the captain that they would not be abandoned, pushed through the crowd and persuaded the jailer to let him talk to the men.[25]

Hamlin reported the events at the jail for his newspaper, giving accounts both of the formal charges lodged against the captains and the identification of the fugitives by their owners. He said that a number of women had infant children in their arms, and they were asked the name of each child. One woman was asked how she could leave such a good home and replied, "I wanted liberty, wouldn't you, sir?" Another young woman turned to the ship captains, who had been formally arraigned in the same room and, while shaking each of their hands, said "God bless you sirs, you did all you could; it is not your fault that we are not free." Once they had identified their property, those few owners who decided not to sell their captured slaves took them home, while the rest began making arrangements to sell their property to the waiting slave traders.[26]

As the traders were negotiating deals with the owners of the fugitives at the D.C. jail, friends and family of some of the fugitives scrambled to raise money to purchase their loved ones. Members of the Edmonson family— there were four older free sisters in the city married to free men—pled with the man who represented the interests of their siblings' owner to allow them time to collect a sizable down payment toward their purchase. He grudgingly agreed, but when they returned to the jail the next day, Mary, Emily, and their four brothers were gone, sold to Joseph Bruin, a slave trader from Alexandria, Virginia.[27] When Bruin had assembled a sufficient number of slaves to make up a transport, he took them to Baltimore, where they were shipped to New Orleans on a brig named the *Union*, along with ten other fugitives from the *Pearl* and slaves belonging to other traders.[28]

William Chaplin temporarily left Washington after the fugitives were captured. In mid-May, he wrote a surprisingly candid column in the *Albany Patriot*,

[24]Drayton, *Memoirs*, pp. 45–46; *Daily True Democrat* (Cleveland), Apr. 25, 1848.

[25]*Daily True Democrat*, Apr. 25, 1848.

[26]Ibid.

[27]Harriet Beecher Stowe, *The Key to Uncle Tom's Cabin* (1853; reprint ed., Port Washington, N.Y., 1968), pp. 159–60.

[28]Slave Manifests, Baltimore to New Orleans, RG 36, National Archives, Washington, D.C.

over his own name, soliciting money to purchase some of the fugitives from the traders.[29] He profiled the Edmonsons and a number of other captured men and women and asked, "Are there not great hearts at the North, which will leap for joy to co-operate in the redemption of these brothers and sisters?[30] Apparently, there were not. The money raised could only free a small handful of the fugitives. John Jacob Astor sent the unusually generous donation of $900, over $20,000 in today's money, earmarked for the Edmonsons. But that was sufficient to purchase the freedom of only one of the Edmonson brothers; the asking price for attractive young women like Mary and Emily was closer to $1,200, a sum that eclipsed the value of their father's forty-acre farm. Richard Edmonson, with an ailing wife and children, was freed with that money.[31]

The three other brothers were sold in New Orleans, but Mary and Emily were returned to the Washington area when yellow fever broke out. The family and their supporters had another chance to free them. Washington's Underground Railroad cell worked closely with them and became deeply involved in a new plan to free the sisters. In a letter dated September 25, 1848, Chaplin wrote his colleagues in New York to suggest that they target the many churches of New York to help raise the money. He advised them to pursue the plan with "cool determination" and tell "every church and congregation" that two young Methodist girls are to be "sold for prostitution."[32] The Reverend Henry Ward Beecher led an ecumenical fund-raiser at the Broadway Tabernacle, which left people visibly shaken. They raised the bulk of the money needed to free the sisters that night, and Beecher later said that "of all the meetings I have attended in my life, for a panic of sympathy I never saw one that surpassed it."[33]

A few other fugitives were freed. Ellen Steward was purchased from the Baltimore slave trader to whom Dolley Madison had sold her. Another young woman, Grace Russell, was purchased by a mix of funds raised by her free relatives in New York City and antislavery activists.[34] Daniel Bell, a free black-

---

[29]*Albany Patriot* (New York), May 24, 1848

[30]Ibid.

[31]Stowe, *Key*, p. 160.

[32]*Anti-Slavery Bugle* (Salem, Ohio), Nov. 17, 1848.

[33]Ricks, *Escape on the Pearl*, pp. 185–87, 192–94; *Utica Liberty Press*, Nov. 30, 1848; (quotation) Paxton Hibben, *Henry Ward Beecher: An American Portrait* (1927; reprint ed., New York, 1942), p. 112.

[34]*North Star* (Rochester, N.Y.), Aug. 25, 1848.

smith with eleven family members on board, managed to borrow funds from a wealthy Washingtonian to purchase his wife and youngest child.[35] There simply was not enough money to free his whole family. At least one of his daughters was retained in the city by her owner and is listed in the U.S. Treasury's list of slaves freed by act of Congress in April 1862.[36] A son, Daniel Bell, Jr., ended up on a plantation in Natchitoches, Louisiana. The 1870 U.S. Census lists him living there with his wife and children, and probate documents show that after his father's death, his mother withdrew money from her husband's estate to send to him in Louisiana.[37]

Samuel Edmonson escaped from New Orleans and made his way to England and Australia with his wife before returning to Washington after the Civil War.[38] The U.S. Census of 1870 states that his eldest child was born in England and his two younger ones were born in Australia. In 1855 Ephraim Edmonson was purchased after money had been collected by his family, which included his sister Emily making a fund-raising trip to Rochester, New York.[39] There is no evidence that John Edmonson ever returned to Washington. A forty-five year-old man of that same name, described as a Maryland-born farmer, appears in the 1870 U.S. Census as a resident of Bellevue, Louisiana, in Bossier Parish. Little is known of the other fugitives sold south after their capture.

Washington's Underground Railroad Cell

It was rare for white northern abolitionists to enter into slave territory to aid slaves' escapes. Typically, it was only when fugitives managed to make their way into a free state that white activists in the Underground Railroad network stepped in to aid them in the still dangerous efforts to reach safer land farther north. It was extremely dangerous for easily identified white northerners to operate in slave territory, but such forays did occur, with at least one conductor, Seth Concklin, losing his life for his efforts.[40]

---

[35]Ricks, *Escape on the Pearl*, pp. 107–8.

[36]U.S. Treasury Secretary Salmon P. Chase, "Report of the Commissions on Emancipation in the District of Columbia," Jan. 14, 1863, National Archives, Washington, D.C.

[37]Probate Records of the Orphans Court of the District of Columbia Circuit Court, RG21, National Archives, Washington, D.C.

[38]Paynter, *Fugitives*, pp. 170–75.

[39]Frederick Douglass Papers, Jan. 4, 19, and 27, 1855.

[40]William Still, *Underground Railroad* (1871; reprint ed., Chicago 1970), pp. 1–17.

Most escapes took place in the Upper South, close to free states, but even there running away was difficult.[41] Most of the escapes that did occur were the work of blacks, with some aid from resident Quakers and a few other sympathetic whites in North Carolina, Maryland, Delaware, and other parts of the Upper South.[42] Harriet Tubman made her way back to Maryland, a territory she knew and where she could melt more easily into the background than a northerner could. Thomas Garrett, who worked with Tubman, operated almost openly in his home slave state of Delaware, enlisting help from black and white sympathizers around him. In the same year as the *Pearl* escape, however, he was fined $1,500 for helping six slaves escape, and his business suffered for it.[43]

But Washington was different. The nation's capital, in contrast to other cities in slave territory, by definition included northern legislators, journalists, federal clerks, and anyone with long-term interests in the federal government. Antislavery activists were able to more easily insinuate themselves into the city on a regular basis. When Charles Torrey, a Yale-educated minister turned passionate abolitionist, arrived in Washington in 1841 to participate in antislavery activities and also to report back to the *Tocsin of Liberty* (which later became the *Albany Patriot*), he soon formed a partnership with a free black man named Thomas Smallwood.[44] With the assistance of a small cadre of associates, including Smallwood's wife, Elizabeth, and Torrey's white landlady, the two men organized escapes of groups of fugitives led north by Smallwood, who took the partnership a step further; he too became a correspondent for the *Albany Patriot*. In November 1842, using the pseudonym of Samivel Weller, Jr., a name plucked from Charles Dickens's *Pickwick Papers*, Smallwood reported that they had assisted 150 fugitives in their escape from Washington.[45]

Underground Railroad activists in Washington were in touch, if not in league, with sympathetic members of Congress, including Representative

[41]John Hope Franklin and Loren Schweninger, *Runaway Slaves, Rebels on the Plantation* (New York, 1999), p. 116.

[42]See Fergus M. Bordewich, *Bound for Canaan, the Underground Railroad and the War for the Soul of America* (New York, 2005); Larry Gara, *the Liberty Line* (Lexington, Ky., 1967).

[43]Bordewich, *Bound for Canaan*, pp. 353–54.

[44]Harrold, *Subversives*, pp. 64–93; see, generally, C. J. Lovejoy, ed., *Memoir of Rev. Charles T. Torrey, Who Died in the Penitentiary of Maryland, Where He Was Confined for Showing Mercy to the Poor* (1847; reprint ed., New York, 1969); Thomas Smallwood, *A Narrative of Thomas Smallwood (Colored Man)* (Toronto, 1851).

[45]Harrold, *Subversives*, p. 82.

Giddings and Representative Seth Gates of New York, both of whom stayed at Mrs. Sprigg's boardinghouse—dubbed "Abolition House" for its like-minded residents.[46] In 1842, when Gates learned that John Douglass, one of the enslaved servants in the house hired out to Mrs. Sprigg by his owner, was about to be sold south, the congressman put him in touch with Torrey. Six years later, Gates wrote to Giddings to say that he had seen the fugitive in New York and had learned that Smallwood had taken him in a group of eighteen to make their way on foot to Philadelphia, where they were "boldly taken on board the [railroad] carrs [sic]" and delivered safely to Canada.[47]

When Smallwood came to believe that he was on the verge of being ex-posed, he left for Canada with his family. Torrey continued the operation but began to show signs of erratic behavior and a singular lack of judgment. With outstanding charges of aiding slave escapes against him in several ju-risdictions, he was captured by the Maryland authorities while attempting to negotiate the freedom of a slave from a Baltimore slave trader.[48]

As Torrey lay dying of tuberculosis in the Maryland penitentiary, William Chaplin arrived in Washington to take his place, both as journalist and Underground Railroad operative. The cell would continue. By 1848 Chaplin was in the epicenter of an expensive, bold, and dangerous plan to move an extraordinary number of fugitives out of Washington on a schooner.

Several letters strongly suggest that the financial backing for the *Pearl* escape and smaller ventures in Washington came from Gerrit Smith, the enormously wealthy abolitionist who was a leader both of the Liberty party and the New York Anti-Slavery Society, organizations of which Chaplin was also a part. Chaplin wrote to Smith on several occasions to detail the costs of purchasing the freedom of a number of people. He also kept him apprised of his dramatic escape plan with particular detail. On March 25, 1848, three weeks before the escape, he wrote to Smith to say that "there are not less than 75" enslaved Washingtonians who were ready to leave and that he was "expecting the arrival of a vessel from Philadelphia" that could hold fifty or more runaways.[49] What had been described as an escape for a small group of people in the initial contact with Professor Cleveland had, in the short

[46]Ibid., p. 66.

[47]Seth Gates to Joshua Giddings, Dec. 5, 1848, Joshua Giddings Papers, Ohio Historical Society.

[48]Harrold, *Subversives*, pp. 83–87.

[49]William Chaplin to Gerrit Smith, Mar. 25, 1848, Gerrit Smith Papers, Library of Congress, Washington, D.C.

period of a month, perhaps after the strategy meeting between Drayton and the Washington organizers, increased significantly, and certainly did so with Gerrit Smith's knowledge.

The second important factor that enabled the Underground Railroad cell in Washington to plan such a complicated escape was the organization's strong roots in the black community, particularly the links it had forged with the black churches in the city. Torrey and then Chaplin attended black churches in the city, one of the most important institutions in the black community. Churches, as well as other black organizations, sometimes became involved in raising money to help purchase loved ones who were about to be sold south.[50] Black codes proscribed all blacks, free or enslaved, from assembling in groups larger than seven without obtaining a permit, but church services and prayer groups were the few exceptions. Black ministers, exhorters, and preachers were powerful leaders, and though not all supported the illegal activities of the Underground Railroad, there is evidence that many did. When Mr. Cartwright, the "colored minister" from the Methodist congregation in Georgetown, traveled north to raise money to free two enslaved members of his family, he stayed at Torrey's home in Salem, Massachusetts.[51]

Prominent figures in the black clergy had connections with the cell. Daniel A. Payne, a leading minister with the African Methodist Episcopal churches, was associated with antislavery activists in Washington for two years during the 1840s. Presbyterian minister and teacher John F. Cook had long been active in community affairs. In 1833 he was the manager of a program "For the Benefit of a Young man, about to disenthrall himself from Slavery."[52] Forced to temporarily flee Washington after a proslavery riot burned his school for black children two years later, Cook taught in a school in Philadelphia and was well known in antislavery circles, both black and white.[53] He returned to continue his school.

Many of the fugitives had strong links with the churches. Two were listed as members of the Mt. Zion Methodist Church in Georgetown, the only black church with extant records of that time. Mary and Emily Edmonson's

[50]Letitia Woods Brown, *Free Negroes in the District of Columbia, 1790–1846* (New York, 1972), pp. 117–18.
[51]Lovejoy, *Torrey*, p. 90.
[52]Cook Family Papers, Moorland-Spingarn Research Center, Howard University.
[53]Ibid.

brother-in-law was a class leader for that church as well as an exhorter and, for a brief time, a preacher.[54] Other members of the Edmonson family, including Mary and Emily, worshiped at the Asbury Methodist Church in Washington.[55] Undoubtedly, fugitives of the *Pearl* attended a number of other churches in the city, but few records or other documents have been found with any details.

By 1848 the cell had reached the point where it could send word out to more than seventy-five people waiting to escape and even assist a number of them in reaching the schooner, which had been moved to a secluded spot to await their arrival.[56] There is one report that a black couple by the name of Bush helped lead people to the schooner. Lucinda Bush, a free woman of color, is reported to have gone to a number of homes in Washington "to retrieve the slaves under some ruse and to have taken them to the *Pearl.*"[57] She would have proved an invaluable operative. Not only were she and her free property-owning husband, William, well versed in the cautionary ways of the Underground Railroad in Washington, but Lucinda could easily pass for a white woman and move unquestioned through the streets of the city in the company of black people, who would be presumed to be her slaves. It is also quite likely that William Bush might have been the black man who approached Daniel Drayton to carry a woman and a few relatives to Philadelphia the summer before. Nine years later, William Bush would be the last friend to visit with Daniel Drayton before his suicide in New Bedford, Massachusetts, where the Bushes had moved shortly after the *Pearl* was captured.[58]

Other operatives were involved in the Underground Railroad cell that planned the escape, but only a few of their names are known. In Chaplin's March letter to Gerrit Smith, he reported that the Carters, a black couple, were hiding three women who had been sold to a slave trader by a wealthy Georgetown shipping merchant but had managed to escape.[59]

---

[54]Mt. Zion United Methodist Church Records.

[55]*Anti-Slavery Bugle,* Nov. 17, 1848, citing Oct. 5, 1848, letter of Reverend Mathew Turner, minister of Asbury Church.

[56]Drayton, *Memoirs,* p. 29.

[57]Kathryn Grover, *The Fugitive's Gibraltar: Escaping Slaves and Abolitionist in New Bedford* (Amherst, Mass., 2001), p. 192.

[58]Ibid., pp. 287–88; see also Brian Murphy, "A Martyr for Freedom: The Story of Daniel Drayton and the Schooner Pearl," MS in author's possession, pp. 44–46.

[59]Chaplin to Smith, Mar. 25, 1848.

Family historian Paynter states that three black men were central figures in the planning of the escape. One was Mary and Emily Edmonson's enslaved brother, Samuel, who carefully guided his two sisters to the schooner. Another was Daniel Bell, a free man, who delivered eleven members of his family to the *Pearl*. The Bell family had struggled to establish their freedom in the District of Columbia court and, fearing the imminent breakup of their family by the widow of the owner who had freed the mother and reduced the term of slavery for her children, turned to the Underground Railroad. At the trial of the two ship captains, defense attorney Horace Mann, the Massachusetts educator who had been elected to fill the congressional seat vacated by John Quincy Adams's death, Mann stated that Bell had organized the escape after his family had failed to win their freedom in court.[60]

The third man, Paul Jennings, had been brought to Washington years earlier as a slave of President James Madison.[61] Jennings had been sold by Dolley Madison the year before, after working for years to save enough money to purchase his own freedom. The balance of his purchase price was paid by Senator Daniel Webster, who then hired Jennings as his butler and deducted sums from his pay to repay that money.[62] Jennings may well have escorted a young woman named Mary Ellen Stewart to the *Pearl* that night. Stewart was owned by Dolley Madison, who had attempted to sell her to a slave trader waiting at a water pump in Lafayette Square. But Stewart had managed to escape and went into hiding. Jennings was certainly known to the Underground Railroad cell. A profile of the former White House slave had appeared in the *Albany Patriot* before the escape took place.[63]

There were others in the city with known connections to the Underground Railroad cell. Jacob Bigelow, a patent lawyer from Massachusetts who also filed reports of slavery to an abolitionist newspaper in Boston under a pseudonym, may have had a hand in planning the escape. He was involved in assisting the Edmonson family after the *Pearl* was captured and would become even more active in moving people to freedom in the North from the Wash-

---

[60]Paynter, *Fugitives*, pp. 20–29.

[61]Paul Jennings, "A Colored Man's Reminiscences of James Madison," and "Commentary: The Washington of Paul Jennings—White House Slave, Free Man, and Conspirator for Freedom," by G. Franklin Edwards and Michael R. Winston, *White House History Journal* 1 (1983):46–63.

[62]Signed Statement of Daniel Webster, Mar. 19, 1847, Moorland-Spingarn Research Center, Howard University.

[63]*Albany Patriot*, Mar. 15, 1848.

ington area in the following years.[64] Ezra L. Stevens, a correspondent for the *Daily True Democrat* and a clerk in the Bureau of Indian Affairs, wrote about events concerning the *Pearl* escape and became a supportive fixture on the network to freedom.[65]

This resident cell, composed of a few white northern antislavery activists well connected to networks in the North and free and enslaved Washington blacks, functioned from 1841 until slavery was abolished in the District of Columbia in the city in 1862. Without that Underground Railroad cell in situ, the escape on the *Pearl* would have been impossibly difficult to organize.

Motivation of the Fugitives

The attendant risks for such an unusual escape attempt raise the question of what motivated the fugitives, most of whom were living in what would be some of the least oppressive circumstances of slavery, to participate. They all knew that if the escape went wrong, most of them would be sold to a slave trader for the lucrative southern market. On their way to the schooner that April evening, many of the fugitives likely passed near William H. Williams's slave pen. It was Washington's most infamous slave pen at that time, located near where 7th Street crossed Maryland Avenue, just south and east of the construction site for the Smithsonian Institution on the National Mall. Its exterior differed little from the other houses around it, save for the high wall that rimmed its backyard, the fierce bark of his dogs, and the shackles and whips inside.[66]

Nearby, another pen was operated by Joseph Gannon, who was waiting outside his slave pen when the captured fugitives and the ship captains were marched up from the river to the jail. As they passed Gannon's establishment, the slave trader attempted to stab Daniel Drayton.[67] Other traders operated openly in Washington as well as in Baltimore and Alexandria. They

[64]Stowe, *Key*, p. 163; Harrold, *Subversives*, pp. 162, 167; Still, *Underground Railroad*, pp. 174–188; Hilary Russell, "Underground Railroad Activists in Washington, D.C.," *Washington History* 13 (2001–2):35.

[65]Harrold, *Subversives*, pp. 111, 132–33, 149.

[66]Solomon Northup, *Twelve Years a Slave*, ed. Sue Eakin and Joseph Logsdon (1852; reprint ed., Baton Rouge, 1968), pp. 21–29.

[67]Drayton, *Memoirs*, pp. 39–40; Paynter, *Fugitives*, pp. 109–110; Stowe, *Key*, p. 159.

often employed agents to prowl the countryside and smaller town to solicit sales. The threat of sale was widely known to all slaves.

The extent of this domestic slave trade had not been anticipated. The late eighteenth-century invention of the cotton gin redefined and expanded agriculture in the Lower South, while the 1808 federal ban on the trans-Atlantic slave trade forced planters to look elsewhere for plantation labor. They found it in the Upper South, where a decline in tobacco production had left slave owners with an excess of slaves whose value was rising with the new demand. Thus began an interstate slave trade that resulted in an astonishingly large forced migration from the Upper South, an area that included Maryland, Virginia, and the District of Columbia, in which some one million slaves were transferred to the Lower South. The majority were sold directly to slave traders, while the others were walked to the Lower South by owners who had purchased land for themselves. In either case, families were often split. Historian Robert H. Gudmestad states that "forcible separations destroyed about one-third of all first slave marriages in the Upper South, and cut the ties between spouse and spouse, between parent and child, between sibling and sibling, and between others in the kindred network."[68]

Slave traders in Washington stowed their purchases in public jails, privately owned slave pens, also known as "Negro jails," holding cells provided by small inns and hotels, and attics and basements of their own homes. They collected slaves until they had assembled a sufficient number to make the trek south, with the overland coffles usually consisting of thirty or forty people strung together by chains. However, a visiting Englishman reported seeing a three-hundred-person coffle making its way south from Alexandria, Virginia, where the Edmonsons were taken after their sale.[69] Coffles could be marched as far as Natchez, Mississippi, or across to Wheeling, Virginia, and then shipped down the river. Like the Edmonsons, a large number were shipped south. Washington area slave traders took their slaves to Alexandria and Baltimore for long-distance shipping.[70] Joseph Bruin of Alexandria used a partner in Baltimore but also took coffles overland.[71]

---

[68]Robert Gudmestad, *A Troublesome Commerce: The Transformation of the Interstate Slave Trade* (Baton Rouge, 2003), p. 8.

[69]Steven Deyle, *Carry Me Back: The Domestic Slave Trade in American Life* (New York, 2005), p. 146.

[70]See Ralph Clayton, *Cash for Blood, the Baltimore to New Orleans Domestic Slave Trade* (Bowie, Md., 2002).

[71]Ricks, *Escape on the Pearl*, pp. 87–90, 129–132, 137.

The slave pens were well known in the white community. Who could mistake their purpose when slave coffles were led out and through the streets of Washington on their way south and slave traders placed advertisements in the local papers?[72] And they were well known in the black community, where many found themselves suddenly separated from their families and sold. The trade was often described in the abolitionist newspapers and commented on by northern visitors and the diplomatic corps, who were shocked to view coffles in the nation's capital. And the slave pens were known in Congress, although a few proslavery senators claimed never to have seen them. In a speech attacking slavery in the late 1850s, Abraham Lincoln, who proposed a gradual end to slavery during his one term in Congress, which coincided with the time of the *Pearl* escape, remarked on what he had seen during that time. Very likely describing the Williams pen, he said that "a peculiar species of slave trade in the District of Columbia, in connection with which in full view from the windows of the capitol, a sort of negro-livery stable, where droves of negroes were collected, temporarily kept, and finally taken to Southern markets, precisely like droves of horses, had been openly maintained for fifty years."[73]

Occasionally, politicians became entangled with slave traders. Representative Joshua Giddings tried to help a hired slave, working in his boardinghouse, who had nearly finished buying his freedom when he was suddenly seized by armed agents of slave trader Williams because his owner had abruptly decided to sell him. Giddings took his objections inside the slave pen but left empty-handed, told that the seized man had already been sent to New Orleans. The congressman then turned for help to Duff Green, the proslavery owner of the building in which his boardinghouse was located. The kidnapped man was eventually found in Alexandria, where he was probably awaiting shipment, and a deal was worked out for his freedom.

While the fear of being sold theoretically hovered over all the fugitives on the *Pearl*, it was a concrete reality for Mary Ellen Stewart on Lafayette Square and the three women from Georgetown, who had already been sold and had escaped from slave traders. In the case of the Bell family, the mother had been freed and the children had had their term of slavery reduced by their dying owner in 1835. But his widow refused to recognize those manumissions

---

[72]See Mary Beth Corrigan, "Imaginary Cruelties? A History of the Slave Trade in Washington, D.C.," *Washington History* 13 (2001–2):5–27.

[73]*Abraham Lincoln: Speeches and Writings, 1832–1858* (New York, 1989), p. 313.

and had applied to the probate court to have the family's value appraised so that she could have them "divided" among her children. The Bells filed petitions for freedom in the District of Columbia court.[71] After several jury trials, all of which supported the widow's contention that the Bells were her slaves, the family turned to the Underground Railroad.

The Edmonsons may have believed that they were at risk for being sold. Their mentally deficient owner was aging, and, two years earlier, one of their owner's nephews sold his future share of the family to his brother.[75] They had already seen a loved one sold to a trader. Fifteen years earlier, Hamilton Edmonson, an older brother, was sold to a trader after an unsuccessful escape attempt. Caught before he left Maryland, his name was logged into the runaway slave ledger at the Baltimore jail on July 1, 1833.

The constant threat of sale due to an owner's death, debts, or need for quick cash hung over the entire black community—the enslaved and those intermarried and close to them. It could propel slaves to leave an area where generations of their family may have lived to face a new life in the North, where they had few contacts or support. Many families, like the Edmonsons and Bells, were an amalgam of free and black. In the District of Columbia, the free black population had increased dramatically since the capital's formation, due in part to the city's relative attractiveness for free blacks in Virginia and Maryland. Work was available in the growing capital, there were no legal prohibitions against schools for free black children, and black churches had been established as early as 1816. By 1830 free blacks slightly outnumbered the enslaved. By 1850 nearly three times as many free blacks as enslaved were living in the nation's capital.[76] Although we have no records from which to extrapolate exact numbers, those population figures also represent the fact that the number of slaves was reduced because they were sold, not because they were freed. While many owners were pleased both with the profits these sales brought and the increase in field hands it brought to plantations in the Lower South, others could foresee a coming political problem in this mass transfer of slaves. A number of southern newspapers lamented that if the Upper South sold off all of its slaves, its interests would no longer be allied with the slave states.[77]

---

[71]*Mary Bell v. Susan Armistead and Eleanor Bell by William Simms, her next friend, v. Susan Armistead*, Trial Records of the United States District Court for the District of Columbia, 1838–1861, RG 61, National Archives, Washington, D.C.

[75]Montgomery County Land Records, STS 1, 544–45, Montgomery County Courthouse, Rockville, Md.

[76]Brown, *Free Negroes*, p. 11.

[77]Deyle, *Carry Me Back*, p. 74.

There is one other factor that might have played a role in the fugitives' willingness to take a chance on a schooner. It afforded an opportunity for families to take their children on a journey that would be very difficult for them otherwise.

Political Implications of the Escape

The enormity of the escape strongly suggests that it had evolved into a grand political gesture designed to reinvigorate national and international outrage to the presence of slavery and the slave trade in the capital. Such an audacious event should have attracted attention whether it succeeded or failed.

It also reflects the frustration felt by antislavery activists who had been unable to win support to end slavery in the District of Columbia. In the 1830s, when a more sharply focused and more militant phase of antislavery activity had risen, a campaign to end slavery in the District of Columbia became a major focus of abolitionists. Local antislavery societies that were springing up across the North exercised their constitutional right to petition the federal government to end slavery and the slave trade in the District of Columbia. Since the capital fell solely under federal jurisdiction, the argument that slavery came under the sole jurisdiction of the states, as most northerners conceded, was irrelevant.

But the new antislavery passion was met in kind by a growing militancy of the southern legislators' opposition to losing any ground on slavery. Their outrage over the petition campaign and the abolitionists' increasing attacks on the immorality of slavery resulted in the passage of a gag rule that banned all slavery-related petitions.[78] It could not have passed, and have lasted for eight years, without the support of a large number of northern congressmen. The campaign to end slavery in the capital found few converts in Washington and soon lost steam.

Even though the gag rule had been removed by 1848, there was still resistance in Congress to any discussion of ending slavery or the slave trade in the federal enclave. But on the Tuesday that the *Pearl* arrived back in Washington, a remarkable political debate ensued. Representative Joshua Giddings of Ohio asked leave to introduce a resolution on the captured fugitives, to which several southern congressmen objected.[79] Three years earlier, Giddings

---

[78]See William Lee Miller, *Arguing about Slavery: The Great Battle in the United States Congress* (New York, 1996).

[79]*Congressional Globe*, 30th Cong., 1st sess., 1848, p. 641.

had already been accused of being involved in the Underground Railroad by Representative Junius Black of Georgia, who accused him of working directly with Charles Torrey in organizing slave escapes from Washington. There is no evidence that he did. However, he did know where to direct people who came to him looking for help. Not long before the *Pearl* escape, a correspondent for the *Daily True Democrat* reported that he was in Giddings's room when several free men of color arrived separately to ask the congressman to help save loved ones from being sold south.[80] It is doubtful that Giddings had been actively involved in planning the escape on the *Pearl*, but he may very well have helped to increase the number of passengers awaiting a vessel from Philadelphia by sending those men to the people who could help them.

Giddings was finally allowed to read his resolution, which stated in part: "Whereas, more than eighty men, women and children are said to be now confined in the prison . . . without being charged with a crime," Congress should appoint a select committee to investigate these circumstances. In particular, Giddings wanted the committee to examine why a prison that was erected and sustained by federal funds—generated from free as well as slave states—was being used to contain slaves. He added that these fugitives were doing no more than attempting "to enjoy that liberty for which our fathers encountered toil, suffering, and death itself."[81]

Southern congressmen were enraged, and Isaac Holmes of South Carolina moved to amend the resolution by adding an inquiry to ask "whether the scoundrels who caused them to be there ought not to be hung." The resolution was rejected but the debate had only just begun.[82]

In the following days, John Palfrey of Massachusetts pursued the question of whether Joshua Giddings's right of privilege as a U.S. congressman had been violated by the physical threats hurled against him by rioters. Robert Toombs of Georgia, one of two southern politicians whose slaves would be captured while escaping with William Chaplin two years later, charged that Giddings was clearly trying to protect himself from prosecution for aiding the illegal escape, and William T. Haskell of Tennessee proposed an investigation to determine if antislavery members of the house had been involved. Haskell claimed that the abolitionists, unable to convince Congress to pass

---

[80]*Daily True Democrat,* Jan. 24, 1848.
[81]*Congressional Globe,* 30th Cong., 1st sess., 1848, p. 641.
[82]Ibid.

legislation to end slavery in the District of Columbia, were now undermining slavery by conspiring with slaves to run away from their masters. He was right.

With the attack on the *National Era* clearly in mind, Senator John Hale of New Hampshire proposed a law that would hold the city of Washington responsible for any damages to property caused by mob attacks. A furious Senator John C. Calhoun of South Carolina, a leading southern voice and former vice president of the country, rose to say, "there is but one question that can destroy this Union and our institutions, and that is this very slave question." Calhoun condemned any bill that would thwart the "just indignation of our people from wreaking their vengeance" on the perpetrators of the attempted slave escape. Proslavery congressmen had been put in the position of defending a mob's rampant disregard for law while at the same time defending the rights of slave owners based on the letter of the law.

Kicking off the campaign for a more forceful federal fugitive slave act, Calhoun warned the Senate that the country was approaching a crisis. He suggested passing new laws that would "prevent these atrocities—these piratical attempts on our own rivers . . . these robberies of seventy odd of our slaves at a single grasp." Calhoun defended the "great" institution of slavery, "upon which not only [the South's] prosperity, but its very existence depends."[83]

Senator Jefferson Davis suggested that a federal law was needed to punish anyone who would come into the District of Columbia "to steal a portion of that property which is recognized as such by the Constitution of the United States."[84]

But it was left to Senator Foote of Mississippi to propose a lynching. After accusing Hale of direct involvement in a "covert and insidious" attempt to discourage anyone from holding slaves in the District of Columbia, Foote encouraged Hale to come to Mississippi, where his body would "grace one of the tallest trees of the forest," and assured him he would join in the effort along with the patriotic citizens of his state.[85]

An abolitionist newspaper in Utica, New York, remarked that before the escape "the District was forgotten" and the old agitation of years before, when slavery in the nation's capital was "the battleground," had died away.[86]

---

[83]Ibid., pp. 501–2.
[84]Ibid.
[85]Ibid., p. 653.
[86]*Utica Liberty Press,* May 4, 1848.

It concluded that the extensive debate generated by the attempted escape on the *Pearl* has again riveted attention "upon slavery in the ten-mile square."

There was another incident, wholly unanticipated, that brought the horrors of the slave trade in Washington to national attention. After the majority of the *Pearl* fugitives were purchased by Baltimore slave trader Hope Slatter, he put iron shackles on the men and the older boys and assembled them in a line with the unfettered women carrying the younger children and the older ones walking with them. Slatter marched them about three blocks to the railroad depot adjacent to the grounds of the U.S. Capitol. At the depot, Slatter loaded the fugitives into a railroad car to wait for the journey to his slave pen in Baltimore to begin.

A small crowd gathered around the waiting railroad car. Observers, including several of Washington's antislavery journalists, watched as family and friends of the passengers surrounded the car to say sorrowful good-byes to loved ones they knew they would likely never see or touch again. John I. Slingerland, serving a first term as member of Congress from Albany, New York, arrived on the scene and witnessed the harrowing picture of misery and grief under the shadow of the U.S. Capitol.

In a letter written for an Albany, New York, newspaper, which Underground Railroad operative and journalist Ezra Stevens published in virtually the same form under his own name in the *Daily True Democrat*, Slingerland reported that he watched visibly upset people of color struggling to say good-bye to their loved ones and quickly realized that most of the people inside the car were fugitives from the *Pearl*.[87]

While they waited for the train to leave Washington, Henry Slicer, the chaplain of the U.S. Senate, happened on the site. The well-known Methodist minister entered the railroad car and, as Slingerland and others watched, offered his hand to Hope Slatter and chatted with the slave trader. Slingerland accused Slicer of appearing "to view the heart-rending scene before him with as little concern as we should look upon cattle."[88]

That letter was printed in a number of newspapers in the North, and the horror of the slave trade in the shadow of the U.S. Capitol left its mark both locally and nationally. In December 1848 the *Georgetown Advocate* stated that "if the public would make provision to purchase out the slaves now held in

---

[87]Letter published in *Albany Evening Journal*, reprinted in *Albany Patriot*, May 3, 1848.
[88]Ibid.

the District, compensating the owners of them therefore, we do not suppose that the slaveholders of the District would have any serious objection. . . . From the increasing insecurity, and the unsatisfactoriness of this kind of property, the pecuniary advantage of slave owners would probably be promoted by such a course."[89]

But any change in the status of slavery in the District of Columbia would have to be passed by Congress, and the opposition to any kind of federally sponsored emancipation was still very strong, strong enough that antislavery legislators decided to focus solely on ending the slave trade. In December 1848, about the same time the *Georgetown Advocate* article appeared, Representative Daniel Gott of New York offered a resolution asking the Committee for the District of Columbia to report a bill prohibiting the slave trade in the district. In that same month, the Reverend Henry Ward Beecher wrote in the *Independent,* a new religious antislavery newspaper published in New York, that "recent events, especially those connected with the affair of the sale and redemption of . . . the Edmonson family, have greatly aroused the public mind with regard to the atrocities of the trade in human beings, now greatly carried on at Washington City."[90]

In response to Gott's resolution, a southern congressman moved that it be laid on the table to end any further discussion. During the lengthy and contentious discussion that followed, Abraham Lincoln proposed that the resolution be amended to instruct the Committee on the District of Columbia to include a provision to gradually free the slaves in the capital and to compensate their owners from federal funds. Lincoln added that he had already submitted his proposal to a number of leading citizens in the city, one of whom was quite likely the editor of the *Georgetown Advocate,* and they all supported it. Lincoln's proposal quickly sank with little discussion. Southern politicians had no interest in such a proposal; nor did most abolitionists, who rejected any proposal that called for a gradual program of emancipation. In the end, the resolution addressed only the slave trade and, to the shock of southern legislators, the motion to suppress the resolution failed.[91] The Committee on the District of Columbia was instructed to prepare a bill to end the slave trade in the capital.

[89] *Georgetown Advocate,* Dec. 30, 1848.
[90] *Independent* (New York), Dec. 7, 1848.
[91] *Congressional Globe,* 30th Cong., 2d sess., 1849, pp. 210–16.

The recent coverage of the *Pearl* fugitives being paraded through the streets of the District of Columbia to be jailed and then sold to traders, the proslavery riot, the attack on the *National Era*, and the widely circulated story about the railroad car of fugitives waiting to be transported to Hope Slatter's slave pen in Baltimore appears to have contributed to a change of heart in a number of congressmen. For the first time, a growing number of once reluctant northern congressmen had finally found the backbone to stand up to the proslavery forces. On December 30, the *Pittsburgh Commercial Journal* reported that "the first practical step on the part of the North, has therefore been taken."

A month later, the bill to end the slave trade in the capital was introduced in the House, but it failed to pass. However, antislavery forces continued to push for its passage while tensions over the extension of slavery into the new western territories increased. A similar bill became a part of the Compromise of 1850, designed to resolve those sectional tensions over slavery. But so did a new Fugitive Slave Act that would dramatically strengthen federal support to retrieve runaways from the North and return them to their owners.

The slave pens in the nation's capital closed. Residents and visitors would not have to view slave coffles walking through the city on their way south. But the traders simply moved their operations to Maryland or Virginia. Slave owners in the District of Columbia could still sell their own slaves in the District of Columbia, and the federally appointed U.S. Marshal could still publicly sell slaves in the capital to satisfy legal judgments.

But it was the first time that any kind of limitation on slavery in the District of Columbia had succeeded, and antislavery activists, both in and out of Congress, expected to follow that Pyrrhic victory with a bill to bring slavery itself to an end in the capital. The Compromise of 1850, however, failed to resolve the tension over slavery and the volatile and deeply polarizing struggle over whether slavery could be extended to federal territories overshadowed the issue of slavery in the capital. The abolition of slavery would have to wait until the outbreak of the Civil War. When the confederate legislators left the city, there were finally enough votes to pass a bill compensating slave owners for the loss of their "property." The slaves received no compensation.

THE *PEARL* MAY not have succeeded in its goal of moving nearly eighty enslaved African Americans out of bondage; but the escape, and the events that surrounded it, did shine a brighter light on slavery in the District of

Columbia. Just as it led to more antislavery votes in Congress in the push to end the slave trade in Washington, it may have influenced more people in the North to reject the expansion of slavery in the new western lands.

Ironically, the passage of the Fugitive Slave Act, which the South wanted in part due to its reaction to the *Pearl* affair, may have furthered the antislavery cause. Some have argued that the draconian new law created new abolitionists in higher numbers than the slaves it returned to the South.

The attempted escape in Washington did one other thing. It generated an unusual amount of documentation on the workings of the Underground Railroad and the political campaign to end slavery in the capital. In addition to the Paynter accounts of his family's involvement and the chapter in Stowe's *Key to Uncle Tom's Cabin*, Daniel Drayton, with the assistance of one of the lawyers on his defense team, published his memoirs in 1854, which carefully charted his role in the escape without naming any of the Washington operatives. Both antislavery and proslavery newspapers recorded the events surrounding the escape, the campaign to free Mary and Emily Edmonson, Drayton and Sayres's trial and conviction, and their eventual presidential pardon, orchestrated by Senator Charles Sumner. Letters written by Drayton, Professor Cleveland, and William Chaplin reveal much of the planning and involvement of northern abolitionists in the escape. The trials of the two ship captains left court records that detailed the capture of the *Pearl*. It is a surprisingly rich legacy that fleshes out the details of an almost forgotten chapter of American history.

Mitch Kachun

Celebrating Emancipation and Contesting Freedom in Washington, D.C.

WASHINGTON, D.C., CAN CLAIM a venerable and illustrious association with African American history. The site of the future capital contained a population of enslaved and free blacks even before the city existed. Free African American mathematician, astronomer, and almanac author Benjamin Banneker assisted in laying out Pierre Charles L'Enfant's distinctive grid for the city. And, as other essays in this volume remind us, the labor of enslaved blacks was instrumental in constructing not only the major governmental buildings but also much of the city that grew around the seat of government. The second U.S. Census in 1800 shows that the district as a whole included 3,244 slaves and 783 free blacks among its 14,093 inhabitants.[1] Over the first half of the nineteenth century, free black Washingtonians established churches, schools, fraternal orders, literary societies, and other institutions to foster a degree of solidarity and stability in a federal district that remained firmly committed to the continuation of racial slavery.

In fact, Washington and Alexandria quickly became major centers for the purchase of slaves intended for the lucrative markets of the Deep South, where demand for bonded labor in the expanding Cotton Kingdom increased dramatically in the first decades of the century. The 1808 abolition of the Atlantic slave trade made the Upper South an even more important

---

[1] Constance McLaughlin Green, *The Secret City: A History of Race Relations in the Nation's Capital* (Princeton, N.J., 1967), p. 33.

source for laborers bound for the cotton states and territories. In this context, it should not be surprising that an 1805 resolution to emancipate all district slaves when they reached the age of twenty-five went down to defeat.[2]

Life for those already free was constrained by legal proscriptions that limited their mobility and their pursuit of social, intellectual, and economic advancement. Still, the district's free black population grew dramatically during the first half of the century. By 1850 the original 783 free blacks had grown to over 10,000—about 20 percent of the city's total population. The slave population, which had exceeded 6,000 during the 1820s, had declined by 1850 to 3,687—only a few hundred more than in 1800.[3] Despite this apparent decline in reliance on slave labor, on the whole Washington remained a staunchly proslavery city.

As historian Stanley Harrold has observed, however, Washington also saw a steady increase in black and white cooperation in the antebellum abolitionist movement. These "subversives" aided fugitives, lobbied the government, published newspapers, and otherwise worked to move both government policy and public opinion in an antislavery direction.[4] By midcentury, the annexation of Texas and the acquisition of immense western territories through the war with Mexico had thrust sectional disputes over slavery to the forefront of national affairs. In Washington the 1848 *Pearl* incident and other local events added to the general agitation surrounding slavery and abolitionism. Congress attempted to alleviate sectional tensions with the Compromise of 1850, an omnibus bill offering specific actions that would mollify the contending factions and thereby avert a national crisis.

Two components of the compromise pertained specifically to the lands ceded by Mexico at the 1848 Treaty of Guadalupe Hidalgo: proslavery proponents welcomed the possibility that slavery might take root in the New Mexico territory, while antislavery forces applauded the admission of California as a free state. The other two provisions of the measure had a far more direct bearing on life in Washington. The increasing—and, judging by the *Pearl* incident, increasingly bold—efforts of abolitionists to move fugitive slaves northward served to legitimize southern calls for a stronger fugitive slave law that would impede flight and facilitate the recapture of fugitives. At the same

---

[2]Green, *Secret City*, pp. 19–21; Stanley Harrold, *Subversives: Washington, D.C., 1828–1865* (Baton Rouge, 2003), p. 30.

[3]Green, *Secret City*, p. 33.

[4]Harrold, *Subversives.*

time, antislavery advocates continued to be appalled by the sight of slave pens, slave coffles, and slave auctions in the nation's capital—practices that were on the rise as slaveholders sold slaves into the Deep South rather than see them join the steady stream fleeing northward. The compromise's provisions for a strong fugitive slave law and the abolition of the slave trade in the federal district were intended to appease each side.[5]

One might expect that the slave trade ban would occasion great celebrations among abolitionists. After all, the first public commemorations organized among free blacks in the North were held in observance of the 1808 abolition of the transatlantic slave trade. From the date the act went into effect, on January 1, 1808, until the end of the 1820s, free blacks in several northern cities held annual public commemorations celebrating what they saw as an important step toward the destruction of slavery and the recognition of the rights of black Americans as free people and as American citizens. These slave trade celebrations initiated a tradition of African American public commemoration that would serve as the foundation for black commemorative traditions into the twentieth century. The slave trade celebrations ended by the late 1820s for a variety of reasons: slave-traders' blatant disregard for the law in the continued importation of Africans; the burgeoning domestic trade that intensified with the growth of the southern Cotton Kingdom in the 1820s; the failure of civic authorities to protect black celebrants from white harassment and violence; and the absence of any indication that American government or society was about to act more forcefully against slavery.

While celebrations of the transatlantic slave trade did not continue past 1830, antebellum abolitionists continued their public commemoration of the expansion of freedom, most conspicuously through annual commemorations of Great Britain's abolition of slavery in its West Indian colonies, which went into effect on August 1, 1834. By 1850 a vibrant commemorative tradition centered on First of August observances of West Indian emancipation had taken shape throughout the free states, and these celebrations became important institutions in African American political culture. Hundreds of large, biracial events were held in northern communities large and small during the antebellum decades, establishing a black presence in an expanding public sphere, articulating positive interpretations of black history and

---

[5]National Archives and Records Administration (NARA), "Transcript of Compromise of 1850," *100 Milestone Documents*. http://www.ourdocuments.gov/doc.php?flash=true&doc=27 &page=transcript.

heritage, creating a sense of cultural identity and group solidarity, and establishing emancipation celebrations as important annual opportunities for black Americans to gather together for social conviviality and to mobilize for political activism.[6]

However, the abolition of the slave trade in the District of Columbia did *not* inspire any great rejoicing or public commemoration, either at the time of its passage or thereafter. In fact, the act was very limited in its effect and aroused only cautious optimism among abolitionists. Not only did the act disregard the ultimate objective of Washington's activists—the abolition of slavery in the district—neither did it completely eliminate the *trade* in human flesh. Indicating only that "it shall not be lawful to *bring into* the District of Columbia any slave" for the purpose of sale, it permitted the continued buying and selling of the thousands of slaves living in the district, including the sale of slaves to be sent further south.[7] Washington abolitionist Gamaliel Bailey's weekly newspaper, the *National Era,* initially seemed encouraged by the slave trade ban, which gave the editor cause to "look forward to the time, not far distant, when the soil of the District shall be consecrated entirely to Free Labor."[8] But in October 1851 Frederick Douglass publicized a district clergyman's sale of a "young woman" who "was carried off to the South in a gang or coffle last week," even though "the slave trade at Washington [had been] abolished by the 'compromise.'"[9] In February 1853 Bailey confirmed for his readers that, indeed, "a slaveholder here may put up his slaves at auction, and a negro trader may buy them and carry them out of the district, without violating any law, except the 'Higher Law,' which is not much in vogue where Congress sits." Still, two weeks later, he contended that the compromise had succeeded "in rescuing the city from the disgrace of being a mart for slaves. More will yet be gained: let us be patient and hopeful."[10] While counseling patience and expressing hope, Bailey surely recognized that public slave auctions still were held in Washington, and even the interstate traffic that had been removed from the city still thrived just across the river in Alexandria, Virginia.[11]

[6]On the development of early national and antebellum African American commemorative traditions, see Mitch Kachun, *Festivals of Freedom: Memory and Meaning in African American Emancipation Celebrations, 1808–1915* (Amherst, Mass., 2003), esp. chaps. 1 and 2.

[7]NARA, "Transcript of Compromise of 1850" (emphasis added).

[8]*National Era* (Washington, D.C.), Oct. 3, 1850.

[9]*Frederick Douglass' Paper* (Rochester, N.Y.), Oct. 2, 1851.

[10]*National Era,* Feb. 3, 17, 1853.

[11]Harrold, *Subversives,* pp. 164–66.

Of course, the fugitive slave law was the one component of the compromise that attracted the most attention from abolitionists, and that ultimately played the greatest role in moving the nation toward civil war. But as they and their counterparts elsewhere did their utmost to hinder the new law's implementation, Washington's abolitionists did not give up their goals of ending slavery, either in the district or in the nation as a whole. In 1861, when southern congressional representatives and senators left Washington upon their states' secession, the remaining antislavery majority recognized an opportunity to act against slavery where they could. On April 10, 1862, Congress passed a law stating "that the United States ought to cooperate with any State which may adopt gradual abolishment of slavery, giving to such State pecuniary aid, to be used by such State in its discretion, to compensate for the inconveniences, public and private, produced by such change of system."[12] They could act more decisively in those areas over which Congress had direct jurisdiction: in the territories and in the federal district. On April 16, 1862, Abraham Lincoln signed the congressional bill abolishing slavery in the District of Columbia, and in June of that year Congress prohibited the existence of slavery in any of the nation's existing or future territories.[13]

In one sense, district emancipation fulfilled a goal that had been pursued by antislavery Washingtonians since the city's founding (recall the failed emancipation bill of 1805). But the act's emancipatory impact was tempered by provisions dictating the compensation of slaveholders and encouraging the freedpeople to emigrate out of the country. Slaveholders who demonstrated their loyalty to the United States would be paid $300 for each freed slave, and freedpeople choosing to emigrate would be paid up to $100 each. By early 1863 approximately 3,100 slaves had gained their freedom, at a cost to the government of nearly $1 million.[14]

Despite the act's concessions to slaveholding interests and its encouragement of colonization, black Washingtonians reacted enthusiastically. One resident wrote to a friend in Baltimore, describing the extent of the "rejoic-

---

[12]Freedmen and Southern Society Project, "Chronology of Slavery during the Civil War," http://www.history.umd.edu/Freedmen/jtres.htm.

[13]NARA, "Transcription: An Act for the Release of Certain Persons Held to Service or Labor in the District of Columbia," http://www.archives.gov/exhibits/featured_documents/dc_emancipation_act/transcription.html.

[14]NARA, "Featured Documents: The District of Columbia Emancipation Act," http://www.archives.gov/exhibits/featured_documents/dc_emancipation_act/.

ing around me" and suggesting the range of African Americans' reactions to the news: "Were I a drinker I would get on a Jolly spree today but as a Christian I can but kneel in prayer and bless God for the privilege I've enjoyed this day." In New York, Robert Hamilton, editor of the *Anglo-African* newspaper, emphasized "the boon to the nation at large" in ridding its capital of slavery. This purifying of the nation's "physical heart," Hamilton claimed, would ensure "the return of health and vigor and freedom to the whole national body. . . . It is an act of emancipation which frees a hundred thousand white men for every individual black man."[15]

Anticipating the legislation's implementation, the city's black churches set aside Sunday, April 13, "as a day of Thanksgiving and Prayer, in view of Emancipation in the District." African Methodist Episcopal (A.M.E.) Bishop Daniel A. Payne, who had met several days earlier with a hesitant President Lincoln to urge him to sign the bill, delivered a prescriptive sermon at Georgetown's Ebenezer A.M.E. Church. Well aware of the misgivings held by many in both races regarding the freedpeople, Payne advised those "ransomed ones" to work hard, save their earnings, educate their children, aspire to honesty and godliness, and avoid "the gambling hells, and groggeries, which gradually lead their votaries to infamy and the pit that is bottomless." "Enter the great family of Holy Freedom," he admonished, "not to lounge in sinful indolence, not to degrade yourselves by vice, nor to corrupt society by licentiousness, neither to offend the laws by crime, but to the enjoyment of a well regulated liberty, the offspring of generous laws . . . a liberty to be perpetuated by equitable law, and sanctioned by the divine." Regarding the war effort at a time when black volunteers were still being turned away, Payne recommended "supplications, prayers, intercessions, and thanksgiving" in the knowledge that "the hand of God" would direct "this nation [to] . . . do right, administering justice to each and all, protecting the weak as well as the strong, and throwing the broad wings of its power equally over men of every color."[16]

---

[15]Unidentified letter-writer and *Anglo-African* editorial, both cited in James M. McPherson, *The Negro's Civil War: How American Blacks Felt and Acted during the War for the Union* (New York, 1991), p. 45.

[16]Daniel A. Payne, *Welcome to the Ransomed; or, Duties of the Inhabitants of the District of Columbia* (Baltimore, 1862), reprinted in Payne, *Sermons and Addresses, 1853–1891*, ed. Charles Killian (New York, 1972); John Hope Franklin, *The Emancipation Proclamation* (Garden City, N.Y., 1963), p. 19.

Daniel Payne, like many whites and blacks around Washington, was deeply concerned about the confusion and conflict that could result from the expected inundation of the capital by thousands of fugitive slaves from neighboring states—concerns that turned out to be well founded. On the eve of the Civil War, more than 75 percent of district blacks were free, and many of those individuals' families had been free for generations. Almost overnight most of Washington's rapidly growing black population consisted of former slaves or the descendants of slaves. This new reality forever changed the demographic and social arrangement of the community and stimulated the black elite's concern with differentiating themselves from the black masses.[17]

Despite these concerns, district emancipation was welcomed as a portent of things to come should the radicals in Congress extend their actions to the rest of the nation. These sentiments were reinforced over the summer of 1862, when legislation was passed abolishing slavery in the western territories, strengthening the State Department's enforcement of the Atlantic slave trade ban, and, through the Second Confiscation Act, providing for the liberation and enlistment of rebel-held slaves. By July, Lincoln had broached the subject of his more sweeping Emancipation Proclamation with his cabinet, and only Secretary of State William Seward's advice that he wait for a military victory delayed action at that time.[18]

Also during that summer African Americans at various sites in the North began to incorporate district emancipation into the existing Freedom Day tradition. In Philadelphia, the *Christian Recorder* newspaper advocated a joint commemoration of district and West Indian Emancipations on August 1, and "mammoth" meetings to mark the event were held in both New York City and New Haven, Connecticut. Frederick Douglass spoke at a celebration in Ithaca, New York, at which "colored people for hundreds of miles around came in that day to take joyful notice of Emancipation both for this State [New York] and for the District of Columbia."[19] Recent congressional

[17]"Washington, DC: Civic, Literary, and Mutual Aid Associations," in *Organizing Black America: An Encyclopedia of African American Associations,* ed. Nina Mjagkij (New York and London, 2001), p. 91; Jacqueline M. Moore, *Leading the Race: The Transformation of the Black Elite in the Nation's Capital, 1880–1920* (Charlottesville, 1999), pp. 3, 5, 32.

[18]Joseph T. Wilson, *Emancipation: Its Course and Progress, from 1481 B.C. to A.D. 1875* (1882; reprint ed., New York, 1969), pp. 57–60; Franklin, *Emancipation Proclamation,* pp. 17–21, 39–40.

[19]Frederick Douglass, *The Frederick Douglass Papers,* ser. 1: *Speeches, Debates, and Interviews,* vol. 3: *1855–63,* ed. John W. Blassingame (New Haven, 1985), p. xxxiv (hereafter cited as *FDP*); *Christian Recorder* (Philadelphia), June 28, 1862; *Douglass' Monthly,* Aug. 1862.

actions and the perception that white attitudes were growing more supportive of antislavery gave activists like Douglass hope by the summer of 1862.
The emancipation of Washington's slaves was seen as a momentous step,
both symbolic and tangible, in the long march of liberty.

Washington's African American community used district emancipation
to initiate a commemorative tradition that remained an important local institution for decades. As in virtually all other black communities in the slave
states, Washington's antebellum African Americans had been surrounded
by slavery and had had little opportunity or reason to hold freedom celebrations like the August First celebrations that had become a regular part of
African American political culture in the North. Washington's first postwar
celebration of district emancipation, in 1866, was appropriately enthusiastic
and apparently well conducted. Correspondents reporting to the *New York
Times* called the celebration "a very creditable and successful observance of
that first step in the work of emancipation. The colored people, fully com-
prehending its significance, and determined to show their sincere apprecia-
tion of the act, turned out almost *en masse*, arrayed in their very best, and
entirely through their own effort arranged and carried out one of the most
successful celebrations ever witnessed in this city."[20]

The mile-long procession of an estimated four to eight thousand people
included two African American military units, fourteen civic societies, several school and youth organizations, ward clubs, drum corps, and six brass
bands. The "swarthy column" (as it was described) also featured flags, banners, portraits of Lincoln, and other "devices" that made for a "very imposing" sight. Another ten thousand blacks from Washington and its environs
watched from the sidelines, "manifesting their joy and gladness by waving
their hats and handkerchiefs, and cheering lustily the passing procession." It
was mainly an African American celebration, with the "dense mass of colored faces, relieved here and there by a few white ones." So great was the
turnout of the city's black population "that nearly every kitchen, laundry,
barber shop, restaurant, or hotel dependent upon them has been virtually
suspended in its operations to-day." This last comment indicates that, despite
the fact that the city's "black codes" had been rescinded, employment opportunities for African Americans in Washington were still severely limited,

---

[20]"Washington News: The Celebration of the Abolition of Slavery," *New York Times*,
Apr. 20, 1866.

mainly to menial or service-oriented labor. The public display was all the more important in that "the whole affair [was] conducted with remarkable order and decorum. Not an intoxicated or disorderly person [was] seen on the streets. And the colored people have elevated themselves in the estimation of many of the prejudiced whites by their creditable conduct."[21]

The 1866 celebration may have been unrivaled in its demonstration of apparent joy and unity in black Washington's observance of its liberation. This newspaper correspondent's comment about the perceptions of white bystanders at the 1866 celebration is especially telling, as it relates to long-standing, but increasingly contentious, class distinctions among Washington's black residents. Over time these divisions marred the observance of April 16, transforming the celebrations into a site of heated debates over black politics, intraracial class relations, public deportment, and the memory of slavery. Class divisions within black Washington were well established long before the war. The 1862 liberation of the district's slaves and the subsequent influx of fugitives from the surrounding area swelled the black population from about thirteen thousand in 1860 to nearly forty thousand in 1867.[22] This shift elicited an ambivalent response from black Washingtonians. In 1863 the exclusive Lotus Club was formed by a group of mulatto servants, waiters, and coachmen, most of whom were themselves outside of the black elite's inner circle, explicitly to maintain their own distinction above the burgeoning black masses. Though fearful of the expanding numbers of poor and uneducated freedmen, the city's black middle and upper classes nonetheless offered considerable aid and support, even as they maintained their distance from a people they saw as their social inferiors. This ambivalence did not prevent the regular commemoration of district emancipation, but even in the early postwar years these freedom festivals presented conflicting images and messages to the broader public.[23]

In 1867 visiting contingents of African Americans from Baltimore and Annapolis "manifested no little displeasure" when rain caused the Washington organizers "to postpone the celebration until the first clear day." Indecisive leaders aborted and resumed the festivities twice before a truncated

---

[21]Ibid.

[22]Harrold, *Subversives*, p. 226.

[23]Green, *The Secret City*, pp. 59–66; Willard B. Gatewood, *Aristocrats of Color: The Black Elite, 1880–1920* (Bloomington, Ind., 1990), pp. 47, 51–52, 58, and chap. 3; Moore, *Leading the Race*, pp. 13, 14; "Washington, DC: Civic, Literary, and Mutual Aid Associations," in *Organizing Black America*, pp. 691–94.

procession of understandably frustrated marchers finally formed in the late afternoon and wended its way through the muddy streets, passing thousands of spectators on the crowded sidewalks. As the parade returned from George-town toward the Fifteenth Street Presbyterian Church, an altercation arose between participants and the drivers of several streetcars whose progress was "impeded" by the procession. Violence "was prevented by the timely inter-ference of the police," but the fracas further marred an already chaotic cele-bration. Despite "all the disadvantages surrounding" the celebration, the sympathetic observer from Washington's *Daily National Intelligencer* still de-clared that "it was by no means a failure."[24]

That paper's reporter the following year clearly did not share his col-league's respect for the black celebrants. The 1868 affair included a large procession and "speechifying" by various black and white figures on the grounds of the Executive Mansion, but the columnist from Washington's *Daily National Intelligencer* was less interested in describing the event than in mocking it. He implied that the "two fine looking darkies" in the rear of one "open barouche" had displaced a white city councilman from his rightful place. After suggesting that the contingent had acquired a "strong" odor after "tramping through the mud for several hours," the acid critic contemptu-ously noted that "the crowning and most ludicrous feature of the parade was the chariot containing several colored damsels." By contrast, the San Francisco *Elevator* (a black paper) described the procession of "upwards of three thousand persons" in some detail, noting with considerable pride the presence of black military and fraternal organizations, as well as the "light-complexioned colored girl" representing the goddess of Liberty in the ever-green- and banner-bedecked chariot. Wagons carrying a working printing press (reeling off copies of the Emancipation Act), a blacksmith at his forge, and a carpenter at his workbench also were said to have made a fine impres-sion. Even the *Intelligencer*'s snide chronicler had to admit that the affair was well ordered and that all the participants were "satisfied with the style in which they had passed their holiday."[25] If such was the treatment African American celebrants could expect from the mainstream popular press after

---

[24]"Fifth Anniversary of Emancipation—The Celebration Yesterday," *Daily National Intel-ligencer* (Washington, D.C.), Apr. 17, 1867.

[25]"Emancipation Day—The Grand Parade of the Colored Population," *Daily National Intelligencer*, Apr. 17, 1868; "The Emancipation Celebration," *Elevator* (San Francisco), May 15, 1868.

an apparently dignified and smoothly run commemoration, it is not surprising that black civic leaders were concerned with the public face they presented to whites.

The celebration in 1869 must have further reinforced those apprehensions, though this time it was black disorder, rather than white derision, that was to blame. It was a very popular event, the scale seeming to have dwarfed previous affairs. One commentator noted that "it appeared as though the entire colored population of the District had been reinforced by their neighbors from Virginia and Maryland." Addresses at City Hall by distinguished black activists George B. Vashon, John Mercer Langston, and the Reverend J. Sella Martin lent further dignity to the proceedings. Unfortunately, however, the procession, which proceeded from "K" Street, through Georgetown, and down Pennsylvania Avenue to the speakers' platform, was tainted by a skirmish between marchers and spectators, described in detail by the local press:

> While the procession was passing along the avenue, at the corner of Thirteenth Street, several stones were thrown from the south side of the street by colored men, in consequence of one of the crowd having, it is said, been struck with a sword by a man in the procession, a short time previously, and immediately a rush was made for the men who threw the stones; but the police (mounted men and officers of the Fifth Precinct) took three of them in custody, and by great exertions succeeded in taking them down Thirteenth Street into D, where a number of the friends of the captured parties made efforts to rescue them, while others intended to administer mob law to them. At the corner of Twelfth street, one of them broke away, but was recaptured, and finally the officers succeeded in locking them up in the Central Guardhouse.

"With the exception of the above and a trifling disturbance among themselves," the reporter asserted without a hint of sarcasm, "the procession was orderly."[26]

Little wonder then that some African Americans looked forward to district emancipation celebrations with as much trepidation as pride. But the commemorations continued to be conducted through the 1870s and beyond, and black leaders in Washington used these celebrations to promote many of the same ideals and objectives that had been central components of antebellum August First celebrations, and that remained central components

---

[26]"Seventh Anniversary of Emancipation," *Daily National Intelligencer,* Apr. 17, 1869.

of emancipation celebrations around the country during the late nineteenth century. Black leaders recognized the importance of sustaining the Emancipation Day tradition in order to present their case for equality and justice before the court of public opinion and to earn the respect and support of their white contemporaries. They also appreciated the celebrations' social functions, as they gathered together large numbers of blacks from across the region, reinforcing social ties and networks of activism and political mobilization. Moreover, Emancipation Day commemorations served a vital educational function, helping to disseminate a distinctive, black-centered interpretation of history and politics. Perhaps most important of all, the organizers of these events, throughout the nineteenth century, were deeply concerned with the judgment of posterity. From the earliest slave trade observances, black Emancipation Day orators emphasized the need to establish a commemorative tradition in order to leave a legacy for future generations.

Pursuing this agenda remained an important part of district emancipation celebrations through the century, but during the 1880s the social and political rifts in black Washington grew more pronounced and contentious. This division may have been exacerbated by a shift in race relations after the Organic Act of 1879 "effectively disfranchised the District of Columbia by ending home rule." One result of this was that political ties between whites and the black elite were severed. In the wake of this development, historian Jacqueline Moore argues, "Washington became two distinct communities, one white, one black, the black one struggling for identity and control of the few matters that were left in its hands." Given the additional factor that many whites thought district blacks "incompetent to manage their own affairs," these developments set up a crisis of community self-definition for black leaders.[27] If there had been hints of a lack of unanimity in the celebrations during the 1860s and 1870s, during the 1880s signs of discord were overt and incontrovertible. In 1886 these various and vehemently held positions divided black Washington in an embarrassingly public display.

In another publication I have detailed this escalation of discord in the celebrations during the mid-1880s, and I will not review that process or provide great detail on the 1886 celebration here. Suffice it to say that political maneuverings, personal animosities, disagreements over how best to commemorate the end of slavery, and the ongoing class and cultural divisions among

---

[27]Moore, *Leading the Race*, p. 3.

black Washingtonians all played a part. For all these reasons, in 1886 there were two separate African American parades and celebrations on April 16, representing two antagonistic factions of the city's black civic leaders. The chief spokesperson for one faction, Washington *Bee* editor W. Calvin Chase, claimed to represent "the quiet law abiding citizens of this District" while characterizing the competing celebration as one arranged by "a certain element . . . that is determined to degrade the day rather than to celebrate it."[28]

The competing celebration was organized by a black Republican politico and saloon keeper named Colonel Perry Carson who claimed a loyal following among working-class blacks in the northwestern section of the city.[29] Unfortunately for Carson, Calvin Chase had the benefit of being a newspaper editor, so today we must rely largely on his version of events. As the date of the dual celebrations approached, Chase presented the situation as a choice "between respectability and rowdyism," and he continued to denigrate that "notorious class of Negroes" who "were endeavoring to gain power and rob the people." The two camps, up to the day of the celebrations, openly competed for the participation of a variety of bands and military companies, and, perhaps most notably on a symbolic level, the sanction of President Grover Cleveland.[30]

The president's formal review of the Emancipation Day procession was a regular feature of the ceremony, but Cleveland wisely removed himself from the fray by declining to review either procession, though Carson led his contingent past the locked gates of the executive mansion anyway. Carson's group appears to have been the larger, despite Chase's estimate that his own line of march contained some four thousand of "the best element of the colored people." Both ended their respective parades with speeches, Carson's at Lincoln Park and Chase's at the Israel Bethel Colored Methodist Episcopal Church. The editor praised his followers for their patriotism and manliness in the face of opposition from the "maudlin bummers and worthless men" who comprised "the whisky element." Carson in particular was con-

---

[28]"Our Weekly Review," *Bee*, Feb. 20, 1886; "The Emancipation," *Bee* (Washington, D.C.), Mar. 27, 1886; "Progress of the Colored People," *Bee*, Apr. 10, 1886; Kachun, *Festivals of Freedom*, chap. 6.

[29]*Washington Sun*, Feb. 5, 1915, in Tuskegee News Clipping File (microfilm), "Necrology," reel 237, frame 47; *Washington, D.C. City Directory, 1890* (Washington, D.C.: R. L. Polk Co., 1890), http://www.ancestry.com.

[30]"The Emancipation Celebration," *Bee*, Apr. 10, 1886; "Our Weekly Review," *Bee*, Apr. 17, 1886; editor's note, *FDP,* 5:212–13.

demned as an "ignoran[t] . . . man, who puts himself up as a leader of the people."[31]

Frederick Douglass, the featured orator at Chase's celebration, could hardly avoid commenting on the situation. He insisted at the outset "that no apology is needed for these annual celebrations" whose "demonstrations of popular feeling . . . are consistent with and creditable to human nature." He did, however, express remorse and disappointment over "an incident connected with [the celebration], and by which it is greatly marred." His concerns were, like Calvin Chase's, partly about the face black Washingtonians had presented to the larger society. The dual celebrations "have said to the world that we are not sufficiently united as a people to celebrate our freedom together." He personally found the division "unfortunate, disgraceful, and mortifying" and appealed to the tolerance and patience of the "disgusted public" with the excuse "that colored men are but men" who would surely behave better and act more wisely "when we have enjoyed the blessings of liberty longer." Douglass also warned blacks that "a repetition of this spectacle will bring our celebrations into disgrace and make them despicable."

Warming to this tone of rebuke, Douglass continued to upbraid an audience comprised "mainly [of] colored men" for having lost sight of their larger common goal of race progress. In so doing he made clear the importance of carrying on commemorations so as not to call undue attention to the most unflattering elements in the black community:

> The thought is already gaining ground, that we have not heretofore received the best influence, which this anniversary is capable of exerting; [He condemned] that tinsel show, gaudy display, and straggling processions, which empty the alleys and dark places of our city into the broad daylight of our thronged streets and avenues, thus thrusting upon the public view a vastly undue proportion of the most unfortunate, unimproved, and unprogressive class of the colored people, and thereby inviting public disgust and contempt, and repelling the most thrifty and self-respecting among us, is a positive hurt to the whole colored population of this city. These annual celebrations of ours should be so arranged as to make a favorable impression for us upon ourselves and upon our fellow-citizens. They should bring into notice the very best elements of our colored population, and in what is said and done

---

[31]"The Dual Celebration," "Our Weekly Review," "The Emancipation Celebration," *Bee*, Apr. 24, 1886; editor's note, *FDP*, 5:212–13.

on these occasions, we should find a deeper and broader comprehension of our relations and duties. They should kindle in us higher hopes, nobler aspirations, and stimulate us to more earnest endeavors; they should help us to shorten the distance between ourselves and the more highly advanced and highly favored people among whom we are. If they fail to produce, in some measure, such results, they had better be discontinued.[32]

Despite the intense controversy surrounding the 1886 celebration, it was clear that the masses of Washington's black citizens looked forward with great pleasure to this annual day of revelry and were not about to let the festive tradition die. The Washington correspondent of the *Cleveland Gazette* noted in 1887 that "for a month before [the celebration] it is the common topic of conversation, the constant food for newspaper gossip." Not only was April 16 a great opportunity for "real as well as would-be orators," it was also viewed by the military companies as "the best dress parade of the year." "The white people," district blacks felt, "turn out on General Washington's birthday, the Irish have their St. Patrick's day, the Dutchman has his day, and we are going to have ours, too. This 16th of April is our day, and we are going to celebrate it." The social and recreational functions of the day were clearly foremost in the minds of the working classes. It was an opportunity not only to visit with fellow Washingtonians but also to meet with visitors from out of town. "The people living here are up by times on the 16th . . . and all the married sisters, cousins and aunts from the bordering States swarm out upon the streets, sometimes twenty thousand strong, to see the sights and to be seen by sight-seers." In the evening, celebrants could choose between listening to the orations "or else betake themselves to the numerous balls and hops given in honor of the occasion."[33]

I should also note that Chase's *Bee* also lashed out at those who preferred *not* to honor the occasion—as he put it in 1886, the "few in this city who oppose the annual Emancipation celebration." Those who wanted to do away with the tradition found "the custom . . . degrading," primarily because of its "tendency to recall the former condition of the race which should be

[32]"Strong to Suffer, and Yet Strong to Strive," an address delivered in Washington, D.C., April 16, 1886, in *FDP,* 5:219. On the life of the alley dwellers criticized by Douglass and Chase, see James Borchert, *Alley Life in Washington: Family, Community, Religion, and Folklife in the City, 1850–1970* (Urbana, Ill., 1980), pp. 208–9.
[33]"Colored People of the District of Columbia's Recent Emancipation Celebration," *Cleveland Gazette,* Apr. 30, 1887.

forgotten." Chase and his columnists argued that simple respect for "the honest mothers and fathers who have felt the pangs of slavery" demanded that a day be set apart for them to express gratitude for their deliverance. As for that "certain class that are ashamed of their parents, such people should be relegated to oblivion. Let every honest man and woman turn out and celebrate this day."[34]

By the 1890s the district's black leaders were moving away from large celebrations with rowdy street parades. Black Washingtonians continued to debate the propriety of Emancipation Day parading, and in some years dual celebrations split the community. At times a tenuous truce was attained that permitted a single commemoration. Compromises at times even sanctioned a parade so long as rickety carts, wagons, and disorderly persons were prohibited. Often the proceeds from the literary exercises were remitted to a worthy cause, like the Home for Destitute Colored Girls. And always the speeches—by Douglass, John Mercer Langston, Calvin Chase, William Derrick, and others—attempted to instruct and inform the black community about its past, present, and future in America. While some celebrations during the last decade of the century did include both "patriotic addresses" and a parade, Washington's freedom festivals in the 1890s never approached the scale, or attracted the public attention, of similar events in the previous decade.[35]

After the turn of the century, public processions on Emancipation Day were only a memory. In 1906 Chase and most of the other community leaders in the city did not even consider publicly debating the issue of holding a parade. Chase joined the Reverend Francis J. Grimke, Professors Kelly Miller, and others at a subdued, almost private indoor commemorative ceremony. Still, Mrs. Helen A. Davis, who chaired the meeting, noted that "there is no occasion that inspired the colored people of this city more than this day." Kelly Miller presented statistics demonstrating the progress of the race, an increasingly common occurrence at black meetings in the early years of the century. Other speakers emphasized the need for black men to respect black women, to adhere to religious faith, and generally to assert their manhood. When Calvin Chase stepped up to the rostrum he first called for African

[34]"The Emancipation," *Bee,* Mar. 27, 1886; "Louise to Clara," *Bee,* Feb. 20, 1886.
[35]Representative coverage of these affairs can be found in the *Bee,* Apr. 20, 1889; Feb. 22, Mar. 1, 15, Apr. 19, 1890; Mar. 7, Apr. 18, 25, 1891; Apr. 23, 1892, Apr. 15, 22, 1893; Mar. 7, 1896; Apr. 24, 1897; *Richmond Planet* (Va.), Apr. 22, 1899.

Americans to wake up from their slumber of nearly three hundred years and take action to secure their place in American society. Then he pondered the past and "cited amidst applause and laughter the time when he and Col. Carson had two Emancipation Day street parades." He also noted Grover Cleveland's refusal to review either parade "because there was a division among the negroes. However," Chase recalled, "we paraded just the same. To-day we have adopted other methods in celebrating this day. . . . 'We want to be united,' said Mr. Chase, 'and show to the American white people that we are good citizens.'"[36]

Chase and his companions felt sufficiently removed from the heated conflicts of the 1880s to smile and wax nostalgic as early as 1906, even as they remained concerned with the judgment of whites. A quarter century later another journalist pondered "the emotional abandonment with which the masses of people used to 'turn out' to celebrate the anniversaries of the emancipation of slaves in the District of Columbia. There is no gainsaying the importance of the event in the lives of the masses of the people." The editorialist seemed to be well informed regarding the old celebrations despite the broad gulf of time that separated him from the events. He was also cognizant of the class distinctions that still caused dissension within the race. "That the old methods of 'celebrating' should displease native sons and daughters who were slowly arriving at 'middle class status' is to be expected, but that they did not turn the event into a more dignified occasion is cause for comment." This hinting at unrealized possibilities recalls Chase's own unsuccessful attempts to make the tradition do good for the race during the 1890s. The 1931 editorialist's description of the "old methods of celebrating" was unflattering to elite and masses alike but indicated that a great opportunity had been lost when the tradition was discontinued:

> In the former "celebrations," one might witness hordes of the unwashed, partly clothed, slow-dragging to bands with . . . drums and trombones in crescendo while beribboned marshals pranced astride spavined cart horses back and forth along the belated line of march. Prominent citizens, many long since passed into the great beyond, were seen to loll importantly in open carriages bedecked with strings of scanty bunting. Uniformed organizations with every man an officer, and others with greenish frock coats and stovepipe hats of veteran service composed the line which was reviewed by city officials and even Presidents. It was a great occasion for display, emotion, and

---

[36]"Emancipation Celebration," *Bee*, Apr. 21, 1906.

expression. Though it but crudely expressed freedom, it was impressive and had in it the elements of an annual custom for which music could have been written, poems composed and dramas enacted, but were not.

At least those celebrants of days gone by had tried to make a statement that mattered about who they were, what their history was, and what their expectations were of participation in American public life. "As crude as that celebration was," he judged, "it was far superior to the smug, middle class, suppressed life of today." Harshly critical of assimilationist middle-class blacks who aped whites while exploiting the black masses, the editorialist chastised his readers to remember that racial unity is the essential ingredient in the recipe for racial progress. And even in 1931 he believed that Emancipation Day celebrations could play a role in that project. "Emancipation is a continuing process," he wrote; "it should be celebrated."[37]

In 1906 Calvin Chase stood midway in time between the escalation of community conflict over public emancipation festivals during the 1880s and the lamentation for their abandoned potential for community empowerment in the 1930s. During his two and one-half decades of involvement with district emancipation celebrations, Chase absorbed lessons that his journalistic descendent in 1931 probably could not fully appreciate. He had learned what black activists in many communities around the nation had learned—that an era of large, public African American commemorative festivals was coming to an end and that new methods and new strategies were required to address the challenges that faced black Washingtonians in the new century. Now, early in the twenty-first century, the celebration of emancipation in the District of Columbia has once again gained new energy and has been celebrated annually since 2002. In 2005 it was declared an official holiday, and in March 2007 Congress passed legislation establishing April 16 as a permanent public holiday in the district. I am confident that the divisions that marred district celebrations during the 1880s will remain buried in the past. Instead, these annual celebrations will recall the high ideals, expressed by Frederick Douglass in 1886, that were more typical of emancipation celebrations in the nineteenth century, as African Americans met annually to inspire a pride in history, nurture a sense of group solidarity, provide a forum for festive celebration, and work to organize and mobilize in the pursuit of racial justice in the district and in the nation.

[37]"Celebrating Emancipation Day," *Washington Tribune*, Apr. 24, 1931, microfilm reel 240, frame 933, News Clipping File, Tuskegee Institute.

Contributors

Mary Beth Corrigan, an independent consultant, has studied the African American community in Washington for more than twenty years. She completed her Ph.D. dissertation, "A Social Union of Heart and Effort: The African American Family in the District of Columbia on the Eve of Emancipation," at the University of Maryland in 1996. Corrigan currently serves on the board of the Historical Society of Washington, D.C.

A. Glenn Crothers is assistant professor of history at University of Louisville, director of research at the Filson Historical Society, and coeditor of *Ohio Valley History*. A specialist in southern U.S. history before 1865, Crothers has published articles on southern economic development, southern Quakers, and history pedagogy. He is presently completing a book manuscript, "*The Quakers of Northern Virginia, 1730–1865: Negotiating Communities and Cultures.*"

David Brion Davis is Sterling Professor of History Emeritus at Yale University and founder and director emeritus of Yale's Gilder Lehrman Center for the Study of Slavery, Resistance, and Abolition. He served as president of the Organization of American Historians and his many awards include the Pulitzer Prize for General Nonfiction, the National Book Award for History and Biography, the Albert J. Beveridge Award, and the Bancroft Prize. His publications include *The Problem of Slavery in Western Culture* (1966), *The Problem of Slavery in the Age of Revolution, 1770–1823* (1975), and *Inhuman Bondage: The Rise and Fall of Slavery in the New World* (2006).

Jonathan Earle is associate professor of history at the University of Kansas where he also directs programming for the Robert J. Dole Institute of Politics. His primary interests are the antislavery and democratic movements of the nineteenth century and political history more generally. Professor Earle is the author of *Jacksonian Antislavery and the Politics of Free Soil, 1824–1854* (2004), and he is currently working on a book on the election of 1860.

Paul Finkelman is President William McKinley Distinguished Professor of Law and Public Policy at Albany Law School. A specialist in American legal history, race and the law, and First Amendment issues, he is the author or editor of numerous articles and books, including *Slavery and the Founders: Race and Liberty in the Age of Jefferson* (2001), *A March of Liberty: A Constitutional History of the United States* (2002), and *American Legal History: Cases and Materials* (2005).

Stanley Harrold is professor of history in the Department of Social Sciences at South Carolina State University. Professor Harrold is the author of several books on the American antislavery movement and African American history, including *Gamaliel Bailey and Antislavery Union* (1986), *Abolitionists and the South, 1831–1861* (1995), and *Subversives: Antislavery Community in Washington, D.C., 1828–1865* (2003).

Mitch Kachun is associate professor of history at Western Michigan University. His research concentrates on how African Americans during the nineteenth and twentieth centuries used historical knowledge and public commemorations in their efforts to work for equal rights, construct a sense of collective identity, and claim control over their status and destiny in American society. Professor Kachun is the author of Festivals of Freedom: Memory and Meaning in African American Emancipation Celebrations, 1808–1915 *(2003)*.

Mary K. Ricks has written about Washington history in numerous publications, including the *Washington Post*. A former attorney at the Department of Labor, Ricks is the author of *Escape on the Pearl: The Heroic Bid for Freedom on the Underground Railroad* (2007). She lives with her husband and two children outside Washington, D.C.

James B. Stewart is James Wallace Professor of History at Macalester College in St. Paul, Minnesota. His books and articles address the abolitionist movement in the United States and the politics of the conflict over slavery and the struggles for racial justice. Professor Stewart's books include *Holy Warriors: The Abolitionists and American Slavery* (1970), *Joshua R. Giddings and the Tactics of Radical Politics* (1976), *Wendell Phillips: Liberty's Hero* (1982), and *Abolitionist Politics and the Coming of the Civil War* (2008).

Susan Zaeske is professor and chair of the Department of Communication Arts at the University of Wisconsin–Madison. Professor Zaeske's scholarship focuses on rhetoric, gender, and political culture. She is the author of *Signatures of Citizenship: Petitioning, Antislavery, and Women's Political Identity* (2003). Her current book project is "Encountering Esther: Appropriations of the Jewish Queen."

David Zarefsky is Owen L. Coon Professor of Communications at Northwestern University. His many publications deal with American public discourse (both historical and contemporary), argumentation, rhetorical criticism, and public speaking. Professor Zarefsky is the author of *Lincoln, Douglas, and Slavery: In the Crucible of Public Debate* (1990), and he currently is working on a book on the Texas annexation controversy of the 1840s as it affected the slavery debate.

Index

Aberdeen, Lord (George Hamilton-Gordon), 30
abolition, 8, 28, 34, 87. *See also* emancipation
abolitionism, British, 10, 19–35
abolitionists, 25, 99, 100, 116
Adams, Abigail, 109
Adams, Charles Francis, 69, 72, 73, 108
Adams, John, 7
Adams, John Quincy, 20, 26, 37, 41, 44, 52, 94,
 127, 158, 208; and petitions and gag rule,
 87, 99, 106–9, 116, 118–23, 124, 156, 157
Adams, Louisa, 109
*Address of the Female Anti-Slavery Society of Phila-
 delphia, An*, 102
African Methodist Episcopal Church, 206, 225
African slave trade. *See* slave trade
Albany Patriot, 198, 201, 204, 208
Alexandria, Virginia; retrocession of, 11, 141–68;
 slavery and slave trade in, 11, 159, 166, 223
Alexandria Canal Company, 151
Alexandria Gazette, 154, 157, 160, 161, 163
Alexandria Marine Insurance Company, 159
Alford, Julius, 49, 50
Allen, Charles, 94
Allen, William, 72
American and Foreign Anti-Slavery Society, 59,
 62, 71, 76, 89
American Anti-Slavery Society, 28, 60, 61, 87,
 156
American Colonization Society, 60, 77
American Geography, The (Morse), 145
American Revolution, 8, 120
Amis des Noires, 25, 27
Anglo-African (New York), 225
Anglo-American relations, 22
antifederalists, 9
Anti-Slavery Bugle (Salem, Ohio), 78
antislavery petitions. *See* petitions
antislavery politics, 93–96
Archer, William S., 180
Armfield, John, 159
Asbury A.M.E. Church (Washington, D.C.),
 189, 207
Ashtabula County Anti-Slavery Society, 40

Aspasia, 120
Astor, John Jacob, 202
Atlantic slave trade. *See* slave trade

Bailey, Gamaliel, 11, 51, 200, 223; as antislavery
 journalist and lobbyist, 58–82; and coloni-
 zation, 76–77; death of, 80; peaceful eman-
 cipation, views on, 74–76; religious
 conversion of, 59–60; social gatherings and
 lobbying, 71–73, 83–96
Bailey, Margaret, 72, 80, 84, 90, 91, 92, 93,
 95–96
Ball, Eva, 95
Baltimore and Ohio Railroad, 152
Baltimore, Md., 149, 172
Bank of Alexandria, 153
Bank of Maryland, 153
Banneker, Benjamin 220
Barbados, 27
Barnburners, 69, 94
Basch, Norma, 107
Bassett, George W., 71
Battle of Horseshoe Bend, 107
Becraft, Catharine, 188
Becraft, Sarah Ellen, 188
Bee (Washington, D.C.), 232, 234
Beecher, Henry Ward, 202, 217
Bell, Daniel, 202, 208
Bell, Daniel, Jr., 203
Bell family, 211 12
Belser, James E., 130, 132, 134
Belt, Ellen, 187
Belt, Henrietta, 187
Benezet, Anthony, 24
Bennett, Henley, 55
Benton, Thomas Hart, 94, 127, 128, 129, 130
Berrien, John M., 128
Bigelow, Jacob, 208
Bill of Rights, 10
Birney, James G., 60, 77, 90, 91, 131
Black, Edward, 48, 50, 52
Black, Junius, 214
Black Laws (Ohio), 74

CPSIA information can be obtained at www.ICGtesting.com
Printed in the USA
LVOW06*2138031215

465281LV00003B/28/P